Transformation for Life:

Healing and Growth
for Adult Children of Alcoholics and Others

Roland Petit

Bright Horizons Press, LLC

Clifton, New Jersey
www.brighthorizonspress.com

Bright Horizons Press, LLC

1360 Clifton Avenue, P.M.B. #189
Clifton, NJ 07012.

Although the author and publisher have made very effort to ensure the accuracy and completeness of information contained in this book, we assume no responsibility for errors, inaccuracies, omissions, or any inconsistency herein. Any slights of people, places, or organizations are unintentional.

While the examples described in this book are based on interviews and situations experienced by real persons, the names, professions, locations and other biographical details have been changed to preserve their privacy and anonymity. Unless otherwise noted, examples provided in the text do not reflect actual persons, living or dead. Any resemblance to actual persons is purely coincidental.

ISBN 0-9767417-0-9

LCCN 2005903402

Visit us at: www.brighthorizonspress.com

This book is gratefully dedicated to **Rose Petit** and so many others who have been blessings in my life's journey.

Transformation for Life
Contents

PART ONE: Self-awareness

PART TWO: Healing

PART THREE: Self-love

Chapter 1

Turning Your Life Around
Learning New Skills and Exploring Destructive Beliefs

"I never learned how to be a child, much less a functioning adult. I basically became a walking psychological disaster," said Andy at an ACOA meeting. "All I knew was how to survive in a family where my father's alcoholism took center stage. I shut down my feelings, was isolated, violated, miserable and ashamed to be alive. How screwed up did I turn out to be? Today as an adult, I've got lots of problems. My relationships don't last, my job sucks, I think I'm a loser and every day I'm proven right. I'm lost and don't know how to turn my life around."

It doesn't have to be that way – for Andy or for anyone else who was raised with an alcoholic parent. In fact, you can live a life filled with happiness and success if you choose. Your life <u>does not</u> have to be ruined because of your past. But in order to recover from your difficult childhood and reach your potential, new skills will need to be learned, destructive belief systems challenged and a new dream constructed for your life. That's what the *Transformation for Life* program is all about.

Consider this success story: "As a young boy, I lacked nurturing, guidance, self-esteem and the teaching of life skills—but look at me today," Peter said. "I've left behind years of neglect and abuse to live a successful and happy life. Next month will be my 40th birthday and it's taken longer than I wanted, but I feel free from my past, and strong. Looking back, here's how it happened: First I gained understanding and self-awareness by reading about other Adult Children of Alcoholics and answering questions regarding my own experiences. Those actions showed me where I needed to recover and develop. Then I began a healing and growth program that included guided exercises, affirmations and weekly action plans. Soon the increased competencies and resulting self-esteem empowered me to confront destructive belief systems.

I re-parented my inner child, began to take more risks and think positively about myself. For the first time, I started to feel self-love and also pursue healthy relationships without being paralyzed by the fear of abandonment. And I knew that a power greater than I was always there helping me. Finally, I constructed a mission statement, began to set life goals, and developed detailed plans on how to achieve them. And here I am—surrounded by love, success, spirituality and unlimited potential." The steps recounted by Peter comprise the *Transformation for Life* Program.

"I know from experience that Adult Children of Alcoholics need to heal," said Peter. "*Transformation for Life* empowers us to overcome anxiety, guilt, shame, loneliness and abandonment and to change destructive patterns. What I found most therapeutic was the *audible* self-interview process, but the workbook also provided action plans and skill-building exercises as well as techniques to alter destructive belief systems. It was easy to read and contained personal examples I could relate to. Meaningful change can happen by following this program."

The difference between recovery, success and emotional well-being and living a painful, ineffective life can be traced to the issues addressed in this book. Many of the 28 million Adult Children of Alcoholics (ACOAs) in the U.S. suffer crippling self-esteem difficulties, troubled relationships, loneliness and a multitude of other problems by the time they reach adulthood. ACOAs often are unaware of their feelings, don't get their needs met, react inappropriately, believe they'll be rejected and have limited career potential. *Transformation for Life* acknowledges that we suffer difficulties because of our past but immediately launches a program to help turn scars into strengths. An *audible* self-interview process is used to empower you to act like your own personal therapist. The resulting insight combines with recovery techniques, revealing exercises and homework that heals. Here's how the program works:

1. **Awareness** through a process of self-interview analysis.
2. **Healing and growth** from skill-building exercises, action plans, affirmations and insight.
3. Changing of destructive **belief systems** through guided introspection leading to increased self-love and a formation of healthy relationships.
4. Positive **spirituality** and a connection to God.
5. A look into the future, establishment of a personal **mission statement.**

Dynamic personal empowerment can be yours *if you choose to do the work*. Life-changing healing, growth, skill development and a new, constructive belief system combine to help free you from emotional chains of the past while leading you to the best years of your life.

The Building Blocks

The chapters in *Transformation for Life* are grouped into six major growth and recovery categories: self-awareness, healing, self-love, relationship-building, spirituality and goal achievement. They serve as building blocks that comprise an overall program that provides healing and teaches important life skills.

Self-Awareness

Katie, an ACOA who was raised by an alcoholic father, regularly saw her relationships abruptly end. "I was never sure *why* until attending a 12-step support group," she said. "I soon discovered how certain events could 'trigger' reactions that were developed during childhood. Some were strong reactions that were inappropriate for current events. In my case, I once dumped a pot of spaghetti over my boyfriend's head. He was ignoring me, just like my father used to and I felt angry and hurt so I wanted to hurt him. It turned out that my boyfriend came for dinner with a 101-degree fever because he wanted to see me, but wasn't responsive because of being sick. He responded to the spaghetti all right, but not in a good way. These days I'm trying to become aware of when events 'trigger' the behavior I learned in childhood and react more appropriately."

Healing can't begin until self-awareness identifies problems. Exercises and Five-day action plans in *Transformation for Life* enable you to acquire self-knowledge, understand what happened in childhood, and discover the connection between current behaviors and past experiences. You'll get in touch with personal strengths, attributes, beliefs, values, needs and priorities, and finally begin to learn how to move beyond "survival mode" to live in the present.

Children with an alcoholic parent often shut down feelings as a survival technique, a tendency that can continue into adulthood. As a result, ACOAs often have a reluctance to allow them to feel or, if they do, are unsure of what they're feeling. To address this, you are presented with a "feelings checklist" along with an explanation of how certain emotions lead into others. You'll see how best to overcome negative feelings and enjoy positive ones.

Healing

"From being constantly put down as a child, I became convinced that I was defective and a mistake," said Peter. "I tried to tell myself that it was the alcohol talking but after all, this was my mother saying these things and I was just a kid. She's been sober for eight years now, but I still sometimes hear those damaging tapes playing in my head. My therapist is helping me, but it will take time before I really feel worthy of happiness."

With increased self-awareness, you can identify areas requiring attention so the healing process can begin. The second segment of the book focuses on recovery and healing. One common characteristic of ACOAs is low self-confidence because we received minimal nurturing, were often verbally abused and were taught to place our needs last. In some instances there is physical or emotional abuse that further affects self-esteem. Transformation for Life addresses this by providing exercises to increase self-confidence and self-worth as part of a rebuilding process that walks you through incremental steps in personal achievement.

Anxiety is a condition very familiar to an ACOA. It stems from the unpredictability of an alcoholic parent's behavior. A child in such an environment lives in a constant state of tension. Transformation for Life will show what types of anxiety you may be most susceptible to, and where unnecessary worry may be originating, then it offers techniques to aggressively fight fear.

Children in alcoholic homes frequently blame themselves for their parent's drinking, feeling guilty for the resulting turmoil. Unexpressed guilt often evolves into shame with a general belief that we are defective or inadequate. You will learn why these beliefs are irrational, what to do about them if they remain with you as an adult, and see how to break the "shame cycle" to heal unwarranted guilt.

Self-Love

"I was told by my alcoholic father to keep quiet about what goes on in the house, or else—so I remained silent and built emotional walls," remembered Thomas. "As a result, I never developed a way of relating to others and became very shy. Last year I thought I met my soulmate at work, but every time she tried to talk to me, my shyness would kick in and I'd say nothing. Then I'd tell myself that she's way out of my league anyway. I guess I'll just never find love."

Children raised in an alcoholic home can easily become withdrawn and shy. They often feel different from others, are critical of themselves and lack social skills. This portion of the book will work to alleviate these conditions. Specific information and exercises are presented to minimize shyness. Several different conversational techniques are explained to build social confidence and eliminate excessive self-consciousness. You'll be introduced to a technique called free-flowing association and learn how to keep conversations interesting. Active listening skills also develop your competencies and help you become more confident.

Non-verbal ways to effectively communicate and attract friends are also explored. You will learn how to constructively express anger and stop feeling guilty about feeling angry. An overall self-acceptance develops as a result of positive self-talk and the natural law of displacement (which is explained in a later chapter).

Relationship-Building

"Every time my dad would promise to take me to the park, he'd first want a few drinks and then be too drunk to move," remembered Eric. "I could never trust his word and I learned a valuable lesson—never trust anyone. It seems like a lot of other people haven't learned that yet and get screwed as a result. Personally, I think you can only count on yourself, but have to admit I often feel lonely. Keeping people at arm's length limits my disappointments but comes at a great cost."

ACOAs are more susceptible to experiencing loneliness for a variety of reasons. You will learn how to build a support system that works and how to overcome feelings of being alone. Several categories of loneliness are identified and solution-based remedies illustrated for each. Trust-building actions, beliefs and attitudes are all explained in detail. You are empowered to develop a solid plan that will help you feel comfortable in various types of relationships. The positive effects of change are considered along with ways to move beyond resistance so you can progress toward a positive, all-encompassing life change.

Spirituality

"Now that I'm attending ACOA groups, I've come to realize that God didn't bring the suffering to my childhood," said Ellen. "In fact He helped me through it, giving me comfort when my parents were fighting, hope each time a friend stood by me and strength to work on myself to become the good and capable person I am today."

God/Spirit is perhaps the greatest of all sources of hope for a wonderful future. But living through a traumatic upbringing, an ACOA can form a negative opinion about God/Spirit. "How can there be a God if He allows this to happen?" That's a question often asked, and there are no easy answers. But regardless of your angry rejection of God, you <u>are</u> a spiritual being. You do have a soul and it's important to plug in to the divine source—because the ability to connect can often make the difference between complete healing and moderate success. This segment of the *Transformation for Life* offers you many different options and leaves it up to you to decide what resonates. It doesn't preach but rather presents constructive ways to nourish your soul and get in touch with God/Spirit. Traditional and non-traditional ways to awaken a person's spirituality are presented.

Goal Achievement, Success and Joyfulness

"I've established a mission statement and am very close to achieving my goals," said Jennifer. "Completing projects were tough as a child because of the unpredictable behavior of my parents when booze entered the picture. My parents never completed anything of substance and they were my models. But I've learned new skills and have a clear direction on what I'd like to do with my life. I visualized a Doctorate and new home three years ago and planned the necessary steps to get there. Next year I'll reach both goals and am feeling pretty good about myself."

In the concluding chapters, you'll establish a mission statement, goals and priorities, and then plan the necessary steps needed. Through self-examination, positive self-talk, and acquiring new skills and beliefs, you will have everything needed to claim, create and constantly improve a happy life.

Transformation for Life is about where you are now, where you'd like to be, and how to get there. The roadblocks to achieving your potential can be overcome. You can change your scars into strengths, turn your life around and move toward a bright future.

What Is Necessary & What You Will Gain

Willingness to change, time, short-term discomfort, examination of your belief system, effort and perseverance will be needed. Once you become aware of and address issues from your past, their influence over you will be minimized. Learning and practicing skills will open new opportunities. Acquiring a reality-based belief system will change the way you view yourself and others. And you'll have the self-worth, positive beliefs, and skills to reach your potential. There's a valuable prize for thoughtfully working through your issues: a new and improved life. And by adding new skills, you'll emerge with self-acceptance, competencies and a new belief in yourself.

Only you know where you are today and where you'd like to be. If certain chapters concentrate on issues you'd like to improve immediately, feel free to skip to those areas. You're fully in charge of your healing and development. But some caution is advised here: by doing too much too soon, you can become overwhelmed. And reversing what's happened in your past can't happen overnight. Take the time necessary in each chapter. Be patient, be kind to yourself and be assured that healing and the inevitable rewards will be worth your time and effort.

Audio "Superhealing:" An Active versus Passive Approach

"Don't talk about your feelings or what's happening in this house" is a common demand by an alcoholic parent, so perhaps your voice was seldom heard. But that chapter of your life is over. You will now be heard: loud, clear and often throughout this workbook as a result of some unique and empowering exercises. A key ingredient to this healing and recovery process is an audible self-interview section located within each chapter.

You'll need a small recorder and a quiet place where you won't be interrupted. When you reach the self-interview exercise, a number of questions will appear for you to record along with your answers. The process moves from a passive event (reading a book) to an active experience. The vocalization of honest answers energizes free-flowing thinking. After answering the questions and rewinding the tape, you'll have a unique opportunity to listen not only to what you said, but also how you said it. To derive the most benefit, listen to the recording, paying particular attention to the emotions and voice intonations **behind** the words. This process will bring considerable insight. It will help you to dig deeply and get to the heart of the matter.

You'll gain self-knowledge and self-esteem. As you learn how to release pent-up guilt and anxiety, you will be able to pursue a productive, realistic approach to life. You'll understand how certain occurrences can trigger overreactions and what to do if that happens. I encourage you not to bypass this approach because it has the potential to bring substantially more healing and self-knowledge than other methods. *But if a lack of privacy or any other reason prevents you from recording*, know that you'll still receive important insights by answering and reviewing the questions in a computer or on paper.

Other exercises will help you interpret current behaviors and you'll see how to build and maintain intimate relationships. But let's begin immediately with the first self-interview exercise. This initial information encompasses many of your earlier years and provides a broad personal history. Take breaks after every few questions if you wish. Just be easy on yourself and leave enough time to reflect on your answers.

Self-Interview Taping Exercise:
Use a tape recorder to record questions and answers to the following. Then rewind and thoughtfully listen for the feelings along with meanings behind your responses. Summarize important insights into a notebook for reflection and/or action. (You may use a word processing computer program to record your answers as an alternative.)

• What was it like growing up in your household? How has that affected you today?
• Describe your parent(s), family members and your experience of growing up.
• How did each family member relate to one another?
• Describe your childhood at ages 6 and 12 including where you lived, your friends, your life. Describe the childhood you wished you had.
• What's your happiest memory involving your parent(s)?
• What was their greatest gift to you, and you to them?
• What did you want most from your parent(s) that you didn't get?
• As a child, what adaptive behaviors did you employ to get by? (being a perfectionist or super-responsible, stuffing your feelings, etc.)
• How have adaptive behaviors affected your relationships as an adult?
• How would you like to change your life?

Your Past is History (but only kind of)

Sometimes the most successful future comes from a forgotten past, but it's simplistic to think that you can just "forget" your history. It's damaging to live in the past but also to hide from it. By briefly revisiting it, recognizing how it might be affecting your present, and dealing with issues, past events will no longer retain the power they once did.

Helen tried to explain to her boyfriend why she reacts so intensely when he's uncommunicative with her. "I tried to get my mother to stop drinking by talking to her about it, but she'd just get angry and give me the silent treatment. I felt so unloved and alone. And now when *you're* angry and shut down emotionally, it all comes back to me. Suddenly I'm a lonely, unloved, inadequate child all over again and can do little else but uncontrollably cry."

Perhaps your parents or caretakers were unable to teach you interpersonal skills as a result of their own difficulties with substance abuse. You may have experienced traumatic events that damaged your self-worth and confidence. Being programmed to believe you're inadequate naturally affects your self-worth and can stay with you if you do nothing about it. The truth is that you are made in God's image, and the <u>fallacy</u> is that He makes defective products. Experiences from your past do not dictate your future—unless you give them the power to do so. Don't give them that power!

On your way to love, self-esteem, success and joy, you have to briefly revisit the past. By doing so, you'll see how your present beliefs and behaviors may still be hampered by the past. And with that realization, you'll be better equipped to deal directly with current issues and move on.

Going Back So You Can Move Forward

It's all part of the healing and growth process. You have to go to the origin of your problems; otherwise you're just dealing with surface-level symptoms.

1. Please understand that when you <u>revisit your past</u>, you may find traumatic events you've been trying to forget. Facing childhood issues is difficult. But without identifying the source of current difficulties, there will be no way to understand, confront and overcome them.

2. After <u>determining how your past and present are connected</u>, you can <u>challenge ill-conceived beliefs</u> and do what's necessary to replace them with beliefs that are constructive and true. For instance, poor self-confidence developed in childhood can prevent you from pursuing a good job today. Did the words or actions of an alcoholic parent make you believe you're inadequate? The world of an alcoholic is warped and so are their teachings. There's an old data processing phrase: garbage in/garbage out. Program the computer with bad information and that's what will be output. Did you absorb some bad programming? It's important to recognize that possibility because if you believe you're a failure, you'll make it so. But the opposite is also true.

To illustrate an incorrectly programmed belief about oneself, consider the old Anthony DeMello fable about an abandoned lion cub that was raised by a group of sheep. He was told that he was a sheep, learned to make "baa" sounds, and acted just like them. Then one day another lion came upon the flock and was amazed at what he saw. He went to this lion/sheep and asked, "What are you doing living with these sheep?" The lion/sheep replied, "I *am* a sheep!" And the lion said, "Oh no you're not – come with me" and he took him to a pool of water. The lion/sheep looked at his reflection, let out a mighty roar, and was transformed forever.

You are not a sheep—and you also are not inadequate or anything other than a child of God who has limitless human potential. Your value as a unique individual is significant, even though in childhood you may have been programmed to believe differently. As you work through this book, you'll become aware of your true self. Like the lion who thought he was a sheep until he saw his true reflection in the pool, you'll finally be free to let out that fierce roar, unencumbered by past programming.

3. <u>Acquiring new skills</u> will expand your world. Knowing how to deal with anger, anxiety and relationships will present you with new opportunities. And knowing how to validate yourself through self-talk will bring courage and self-worth. Understanding how to identify and feel your feelings will increase self-awareness and result in greater intimacy with others.

You can move away from beliefs/behaviors that are limiting your potential or causing pain, alter your adaptive behaviors, and instead move toward enjoying life, living in the moment and having your needs met. You may feel pain and other emotions as you realize certain connections to the past are still present. However as you work through and move on from past issues, the temporary pain will give way to a happier and healthier you.

You're Definitely Not Alone and Not to Blame

You may think you're so different from everyone else, but you're not. With over 23 million Americans raised in an alcoholic household and innumerable others from dysfunctional environments, how you're feeling is not so unusual. And it's important to recognize that you were definitely not responsible for your parent's or other people's alcoholism or choices. Children of alcoholics have a natural tendency to blame themselves and feel guilty. As a result, shame, depression, low self-esteem, troubled relationships or other difficulties can develop and continue into adult-hood. But you have the power and can learn the skills necessary to end the cycle. You deserve nothing less than a happy, productive and success-ful life.

Determining What Your Life's Purpose Is

How do you answer, "Why am I here, what are the special gifts I've been blessed with and how will I accomplish my life's purpose?" With insight gained from the exercises throughout this book, you'll make some very important discoveries. But certainly your life has a purpose, a mean-ing and, when you are willing to believe it, a divine plan to be fulfilled. You've got things to accomplish and important ways you can contribute.

The backside of a quilt looks messy with many different threads crossing in what seems like random directions. It's hard to image that a masterpiece can be the final result of all that apparent chaos – but it is. That may be true of our lives as we experience good and difficult occur-rences, which together help to shape our personalities. You are unique in this world and have life lessons to learn, to teach, and important missions to complete. There's also much fun to enjoy. For now, just have faith that your life is going to dramatically improve. Be patient with your progress. As long as you don't give up, your success is inevitable.

How Does the Growth, Recovery, or Healing Process Happen?

Knowledge brings freedom. Each chapter will deliver insights and information on how to improve yourself through healing techniques or skill development. Self-interview questions will help you revisit your past or expand your self-knowledge. Affirmations also play an important role in replacing self-defeating statements with realistic and positive ones. Finally, there are five-day action plans at the end of each chapter to expand your capabilities. They're designed to be both fun and productive experiences.

Positive Planning for a Tremendous Future

You can transform your life forever by remembering what happened to you as a child and taking action to recover from it. You've already taken charge: you have chosen to improve yourself by working through this book. Counterproductive belief systems or behaviors can yield to new, positive skills. Exercises will help you to master new abilities, affirmations will establish a positive conviction about yourself and a detailed mission statement will lead you to achievement you never thought possible. With increased self-awareness, you'll understand how the past is linked to your present and how to change its influence. And a connection with Spirit will guide you if you wish. You'll be moving beyond past limitations and taking constructive action to heal your emotional and spiritual injuries to pursue a healthier, more joy-filled life. It will take effort and time, but you're headed in a new and positive direction—one that will truly transform you.

The next chapter will help clarify some of your values, needs, beliefs and priorities. You'll also get to know yourself better. Consider how you'd treat your best friend if she or he started a life-altering journey requiring some contemplation and tough moments. Act as your own best friend and be as supportive as possible. Your life can transform into one filled with happiness, meaning and achievement. By pursuing self-awareness, developing skills and confronting various issues and beliefs, you will find that your potential is limitless. Best wishes on the journey toward the best years of your life!

Five-Day Action Plan for Growth & Success:
Place a checkmark in each box as you complete the associated action:
❑ Tell another person what you need from her or him and share something personal.
❑ See if you can identify a current behavior that has its origins in your past.
❑ Do something nice for yourself: eat ice cream, get a massage, and indulge in chocolate. Have some fun and laugh, read the comics, watch a comedian on TV, remember a practical joke.
❑ Using a mirror, look into your eyes, and repeat these affirmations aloud in the morning and evening, as many times as it takes until you feel confident about what's being said:
    • I love and care about you.
    • I'm much more than my past.
    • I am now in control of my life.

Summary:
✔ A child raised by an alcoholic can become an adult who is at a disadvantage, who still needs to learn certain lessons, and who must change incorrect belief systems.
✔ Your potential is unlimited once you free yourself from damaging patterns learned in your past.
✔ Time, effort and tenderness is required throughout your personal development journey.
✔ You can lovingly parent yourself and nourish your spirit.
✔ You're not alone: a large percentage of the U.S. population is trying to heal.
✔ Through the self-interview process, you'll gain insight into your life's purpose.
✔ Your past is history, but you still have to resolve issues that originated from it.
✔ Adaptive behaviors may have been helpful once, but can stifle you now.
✔ Once you've identified counterproductive behaviors or beliefs, you can begin to adopt more realistic ones.
✔ You can determine how to best nurture your inner child through introspection.

Chapter 2

Moving Beyond Survival Mode
Gain Self-Knowledge and Grasp the Big Picture

"I needed attention and would do anything to get it," Robin said. Her mother was an alcoholic and father's focus was on coping with it, so family love and validation wasn't available to her. To avoid emotional starvation, Robin looked to external sources. "Out of desperation, I'd sometimes do horrible things to score points. I beat up girls who weren't accepted as part of the 'in' crowd, shoplifted, and even had contests to see who could get guys into bed faster. Other times I was this sweet, innocent-looking person. Basically, I was a chameleon; ready to change to be whoever the people I was with wanted me to be. After a while I didn't know who I was. As an adult, I became so lost that it took years of recovery work before having any self-identity. After working on my recovery, I finally understand my needs, values, beliefs and stand behind them. I've gained the self-knowledge that was missing. Finally, I am being me and loving myself."

When you're in "survival mode" as a child, there's little opportunity to discover your own identity. As a result, an ACOA often has no clue who she or he really is. Self-understanding becomes a mystery because the childhood focus is almost entirely on getting basic needs met by others. That habit often continues as an adult. And a prolonged condition of "disconnect" from yourself results in feelings of isolation, self-alienation and confusion, as in Robin's earlier years.

This chapter aggressively helps you get in touch with your strengths, attributes, beliefs, values, needs and priorities. All these factors culminate to form your "personal foundation." In his book *The 7 Habits of Highly Effective People*, Stephen Covey suggests that the reader construct a mission statement. That entails identifying different roles you're engaged in and solidifying goals within each based upon your core values, wants, needs, beliefs and priorities. Then you will construct a structured blueprint and organized direction to follow. But first you have to possess sufficient self-knowledge and understanding.

That's not always so easy, because on top of the confusion caused by an alcoholic environment during childhood, there are current external factors that add to self-alienation. For example, we can misplace our beliefs, values, needs and priorities when in a relationship with someone who is domineering, or if we're members of a group that doesn't encourage individuality. And by going through life distracted or with limited awareness, we can lose sight of who we are and what we stand for. Or perhaps you're unsure of who you are in the first place because of the way you were raised. This "disconnect" can result in feelings of isolation, depression and confusion about what's important in our lives. It's not a good place to be. But we do not have to stay there.

It's time to find and connect with the real you. This chapter and the next don't concentrate on building specific skills but rather construct a "big picture" of your life. There will be more self-interview questions than usual, and they'll be intermingled rather than appear together as in other chapters. Be prepared to gain some insight.

Invisibility and You: Not Perfect Together

"I told an 8th grade classmate how my father kissed me on the lips when he was drunk and she told everyone in the class," said Sandra. "They all called me a freak. Rather than comfort from a friend, I received further humiliation and abuse. After that I kept quiet about what happened in my house. I constructed walls that no one could penetrate. They worked well, but left me lonely and isolated… even from myself."

As a child, you may have used several different tactics to keep "secrets" about the family turmoil you experienced or to be safe. Perhaps you maintained a low profile by keeping to yourself, changing the subject if someone asked personal questions or any number of other techniques. Perhaps they were helpful in past circumstances, but to have an emotionally healthy life today, you need to be authentic, open, know yourself and let at least one other person deeply know you. The shadow of your emotional wall reaches into all aspects of your life.

So let's do something about it. The more we express, accept and know about ourselves, the easier it is to authentically share with others and feel mutual love. How well do others know you and how well do you know yourself? Are you maintaining barriers constructed during childhood? You may have many friends, acquaintances and activities. People can know things about you, but perhaps you've become comfortable hiding behind a shield for defense. If that's true, there's a large price to pay because no one can love a mask. Superficial conversations can leave you feeling empty and alienated. And they don't help you build self-love and understanding. Therefore a healthier approach of reasonable self-disclosure should be considered.

Among other things, this healthier approach necessitates the building of your self-esteem, gradual removal of emotional walls and the establishment of an effective communication style. Each will be addressed in subsequent chapters. You're encouraged to enhance your proficiency with skills, to adopt a healthy emotional belief system and to share deeper feelings or values with people you care about. Only when you're visible can you grow, be loved, and have your life filled with support and positive acknowledgments from others.

What are some of your Strengths and Attributes?

You've survived some difficult times and acquired positive attributes along the way. Are you aware of them or do you spend more time acknowledging your shortcomings? If you can forgive yourself for not being perfect and instead appreciate your positive attributes, those strengths will expand in volume along with your self-acceptance.

Conversely, if you're in the habit of being self-critical, you may feel a resistance to recognizing or identifying your positive qualities. Some individuals believe they possess few constructive attributes and dismiss compliments while being consistently willing to receive and believe every criticism. If you can relate to this model, and are more critical of yourself than affirming, that habit should be changed.

Every one of us has desirable attributes. Take a look at the chart below and place a checkmark next to every trait that is descriptive of you. Even if you're not *always* caring, kind or whatever the attribute might be (who is?), give yourself the benefit of the doubt. You can always build from your strengths or attributes, as long as you know what they are.

__ caring	__ honest	__ loving	__ helpful
__ supportive	__ ethical	__ flexible	__ loyal
__ tolerant	__ sensitive	__ interesting	__ creative
__ dependable	__ positive	__ spiritual	__ giving
__ open	__ forgiving	__ connected	__ inspiring
__ kind	__ responsible	__ respectful	__ attentive
__ stable	__ gentle	__ reliable	__ honorable
__ trusting	__ productive	__ smart	__ compassionate

Let's further explore some of your powerfully good attributes in the self-interview process. There have certainly been times when you've been kind and compassionate with others. I encourage you to treat yourself in an equally kind manner by recognizing the good in you.

Self-Interview Taping Questions:
• What are your most valuable attributes?
• Who taught you these qualities? What makes them so important?
• What does your closest friend most appreciate about you?
• How have you impacted someone's life through your kindness and your caring qualities?
• What's been your greatest accomplishment as a result of your personal strengths?
• Who validates you? How can you best validate yourself?

After each succession of questions in this chapter, take the time to listen carefully to your answers and reflect on them.

Perfection is impossible for a human being; there's always room for improvement. But recognizing that you're building from a base of positive and valuable qualities will make your progress measurable. Don't be concerned if you do not advance as far or as quickly as you think you should. Your base of positive abilities and attributes can continue to grow beyond your expectations. Recognize and appreciate where you're coming from, but also know that you'll always be improving, even though you may experience some stumbles along the way.

Values Chart Your Direction

What are your priorities in life? Most of your choices are based on ranking. A simplistic example of prioritization is: *if your house was on fire and you only had time to grab one item, what would it be?* Or *if you were asked to do something unethical by your boss, which ranks higher:*

your code of ethics or your job? Answers to these questions can depend
on many factors, but usually your decisions will be based on how highly
you value each at a particular moment. The decisions aren't always
as clear as you'd like. But by knowing distinctly what your *values* are,
you'll be better able to make the right choices. Let's clarify some of your
values in this brief exercise. Next to each word, rate each item's importance from 1 – 10 (1 = not valued, 10 = very highly valued):

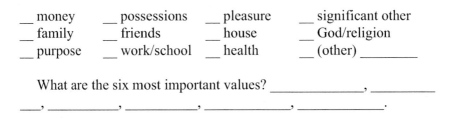

__ money   __ possessions   __ pleasure   __ significant other
__ family   __ friends   __ house   __ God/religion
__ purpose   __ work/school   __ health   __ (other) _____

What are the six most important values? _____ , _____

___ , _____ , _____ , _____ , _____ .

These are some of the highest priorities in your life. This self-examination clarifies your values and provides a direction to follow. If there
are other things requiring your attention or effort, are you wasting your
time with them? Not necessarily; in fact being a well-rounded individual
is quite important. There are volunteer activities, opportunities to learn,
and also many experiences where you can just have fun and unwind.
This exercise simply helps you prioritize what's really important, and by
default what isn't. But that doesn't mean you have to become excessively
intense about your top priorities. Most of your time and energy will
naturally be devoted to what really matters, but it's best to be balanced in
your approach. Your life is constantly evolving, so leaving time for new
interests and priorities to develop may also be quite worthwhile.

Identifying Your Needs is Essential for Living

"I needed to be loved and held but that hardly ever happened," remembered Candice. "My mom was too busy with her true love: a bottle
of booze. To get by, I shut down all my needs that went beyond those
required to survive another day."

When you were a child, some (perhaps many) of your needs weren't
met. At the time there may have been little you could do about it. But
you're an adult now and have all the necessary abilities to ensure that
your basic needs are satisfied. Obviously when you're hungry, food is
what you require, but how about needs beyond that? There's a "hierarchy

of needs" according to Abraham Maslow. It begins with those needs required for survival (physiological or biological) such as food, water and sleep. They must be satisfied before all others. Once they are taken care of, we look for safety and security. When those requirements are met, we desire the sense of belonging, love and sex. Then comes self-esteem or recognition, and finally self-actualization.

You have the ability to satisfy your own physiological and safety needs, even if you have to temporarily use adaptive behaviors to do so. However a sense of belonging, high self-esteem, love and self-actualization can be somewhat elusive at times. Place a checkmark next to some of your current unmet needs:

__ food	__ closeness	__ validation	__ boundaries
__ sleep	__ caring	__ love	__ to know God
__ shelter	__ to belong	__ sex	__ a life mission
__ safety	__ respect	__ to play	__ forgiveness
__ friends	__ appreciation	__ intimacy	__ share feelings
__ nurturing	__ be protected	__ be hugged	__ control

What are the 6 most important needs *not* currently being met? _____ _____, _____, _____, _____, _____, _____. Rank them in order of importance. You probably know which ones need to be satisfied first, but consider Mazlow's hierarchy, if needed. Those related to survival and safety need to be addressed without delay. Consider them urgent necessities and take appropriate and immediate action.

Once those needs are fulfilled, then you can begin to satisfy others in order of your priorities. You've identified goals and it may take some time to achieve them, but they are all attainable. However, keep in mind that too much of a good thing is not a good thing. For example, you may have identified "control" as one of your needs. It's desirable to feel in control of your situation, especially when you're coming from a childhood environment where you had none. But in reality, you can only control yourself and your reactions to what's happening around you. Certainly, you can't control another person—it's fruitless to try. If control is an unrealistic obsession, you can become rigid, inflexible and detached from your emotions. That's when relationships suffer and you end up not only losing the very control you were trying to establish, but also alienating others and perhaps experiencing other losses as a result. Seeking reasonable control may be acceptable, but thinking in terms of "all or nothing" is almost always counterproductive. So take things in moderation and be flexible. Be confident that the actions you take will result in having your needs met. They will.

Your Beliefs Create Reality

We have to be so careful about what we accept into our belief system. There's a lot of truth in the saying, "what you believe, you can conceive (bring into existence)." It's intended to reinforce the universal law that states, "whatever you place into your mind and focus on will come to fruition." But it works for both a positive and negative result. Some of your beliefs may be based upon experiences or things that were said to you in childhood. Perhaps they originated in a polluted environment where parents were affected by alcoholism, children were bullies and/or people were abusive. Negative beliefs about yourself that originated in such a state are beliefs that need to be challenged. They are false in nature and unnecessarily destructive. We call these negative beliefs "stinking thinking." It's time to reexamine them, find their origins and change. Some examples of *stinking thinking* are:

, I'm worthless and will be abandoned if I don't please others.
, When I make a mistake it means I'm a failure.
, No one could love me if they knew the real me.
, I'm going to fail and I won't amount to anything.
, I'm not good enough.
, I can't trust anyone.

All of the above statements are untrue and quite damaging. If friends say such things about themselves, you'd probably correct them. Give yourself that same consideration. You can alter harmful beliefs and adopt correct, rational and truthful ones.

Self-Interview Taping Questions:

Values:

• What do you value?
• What's most important in your life? What are you willing to give up to achieve or protect it?
• What are some qualities you've seen in others that you'd like to also have?
• What things do you like about yourself? What would you like to change?

Needs:
- What unfulfilled needs require your immediate action? How will you go about satisfying them?
- How can you take action to satisfy your less crucial, but still important needs?
- Is there anything missing from your life?
- What are the things you most desire?

Beliefs:
- Describe a few destructive beliefs you have about yourself that need to be changed.
- Where did it originate? How do you think you can change the destructive belief?
- What help would you need, or can you do this yourself?
- What positive beliefs do you have about yourself?

Your Relationships: Great and Not So Great

Everyone alive has had relationships that haven't worked out. Perhaps those previous experiences have come to teach us lessons. If we learn from them, the same mistakes don't have to be repeated. But we ACOAs, have to consider other factors that influence our behaviors with others—including how we choose our mates. For example, a partner who is loving one moment and cold or abusive the next mirrors the behavior of an alcoholic parent. While you may not enjoy being treated that way, it is a familiar way of relating and may seem somewhat intriguing or attractive to you. That's why it's particularly important to look at your past, recognize what still may be guiding you in a wrong direction and change course if necessary. Another consideration is that in order to have and maintain a healthy, meaningful relationship with someone, you first have to enjoy one with yourself. That includes self-awareness, the willingness to work on resolving problems and more. A relationship based on NEEDING to be with each other will inevitably fail. But when two emotionally and spiritually healthy people come together because they WANT to, the foundation is strong for a relationship that will flourish and last. Work on your own recovery first and you'll achieve success.

Many aspects of relationships will be addressed in a later chapter. For now, you can explore some experiences you've had.

Self-Interview Taping Questions:
- Describe your most intimate relationship and how deeply the sharing of secrets was or currently is.

• How would your closest friend describe you?
• What would you like other people to say about you?
• Do you feel you've established and maintained appropriate boundaries with others? How do you react if they are violated?
• Who would you like to have as a friend and why? What's holding you back?

Becoming fully aware of what has or has not worked in relationships will give you clues about where adjustments might be needed. You can learn more about yourself and become successful with your interactions.

What Self-Knowledge Brings

Discover everything you can about yourself because you're the director of your own life, present and future. You can make it joyful or sad. With self-awareness, you can free your spirit from forces that enslave it. If you choose, you can discard unnecessary emotional baggage, say good-bye to being insecure and instead feel truly worthy. With self-awareness and acceptance, you can move forward with increased confidence, hope and direction. You'll have the freedom and strength to be your best.

Finally, give ample thought to the following general, yet insightful, questions. Then replay and consider your answers.

Self-Interview Taping Questions:
• Describe your current living arrangements.
• What's it like at work or school? If you're unemployed or underemployed, what do you do with your day?
• Describe yourself. What are you all about? Do you like yourself?
• What characteristics do you possess? (Are you fun-loving, honest, depressed, sensitive, cautious, fair, distant, needy, loyal, etc.?)
• What makes you happy, sad or upset? What can get you feeling better?
• Recognizing that you're not perfect, describe two mistakes you've made that you'd like to correct if it were possible.
• If money were no object, what would you be doing right now?
• What do you do best? If you could name only one God-given, innate talent that you have, what would it be?
• Make believe you had three wishes. What would they be?
• What would you like to accomplish with your life? What will be your legacy?

I know this chapter has been hard work for you, but it's a necessary step toward wholeness. Understanding yourself becomes easier when you can identify and interpret your feelings. The next chapter will concentrate on those areas. It will offer suggestions on how to overcome resistance to feeling, how to break free from past emotions, and how various emotions relate to one another. You'll discover ways to better express yourself and grasp an understanding of what you're really feeling below the surface. Self-knowledge will bring you increased levels of awareness that can make further growth and recovery possible.

Five-Day Action Plan for Growth & Success:
Place a checkmark in each box as you complete the associated action:
❑ Send yourself a greeting card expressing how much you are appreciated and valued.
❑ Try to be more receptive to receiving from others. If you're given a compliment, a gift, or someone treats you with kindness, simply say "thank you" and acknowledge that you appreciate it.
❑ In a mirror, look into your eyes and repeat these affirmations aloud in the morning and evening, as many times as it takes until you feel confident about what's being said:
   • I have wonderful qualities.
   • I'm getting better every day.

Summary:
✔ By being emotionally invisible, you can lose sight of who you are.
✔ We all have desirable attributes, and you can build from your strengths as long as you're aware of them.
✔ Being authentic and letting another person know the real you is essential to living an emotionally healthy life. Strive to fully know, love and be yourself.
✔ Your beliefs create your reality and if some originated in a polluted environment, they should be replaced with healthier ones.
✔ Needs have to be prioritized; then you can take action to satisfy the crucial ones first.
✔ Performing an autopsy on past relationships that haven't worked may provide you with valuable information.
✔ With increased self-knowledge, you can free your spirit of forces that may be enslaving it.
✔ Your beliefs, values, wants, needs and priorities combine to chart your life's direction.
✔ Your life has not been ruined by your childhood. The best years of your life are coming and now you're in control.

Chapter 3

Understanding the Reluctance to Feel
Overcome Negative Feelings, Enjoy Positive Ones

"I'd walk home from school always wondering if my mother would be there to greet me as a raving drunken maniac or a loving parent," remembered Paulo. "It was scary because I never knew what to expect—and I'd be in a constant state of tension until I saw her. When sober, my mother loved me but I never trusted that side of her, because from experience I knew it wouldn't last. When alcohol ruled her behavior, she was incredibly abusive and her behavior could change quickly. That inconsistency was unbearable. So I dealt with it by shutting down, or at least numbing, my emotions to avoid pain or disappointment. But I eventually became a plastic figure, unloving and unlovable, rather than evolving into an adult human being with feelings. And now my current relationships are superficial at best."

We ACOAs learned to shut down our feelings as children, but that survival technique can cause problems for today's relationships. If emotions are unexpressed or unidentifiable, intimate communication becomes impossible. And then there are times we're so alienated from our feelings that we react strangely to certain situations but have no idea why. When discomfort happens, it can trigger automatic responses learned as a child that are inappropriate in today's environment or situation. Chapter 3 illustrates six main categories of feelings and words associated with each for identification of what you are experiencing. You can explore why there might be a reluctance to feel and see how temporary pain from remembering past events can result in empowerment and recovery. In addition, you can determine where inappropriate responses are coming from and see how to better respond. Most importantly, you'll become aware of your feelings, understand emotions and learn how to express them appropriately.

Burying your True Feelings in Relationships; Perils of Fantasy

"From day one, we had an instant connection as never experienced before in either of our lives," said Rich of his friend Eleanor. "It was like we had one soul in two bodies, but we were both in relationships so simply developed a wonderful friendship. Then after two years, I became available and she was having trouble in her relationship. I started thinking about the potential between us and in the back of my mind, believed if she ever became available, I'd marry her. At the same time, others noticed our closeness and made comments about how we seemed like soulmates. The comments made it easier for me to develop 'in love' feelings, however I mostly denied them to myself and never discussed them with her because I was afraid of ruining everything. And it turned out I had no idea how strong the feelings had become—no idea at all until there was a massive explosion. The day I realized she just saw me as a friend and never to be anything more, I said things I'll regret to my dying day and lost my best friend as a result. My expectations had become much higher. Now if we had only talked earlier, it would have brought me back to reality, increased understanding and dissipated the romantic feelings. We'd still be best friends—but I didn't bring it up and look at the results. Now we don't talk, she has bad feelings about me; I've lost her forever on all levels and feel horrible about myself. By not facing my true feelings or being honest with them, and with her, I've caused the severing of a true soul connection, the destruction of a long-term friendship and hurt a truly wonderful, much loved person."

In general, if you keep emotions buried, they fester and eventually surface. And in this case, Rich's suppressed feelings exploded like an erupting volcano, doing just as much damage. And if you live with a fantasy of what "might be," it can produce disastrous results including the loss of valuable friendships and terribly hurt feelings. *You must be true about who you are, how you feel about others, and sincerely communicate on an ongoing basis to resolve issues and maintain healthy relationships.*

Rich's experience does NOT mean that men and women can't be friends. The lesson to learn is that when soul or other emotional connections intensify, action needs to be taken and resolution pursued or explosions will follow. As an ACOA, he was thinking about "what might be possible" in the relationship rather than focusing and clarifying what was in the present. He was looking for love—this time in the wrong place.

Do you ever find yourself doing the same? We adult children need to be loved very badly. You may sometimes pick up on friendly gestures and misinterpret the depth of the other person's feelings. In addition, if you feel unlovable, you may make more out of a friendship because it makes you feel good. Then you inadvertently build up this fantasy relationship until expectations are more than the relationship will support. That's why it's important to remain current and TALK ABOUT YOUR FEELINGS.

Consider some other dynamics behind your relationships. As an adult child, you may push people away if you think they might be hinting at rejecting you. Abandonment issues kick in and you find yourself dumping the other person before he or she theoretically dumps you. Where is all this coming from? As a child, you may have coped by silently but emotionally saying to your alcoholic parent, "You don't love me - I don't need you - get away," and constructed emotional barriers. Today you perhaps are continuing that behavior and in the process, destroying otherwise wonderful relationships by ending communication or lashing out in hurt or anger. ACOAs can also have the tendency to do the opposite – desperately hang on to a relationship where you're giving or feeling more than the other person is. *Sometimes you can diminish your own needs to fit what you think someone else is willing to give, but in the end will likely lose everything, including self-esteem, identity and the love of people who matter the most.*

How do you go about clarifying and talking about feelings? Request a meeting with the other person and say you have something important to discuss. When bringing up feelings about each other, it's important to be clear and sincere. So if you have extremely raw or intense emotions, delay the meeting and take time to cool down first to avoid saying things you might later regret. When you communicate, try and stay in the "adult you," not the "hurt child you" who might simply sabotage the relationship using the "all or nothing" mentality learned in childhood. There are communication (active listening) skills explained in a later chapter that can help you with such discussions. Do a reality check and eliminate fantasy as much as possible. Be open and honest and if feelings are not reciprocal, readjust your expectations, love yourself, then when you'd like to, look for someone you might be more compatible with.

You have options. If your feelings are unrequited but very strong, you might need to take a breather from a relationship - hopefully in an amicable and loving way. After all, the other person is not offering what you want and there are incompatible aims. You can also ask him or her to call if circumstances change in the future (without promising your availability). If you're able to dissipate your intense but unreciprocated feelings, a friendship can continue—although perhaps at a different level. Consider all your options before taking action.

Finally, burying your feelings or emotionally investing in a fantasy relationship can get you stuck. Potential partners or friends might be all around but you're not looking. You need to get unstuck by directly addressing this issue. There has to be a paradigm shift in consciousness so each of you can see the other differently. It can temporarily hurt to address this, but if you don't, there likely will be grave consequences and lost opportunities.

In the end, what's meant to be will happen. What's NOT meant to be can't be forced and you can't talk people into loving you. Be in touch and communicative with your feelings, realistic with relationships and move forward to reach your highest good—always being true with your most important relationship, the one you have with your inner self.

Benefits of *Feeling* your Feelings

Sometimes, you might feel like two different people: the way you are at your best and worst. A major difference is often how in touch you are with your feelings. You're at your best when you understand and embrace your emotions, at your worst when you avoid them. There are innumerable reasons to break down your emotional walls and awaken your emotions, but to name just a few...

• You'll be empowered to resolve painful or hurtful feelings from your past. No longer will they be lurking in the background, only to be triggered over and over again causing overreactions to present day occurrences. By feeling your emotions, you can finally become aware of past hurts, confront them and move on.

• You'll experience true intimacy, a sense of being appreciated and belonging. Self-awareness leads to self-acceptance and self-love. Once you're able to love yourself, it opens the door to loving and being loved by others.

• You'll build a happier life, discover your inner strengths, and become free of many self-defeating attitudes. Increased awareness means experiencing both good and bad feelings. Emotional discomfort raises a red flag and lets you know that danger is present and action is needed. By being aware, you're empowering yourself to be your own protector.

• By becoming fully in touch with yourself, you're free to be authentic in your present day relationships and have them thrive rather than merely survive or end. You'll experience a sense of well-being, increased self-worth and enjoy relationships by expressing your honest feelings.

• A new life will begin where you'll experience joy - and some pain, too - but one where you will be fully present, real and connected.

As you get in touch with your emotions (possibly for the first time), have faith in the present and future. Remember that any discomfort you might feel is a *temporary* condition. After gaining awareness of your feelings, accepting them and releasing unnecessary emotional baggage, you'll be free to love yourself and love life in a new way. It's only a matter of time and effort to be extricated from the "emotional dead zone" experienced in childhood, to start feeling and to live a fulfilling life.

What Causes a Reluctance to Feel?

When you were growing up, how could you possibly have survived, if you fully felt your emotions?

"I had a *Jekyll and Hyde* mom," remembered Patty. "She'd hug and love me when sober but after a few drinks, she'd turn into a monster. I never knew what to expect. So I stopped feeling, eliminated the highs and lows, to enable me to live through it all."

One lesson commonly learned from a childhood with an alcoholic parent is "*I love you*" one minute, and "*go away*" the next. The survival technique to cope with this quixotic behavior was to shut down feelings and block emotional intensity that resulted from the unpredictability of an alcoholic parent or ongoing traumatic events. As a result, today you might find yourself unable to identify your feelings. In addition, if and when they do surface, you may sense that they are too intense and out of your control.

"I can't tell you how pissed off I was when my father used to slobber over me when drunk," said Maria. "But I was only a kid and couldn't push him away. Today if my boyfriend has a glass of wine and gets any-where near me, I freak out. I scream at him, tell him to get away from me and don't want to see him for days. Why do I overreact like that?"

The easy thing to do is repress/quash your feelings again, just as you did in childhood. It's a cycle that keeps you from fully living, but an understandable choice considering the background of an ACOA.

Emotional Toothaches

Why do we detach from our emotional selves? People gravitate toward pleasure and away from pain. It's a natural tendency. When the dentist drills a tooth for a root canal, most people prefer Novocaine or some other temporary numbing device. And when the discomfort is emotional, numbing from sleeping pills, excessive TV, reading, drinking, gambling, sex, etc., can bring temporary relief. The key word is TEMPORARY. There's an enormous price to pay if numbing, disowning, unawareness of, or not communicating your feelings has become your way of life because of your upbringing in an alcoholic home. In order to understand yourself, to live a fully engaged life and to deal effectively with issues, it's vitally important to be in touch with your emotions.

How to Overcome Reluctance to Feel

Feelings and worms are alike: you can bury them but they'll eventually make their way to the surface. And when repressed feelings resurface, it would be helpful to understand what's happening. Only then can you terminate the cycle that has you reliving past hurts or triggering the endless suppression of emotions through experiences that happen today.

Shelly observed, "Not only have I been hurt in childhood, but I've also had one relationship after another fail. It's easier to simply deaden my emotions." Perhaps like Shelly, you're afraid to feel because you've been hurt. Some people want to be loved but believe they're unlovable, so they avoid the possibility of rejection through emotional distancing. That causes a self-perpetuating cycle. When he or she withholds feelings, eventually the friend/lover finds the relationship too superficial and leaves, proving again the presumption of being unlovable. By not feeling, understanding, and coping with your losses, they unfortunately tend to recur.

Having a reluctance to feel can taint what's positive in life and make it seem like nothing is worthwhile. You deserve better than that. There's no doubt that reawakening buried feelings can cause temporary discom-

fort. When you learn any type of new skill or are surprised by certain
emotions, it's natural to feel uncomfortable. But your emotional self,
your child within and your spirit need to experience feelings in order to
flourish. Using temporary pain to motivate change can help to end the
cycle of not feeling, talking or healing—which in turn will lead to a happier life.

So how do you overcome the non-feeling cycle? First you'll have to
decide this is what you want to do. If you think about the costs of staying
where you are and the benefits of changing, it's not too difficult a decision. Next comes the realization that what worked during childhood may
be inappropriate now. In fact it may prevent love, self-understanding and
success.

If you are unaware of your feelings, the categories of feelings contained in this chapter may be helpful. Each category has an accompanying list of emotions. Refer to them and try to identify which emotions
you are feeling—especially if a current event is causing you discomfort
or pleasure. Consider this an ongoing exercise. Then talk about your
feelings to a friend, in a small group, or to a therapist. Refer often to the
feelings checklist and repeat the five-day exercise at the conclusion of
this chapter when needed. There are other techniques throughout this
book that can help you to feel, and difficult emotions will come up in the
process, so you might consider not doing it alone. ACOA groups, close
friends or therapists are all viable options for collaboration.

How to Break Loose from Past Emotional Events

"Once I let go of the anger toward my father for his past alcohol
abuse, my whole emotional landscape changed," said Shelly. "Suddenly
all of my relationships were more alive and positive. I had to resolve past
negative feelings before there was room for new positive ones."

Unless you are aware of connections that may exist between your past
and present feelings, emotional experiences will continue to take you
to places best avoided. And unless you let go of the negative emotions
encountered as a child, they will continue to affect your life by preclud-
ing many positive feelings. No matter what happened in the past, nothing
can compare to the damage you could do to yourself in the present by
ignoring emotions, retaining old resentments or believing things can't get
better. Emotions felt in the present need to be examined and dealt with in
the present—without returning to a similar feeling perhaps experienced

in childhood within a traumatic event. And there's the question: do you know what you're feeling?

To help identify your emotions, there are several lists of "feeling" words in this chapter. Once the emotion is identified, try to determine its true origin when you're feeling it—especially if the intensity is high. Awareness leads to understanding and resolution.

Gain without Pain?

It would be nice to build muscles without exercising. And it would be great to lose weight while also eating brownies, fudge, chocolate and gallons of ice cream. But that's not the way it works with fitness or weight reduction. Nor is it the way to emotional healing and growth. In fact, the times when you experience the greatest growth and intimacy may occur when pain gets your attention – as long as you are willing to work through the pain to get past it.

In order to get free of past emotional turmoil, we need to confront what happened and consider how it might be affecting our present lives. This process ends the cycle of reliving past hurts. Temporary pain from remembering past events can result in empowerment and recovery. By working through issues, you can see their residual power diminish. This process can be witnessed every day in ACOA groups: participants connect past events to present feelings/beliefs and move forward to recovery.

While all negative feelings are derived from pain, they vary in intensity. In addition, one may lead to another. Author Dr. David Viscott categorized them and described how they interact:

• <u>Anxiety</u> comes from thoughts of a possible future hurt.
• <u>Hurt</u> is a natural response to pain or loss.
• <u>Anger</u> can be a response to being <u>hurt</u> or an attack
• <u>Guilt</u> comes from *unexpressed* <u>anger</u> or feeling badly about something you've done.
• <u>Depression</u> results from pain that remains *chronically* unexpressed.

Consider your experiences as you answer the following questions for each category:

Self-Interview Taping Questions:
Anxiety:
• What are you feeling anxious about? When did you feel this way as a child?
• What could be the worst thing that might happen? Could you live with that?

Hurt:
• What do you feel sad about? What can you do to relieve some of the sadness?
• Describe your two greatest emotional injuries. How did you recover from the experiences?

Anger:
• What annoys you? Are there other feelings behind your anger (for example feeling hurt or unappreciated)?
• How do you express anger? What happens when you do and what happens when you don't?

Guilt:
• What do you feel guilty about? If you could, how would you have done things differently?
• Is your guilt coming from something you've done, not done, or from unexpressed pain?

Depression:
• Why do you think you're depressed?
• What will you do today to get help?

Positive Feelings:
• When have you been the happiest and what makes you happy?
• When have you felt unconditional love?
• What are you most grateful for?

Anxiety: Feeling Afraid

Anxiety is an expectation of <u>future</u> hurt or loss, a sense that something bad may happen. "Coming home from school, as soon as I walked up my block I could tell that my mother was home and drunk," said Trisha. "I expected it every day and usually was correct. I hated that walk home."

Words in the "Anxiety family"

• nervous	• tense	• afraid	• panicky	• fretting
• fearful	• jittery	• anxious	• reluctant	• scared
• concerned	• insecure	• troubled	• confused	• uncomfortable
• hesitant	• flustered	• shy	• helpless	• overwhelmed

How do you cope with anxiety or the fear about something bad that might happen in your near or distant future? Trisha, from experience, learned that her mother would often be waiting for her in an inebriated condition. Today, do you find yourself in a regular state of anxiety without apparent reason? Is it a habit carried over from childhood? If so, try a new perspective and consciously stay in the present. Consider your anxiousness nothing more than a warning signal, similar to the flag that a road worker may wave to get you to slow down. You know that for any motor vehicle to work correctly, you need both an accelerator and brake pedal. Anxiety in this case is just slowing you down and warning you to be cautious. Since you've reduced your speed, there's time to consider what might go wrong and how you could proactively prepare. Another approach is to think about what the worst-case scenario might be and then accept it. Also consider the other possible outcomes. Realize that in almost every case, you'd survive. Realize that you could get through whatever you need to get through and your anxiety level will diminish. Think about what type of loss might result and be willing to accept the worst but proceed with the belief that it will be okay.

If it doesn't work out perfectly, still give yourself credit for trying. After all, you're growing and bound to make some mistakes. Try to accept imperfections, recognizing that you're only human. Making an effort shows that you have the courage to move out of your comfort zone in order to improve yourself.

If your anxiety is coming from a possible loss of love and companionship from someone, remember that you will remain a lovable person, with or without them. Having anxious feelings will change nothing. Even if your relationship does end, you will be loved again.

Hurt: Feeling Sad

This emotion can have you experience present or remembered pain, feel loss or injury, and bring with it the belief that there'll be no one to comfort you.

Words in the "Hurt family"

• sorry	• grieving	• unhappy	• guilty	• discouraged
• different	• loneliness	• ashamed	• foolish	• disappointed
• betrayed	• pessimistic	• rejected	• cheated	• empty
• needy	• neglected	• depleted	• victimized	• unappreciated
• injured	• wounded	• dejected		

How do you cope with feeling hurt or sad? When you feel depleted, betrayed, or experience a great loss, it's hard to think that things will ever get better. But they will when you continually tell yourself that truth. It may take time, some processing of your feelings or a conscious effort to move on. While you're feeling this sadness, acknowledge it as real. You have to identify feelings before being able to deal with the real issues. You may learn valuable lessons, reevaluate your direction in life or simply need to grieve. A caring friend may support you through the process, but if you're feeling a *profound* sadness, it may be best to join a support group, call a hotline or seek the help of a mental health professional. Whatever you choose, talking it through will dissipate some of the emotional clouds. You will get through it, but it will take time and dedication.

Feeling hurt or sad is a natural response when you experience a loss. Those feelings have to be worked through. Be patient with the process and compassionate with yourself.

Anger: Expressed or Unexpressed

This is a particularly hard emotion to deal with and especially scary for those of us raised in alcoholic households where violence or verbal abuse was present. After all, if we expressed anger toward an alcoholic parent, serious repercussions were possible. So the emotion was frequently hidden. That repressive approach often continues after a child becomes an adult. But anger is an honest feeling that may be expressed in productive, constructive, appropriate ways – and it should be. You need to vent those feelings. If one of the following "anger family" words describes your emotional state, you're feeling angry:

Words in the "Anger family"

• irritated	• resentful	• annoyed	• scornful	• enraged
• bitter	• impatient	• pissed	• volatile	• furious
• irate	• mad	• despising	• aggravated	• explosive

"If I expressed the least bit of anger toward my *volatile when drunk* father, it would just make matters worse and I'd get the crap beaten out of me," said Mark. "I just stuffed it and usually do the same today. I don't want to get anyone mad at me. But then I feel like an idiot for not standing up for myself."

Anger is a natural reaction to hurt. When unexpressed, it can be directed internally, causing you additional pain—so it must be released in some manner, rather than ignored. An entire chapter on anger appears later in the book. For now, recognize that if you deal with it constructively, anger can be a motivator and protector.

Guilt: Anger Within

Guilt can result from unexpressed pain or something improper that you've done. When anger is held in and turned against yourself, that's where the punishment will be directed. But you also may feel guilty about causing pain for others or benefiting improperly as a result of your actions.

Words in the "Guilt family"
- remorseful   • sorry   • unworthy   • deserving punishment
- blamed   • regrets   • bad   • at fault

How can you handle guilt? If you've acted improperly, hurt others or were not ethical, you should make amends – the sooner the better. Apologize and do whatever is necessary to try to undo the harm. However, if anger turned into yourself is the origin of your guilt, you'll need to find a way to express the original emotion to get relief. Sometimes it's dangerous to do so directly; or possibly the person who was responsible is no longer accessible, such as a deceased parent. There are many ways of expressing anger without necessarily confronting the person who kindled it. You can write a letter and burn it. You can pencil the person's name on the bottom of your shoe and figuratively walk all over them. Anything is better than directing your fury inward. Some guilt should not be yours to carry and it needs to be let go. For example, you did not cause your parent's drinking or behavior—it's not your fault in any way. Whatever the cause, guilt has to be resolved or it can evolve into depression.

Depression: Chronically Unexpressed Pain

When we are seriously depressed, we feel hopeless, have low energy, want to be left alone in our misery and can almost be at the point of not wanting to live.

Words in the "Depressed family"
- worthless   • empty   • lonely   • miserable   • helpless
- unloved   • abandoned   • valueless   • lifeless   • victimized
- detached   • unaccepted

Depression can originate from a chemical imbalance or emotional factors - but it is treatable. The first step it is to obtain an accurate diagnosis. That's why it's necessary to visit a health professional if and when you experience symptoms of depression such as: persistent sadness, difficulty concentrating, loss of interest in activities you previously enjoyed, excessive sleep time, change in appetite or thoughts of hurting yourself. Whatever you do, don't isolate yourself, even though that's exactly what your inclination might be. Depression is curable but it will not go away by itself. Take care of yourself by contacting a doctor or therapist.

Anxiety, hurt, anger, guilt and depression are emotions associated with real or projected pain. But let us not forget that there are so many other feelings that generate exhilaration and happiness. Let's consider some.

Positive feelings

Ah, this is much better. Positive emotions are the easiest to understand and vary only in degrees of intensity.

Words in the "Positive family"

• glad	• pleased	• excited	• hopeful	• loved
• satisfied	• secure	• playful	• calm	• contented
• optimistic	• trusting	• relieved	• romantic	• thankful
• accepted	• confident	• comfortable	• sexy	• complete

These emotions deserve equal time – in fact the majority of our time. Sometimes we don't pay enough attention to them because we're so preoccupied with what's going wrong instead of what's good in our lives. Try to become aware of what brings you joy. You'll not only have a more positive attitude, but you will also know where to go to experience positive feelings again. By focusing on what brings positive emotions, you many even discover a new personal or professional direction for your life.

How to Overcome Negative Feelings and Enjoy Positive Ones

"I was feeling pessimistic about the job interview I was about to do," said Karl. "Those old tapes formed during childhood kept playing in my head, saying that I wouldn't amount to anything. But I wanted to prove them wrong, wanted to be successful and independent. I knew where my feelings of inadequacy originated and this time left my past history behind me, put my doubts aside and *acted* as though I was already a success and that the company would be lucky to have me. Two days later I was offered the job at an attractive salary."

Emotions are neither good nor bad, they are simply natural human responses. But when negative feelings overwhelm and keep you from living a pleasurable or constructive existence, they are problematic. You can take positive actions instead. The lives we lead will always contain times of joy and sorrow. Our histories will always be with us—traumatic childhood events included. But once you fully understand your feelings and deal with the issues behind them, their negative impact diminishes. That will leave room for positive emotions to take their place. This chapter has provided an overview and identified categories of feelings along with some of their associated words. These words can assist you if there's difficulty in accessing or assigning a description to your emotions. Refer to the lists as we go into more depth in other chapters and until you become more proficient at naming your feelings. Once aware of what your feelings are, look deeper into the cause[s] and possible ways to alleviate your negative baggage. That may include talking to the person who originated a causative event, writing a letter to express your feelings and ripping it up, acting as though you've already let go of negative feels or other constructive actions. Once expressed, the intensity will be diminished and you can move on to more enjoyable emotions.

Feeling, Understanding and Expressing Emotions Electrifies

Feelings can knock your socks off. They can electrify you and cause a positive or negative power surge. Whichever one it is, you become more alive, acquire self-knowledge and become more authentic in relationships. Expressing even *negative* feelings can actually produce *positive* results.

For instance, Jack and Diana spoke on the phone in the afternoon and planned to meet at an ACOA meeting that evening. During the phone call, she told him how he was always on her mind. But at the meeting, Jack perceived Diana to be somewhat distant. The next day he said to her, "We had a great conversation yesterday afternoon, but I was feeling hurt last night when you quickly walked away from me. We barely said hello and you were off to talk with Charlie. I was feeling kind of sad to begin with, and when you did that, I thought it was a true indicator of how insignificant our friendship really is to you. It brought me back to my childhood when I always got the *I love you, go away* routine. There had been closeness in the afternoon and rejection at night. It was history repeating itself and I felt hurt and unloved."

But Diana meant no disrespect. She needed a job and rushed to speak with Charlie about an opening at his company before he disappeared. Jack started the evening in a dejected mood and overreacted to the unintentional interruption of their conversation. They both realized the dynamics of the situation and talked about their feelings. Not only was there resolution, but they also discovered the high degree to which they really cared about one another.

By sharing your feelings, disagreements can be resolved, greater intimacy can be achieved or you can simply feel good about expressing yourself. But identifying your feelings and knowing how to express them doesn't obligate you to do so in every situation, so *discretion* is the key.

Become aware of your feelings, understand emotions and express them appropriately. You can only win by doing so.

Without feeling confident about yourself, it's difficult to openly express your emotions. The next chapter will show how to increase your self-confidence and self-worth.

Five-Day Action Plan for Growth & Success:
Place a checkmark in each box as you complete the associated action:

❏   Make a record of your emotions – every major feeling you have during the next five days. Include every joy, pleasure, satisfaction and contentment along with every hurt, anger, regret, and sadness. *Then determine the cause and what you did to increase or diminish it.* If you're unsure of what you're feeling, consider the emotions listed below or others shown in this chapter.

__ happy	__ glad	__ confident	__ mad
__ contented	__ cheery	__ angry	__ discouraged
__ satisfied	__ exhilarated	__ indifferent	__ fearful
__ peaceful	__ playful	__ distrustful	__ sad
__ joyous	__ grateful	__ tense	__ ashamed
__ ecstatic	__ concerned	__ suffocated	__ embarrassed
__ hopeless	__ uneasy	__ insecure	__ inadequate
__ depressed	__ guilty	__ abandoned	__ trapped
__ nervous	__ hurt	__ humiliated	__ rejected
__ sorry	__ lonely	__ annoyed	__ bored
__ alienated	__ withdrawn	__ irritated	__ depleted

❑ Deliver two compliments a day for the next week, and accept compliments directed to you by simply saying *thank you*. Monitor how you feel when you do this.

❑ Using a mirror, look into your eyes and repeat these affirmations aloud in the morning and evening, as many times as it takes until you feel confident about what's being said:
  • My feelings are important.
  • I understand my feelings.
  • I deserve compliments, and so do others.

Summary:
✔ Emotions can make us feel extremely happy, sad or anywhere in between.
✔ Your emotional self, your child within and your spirit need to experience feelings in order to flourish.
✔ You could do a great deal of damage by ignoring feelings and by believing that your situation will never get better.
✔ Broad categories of negative emotions include anxiety, anger, hurt, guilt and depression. Some feelings evolve into others. Some feelings mask others.
✔ Positive emotions can have far-reaching benefits.
✔ Expressing your feelings is essential to your emotional well-being.
✔ By fully experiencing emotions, a new life will begin where you'll encounter much joy and some pain too, but this new life is one where you'll be fully present, real and connected.

Chapter 4

Rebuilding
Increase Self-confidence & Self-worth, See Your Star Rise

"My father would be up most nights yelling in a drunken rage, so I'd go to school the next day unprepared and half-asleep," said Stephen. "As a result, I did poorly in most classes, was considered stupid by my parents and told that I'd never amount to anything in life. I believed them because they were my parents and the evidence supported their words. So for many years, I lived with my head down and a sense of worthlessness. Now after talking with other ACOAs, I realize that they also received similar messages and that we're all trying to overcome low self-esteem. Each of us is making progress, slowly by surely"

Since there's little nurturing and rather traumatic events during the upbringing of ACOAs, we're deprived of self-value. Often we feel as though we indeed caused the alcoholism and as a result are responsible for the difficult times our sober parent had to endure. All this naturally affects the self-confidence and self-worth of a child who, without some sort of intervention, brings that condition into adult life. And we can also be overly sensitive to experiences that happen outside the family, taking the blame and consistently judging ourselves without mercy.

This chapter examines how self-confidence, which wasn't developed during childhood, can be now. The power of self-talk is introduced, as is the natural law of displacement. Support group participation is considered along with a reassessment of the value you have as a child of God. Progressive relaxation is also explored. Almost all children of alcoholics suffer damaged self-worth; this chapter sets an action plan to start reversing that condition, replacing bad internal messages and beliefs with lasting self-esteem.

Spiritualist Anthony De Mello tells a story about an eagle's egg. It was found by a farmer who placed it in the nest of a barnyard hen. The eagle's egg hatched along with the hen's eggs. The baby eagle clucked, scratched the ground for insects and did everything else the chicks did, believing she was a chicken. One day she looked up and saw a majestic bird soaring across the sky. "Who's that?" she asked and a chicken replied, "That's an eagle, king of all birds. He belongs up there, but we belong on the ground because we're only chickens." And since she believed she was a chicken, the eagle lived and died as one.

Quite a different ending from the story about the lion who thought he was a sheep. Have you bought into the belief that you're inadequate in some way as a result of words or actions from others? Perhaps you're an eagle, ready to learn the truth about yourself and soar. But maybe your self-confidence could first use a boost from where it is now. Self-esteem can affect the quality and effectiveness of your entire life. There are ways to acquire it and reach your true potential.

People with low self-confidence, especially ACOAs, evaluate themselves without mercy. They may be respectful and kind to others, but not to themselves. Why treat yourself so differently? We'll examine that question, offer proven techniques to increase self-confidence, to recognize competencies and to appreciate your attributes in this chapter. What's at stake is almost every aspect of your life: improved relationships, career, health, spiritual connections, prosperity and more. It's extremely important that you know you're competent, and also understand that you're able to increase self-confidence and self-worth. Entire books have been written on the subject, so an overview of techniques will be presented here. We all need to fill our self-confidence bucket because it can become depleted from time to time. But do you know when to do so and how to go about it?

Identifying When Your Self-Confidence Needs a Refill

The characteristics of low self-confidence are many. They include: avoiding people, eye contact or new experiences; relying on others for answers; keeping your opinions to yourself; performance anxiety; experiencing an unlived life; allowing people to take advantage of you; and even tolerating abuse. Everyone makes mistakes, has embarrassing moments, does things to regret later, and experiences rejection - but these events do not mean they're inadequate or undeserving. Let's start from the beginning, determine where self-confidence may have been first sabotaged and see how things can be turned around. Then you'll be able to accurately reprogram your belief systems for increased self-worth. Exercises and new beliefs are essential but will require practice. And more practice: the course of your life can be altered through hard work and the attainment of new skills. Some risks are necessary, but almost every time you take one, confidence will grow and you'll start to believe a little bit more in yourself.

What Happened to You?

ACOAs grow up in a breeding ground for low self-esteem and frequently think they are the cause of all problems. They experience erratic behavior such as "I love you, go away," and it appears that no matter what they do, it's just not good enough. They believe that if only they were better children, better students, or at all lovable, their parent would stop drinking and be happy. Of course, the goal to do everything perfectly is impossible to meet. Then feelings of inadequacy grow. If we experience that negative personal evaluation often enough, it becomes ingrained in our personal belief system.

Destructive experiences to your self-esteem happen outside the family, too. At a sixth grade function, a girl asks a boy to dance, he replies that he doesn't know how and is seen ten minutes later dancing with another girl. A boy in high school is picked on repeatedly and nobody does anything to help. Your partner walks away from the relationship and you look to yourself to assess blame. Whenever someone is ridiculed, rejected, excluded or treated poorly, she or he naturally begins to feel inadequate. They question their own competency or attractiveness, and the reaction may often be undeserved shame. The effect of a current event can be magnified exponentially if you were, as a child, programmed to believe yourself to be inadequate as a result of erroneous messages received by an alcoholic parent.

You can't play "make believe" and ignore your feelings when something bad happens. Emotions need to be felt, processed, dealt with and let go. When you're on solid emotional ground, this is doable. If not, you find it more difficult. When a firm foundation of self-confidence is present, hurts or losses can be overcome more easily by refocusing attention on your strengths and personal value.

Gaining confidence and self-worth, and seeing yourself as successful is what this chapter is about. Whatever happened to injure your self-confidence was wrong and needs to be relegated to the past. Now you can take steps to make repairs that can leave you in better shape than ever. Remember the data processing phrase *garbage in, garbage out*? It's time to take out and eliminate the garbage *beliefs* about yourself, to live with "quality in, quality out" instead. You are lovable, capable, fully adequate and getting better all the time.

Self-Interview Taping Exercise:

Use a tape recorder to record questions and answers to the following. Then rewind and carefully listen for the feelings along with meanings behind your responses. Summarize important insights into a notebook for reflection or action.

• What is the result of having been overly critical of yourself?
• What event caused one of the greatest blows to your self-confidence? How did you react when it happened? Are you still influenced by it, and if so, do you recognize the harm it may be causing? What are some ways you can recover?
• What is one thing you've done over the last week that you feel good about?
• Complete these sentences: I deserve (to be loved, promoted, etc.)_____, and I need more (attention, appreciation, etc.)_____.
• What positive traits do others see in you? Which ones do you see in yourself?
• Describe your current support system.
• Who has had the greatest influence in your life?
• Specifically, what is your next step in increasing your self-worth?

Forgiveness Empowers You

When did you start losing confidence and who or what prompted it? Did it begin during childhood as a result of the actions of an alcoholic parent? Not helping you see yourself as worthy, valued and competent during formative years was a disservice to you. Perhaps your parents didn't provide a framework for building self-confidence or may have even caused feelings of shame. But they themselves were imperfect, as we all are, and their own self-images may have been warped and negative. More importantly, their behavior may have been significantly influenced by alcoholic abuse. They were perhaps horrible teachers of life lessons. Or possibly your parents did a fairly good job, but people outside the family may have affected you. Maybe you were excluded from the "in crowd" or ridiculed by a teacher or rejected by someone you cared about.

Whatever the case might be, it's time to forgive those who injured you. Carrying resentment only hurts yourself. Recognize that the people who hurt you were wrong and had problems of their own. Forgive them for being so harmful to you. Make peace with past events so you can leave them behind and move on to confidence building.

"My alcoholic father treated me like I was worthless all through childhood," remembered Tammy. "He repeatedly humiliated me in front of my friends, told me I was a mistake and never provided any degree of caring. I hated him. Now that he's old, he's looking for grandchildren. At first I decided to give him none, but I've been thinking about it. My spitefulness and anger are more damaging to me than him. I'm going to forgive and move on with my life."

You can say, "I'll never forgive _____ for what she/he did." But they are *not* the ones who will reap the benefits of forgiveness – you are. By going through life holding on to negative feelings, you block positive ones, including those that enable you to feel good about yourself. Let go and give yourself the gift of freedom. Stop imprisoning yourself. By holding on, you empower the person who hurt you by allowing her or him the control to still affect your life. If you insist that they must pay for their actions, know that they will, but leave that to God, or karma, or simply focus on the phrase "what goes around comes around". Forgiveness brings you peace and freedom.

There's an old fable about two Buddhist monks forbidden to touch women, who come upon a beautiful young woman who need to cross a river but is afraid. They both, young monk and older mentor (who takes the lead), pick her up and carry her to the other side of the river. They set her down and silently continue on their way. Hours later, the young monk speaks: "We are forbidden to touch women! How could you allow us to pick up that lady?!" The older monk looks at him and calmly replies, "I put her down at the riverbank – why are you still carrying her?"

Talk Nicely to Yourself

"Wow—that girl is just my type," said Philip. "But she'd never be interested in me so I won't even bother introducing myself. I'm not good looking and don't have the personality to keep her attention." So he just walked away.

Philip lost a potentially wonderful relationship by talking himself out of even trying. Self-talk has an incredibly strong impact on your self-confidence. It impacts how you feel about your competencies and self-worth. With self-talk, you can create confidence or turmoil; you are in control. But don't you deserve high self-worth in your life? Isn't that a better choice? You can develop a positive response to almost anything. That's not to say you should be delusional and not recognize when something bad happens, but you can see or hope for something positive to come out of your experience and choose not to beat yourself up unnecessarily. For example, if you are passed over for a promotion, look for the possibilities that can come out of this disappointment. Don't say to yourself that you're not smart enough, not connected enough, or a failure. Instead, recognize that you were being considered for the promotion because you are well thought of. That hasn't changed. And maybe the higher position simply wasn't a good move for you. What happened has opened many alternatives for you. You're free to seek out other opportunities; you can become motivated to further your education and build your credentials, or to simply take a break for a while. Don't doubt your personal value – be self-supportive instead.

Did you ever call yourself an idiot after making a mistake? If so, it's essential that you develop a new way of communicating: one that is positive, kind, affirming and forgiving. The importance cannot be overstated. Every time this inner dialogue happens, you either build up or tear down your self-confidence. Even negative words said in humor can harm you. They aren't funny and just serve as false evidence trying to prove your inadequacy. So, first of all, eliminate self-critical statements and leave your childhood programming behind. Then flood your mind and spirit with supportive statements. Your attitude, demeanor and sense of well-being are going to change for the better. There's always a door of opportunity waiting to be opened.

Almost every chapter in this book has positive affirmations for a reason. They're intended to affirm your positive qualities, even if you don't yet know you have them. This is a step toward reprogramming your inner child. Be kind and stop beating yourself up with negative self-talk if you happen not to be perfect. Perfection is simply an illusion. Act like a nurturing, supportive and loving parent to yourself through words that heal and encourage. Keep an eye on your potential, and ignore inconsequential blemishes.

Dare to Compare – But Do It the Right Way

There's no such thing as a "perfect package." We are all are God's children, created with attributes, but since we're human, we *also have imperfections.* When you compare *one aspect* of a person to yourself, it's easy to feel inferior. It's only one aspect of a person you're looking at, but in your mind she or he as a *whole* seems superior to you. That just isn't true. Anyone may excel at some things and be inept at others. Someone may have a pretty face and an ugly soul, a nice body but one that smells bad. Behind that person's mask could be the last person in the world you'd want to be. In back of the mask could be ugly, hairy, oozing sores. Comparing yourself to another denies reality. Perfection or overall superiority just doesn't exist.

Instead of measuring your attributes against another person's, compare your progress, improvements, growth and development to the way you were in the past. Do you remember how you were as a teenager? Give yourself credit for improving. If you've been on cruise control and haven't seen meaningful changes, give yourself credit for having the courage and wisdom to begin now. You may need new skills but they can be learned; then as you get better, recognize your progress and affirm yourself.

Positive Friends and Thinking Support Your Self-Confidence

"Jan was always negative and complaining about everything," remembered Michelle. "Even though we had been friends for years, I had to end the friendship because every time we talked, I'd end up feeling down and depressed. She just wasn't an emotionally healthy person to be around and I couldn't change her—believe me I tried. It was lonely for a while but then I met new friends who I still hang around with. They bring me up instead of being obsessed with cynicism and gloom. I'm a much happier person as a result."

Old friends can be comfortable, but they could be dragging you down. If your self-confidence has been low, you may have attracted others with similar beliefs about themselves. Maybe you can work together on becoming more positive, or you may have to seek out people who can be more receptive to positive change. As you become stronger and more optimistic, you will find yourself automatically attracting new people into your life. Do whatever's necessary to be surrounded by individuals who are emotionally healthy. They will support you if you slip, and they will provide encouragement, love and caring. You'll also see a new view of yourself and the world through them.

In addition to your friends, your thoughts may also need some adjustment. Picture a large glass filled with prune juice. Put it under a running faucet and soon there's nothing left but water. That's the *natural law of displacement*, and it works the same with negative and positive thoughts. Make it a habit to concentrate on positive thoughts, to say uplifting affirmations daily, and the negative ones will be soon replaced. There's simply no room for them anymore. That's not to say that you should try to live in la la land. Difficult things happen in life and we have to deal with them. But we don't have to be consumed by an unhealthy bias that multiples negativity and creates a continually downward spiral.

It's a fact: positive thoughts can bring positive results. Athletes often visualize themselves hitting the ball just right or making that perfect basket. The mind can be programmed to accept what we vividly see and believe to be attainable. Visualizing is just like mentally rehearsing. See yourself succeeding at whatever you'd like to accomplish. Feel as a person with high self-confidence would. It's a self-fulfilling prophecy. Make a contract with yourself to absolutely stop negative thinking in its tracks. Replace it with possibility thinking and build your "positive words" vocabulary. Be fully descriptive of your excellent experiences. Your mood and belief system will change along with your self-worth and self-esteem.

Calm, Cool and Collected

"Growing up, I always thought my dad would stop drinking if I was the perfect son," said Gordon. "So I tried to get good grades and do everything faultlessly but I'd always fall short and be ridiculed. My self-esteem was low and I was always on guard, expecting to be put down no matter what. Being that way left me tense and frozen, so I was never able to do my best. But I learned some relaxation techniques that have been very helpful to me. Most effective has been progressive relaxation. It makes me feel better mentally, emotionally and physically. It only takes ten minutes, can be used anytime and anywhere I happen to be."

Especially when self-confidence is low, you may be overly anxious, always on guard and expecting someone to think poorly of you. In reality, people's focus is usually on themselves, but if you still believe anything less than a perfect performance by you will result in ridicule and further destruction of self-confidence, every word or expression seems a matter of life and death. And when your muscles tense up, your mind can also tighten, just like a vice. Then you can't think clearly and aren't at your best. Progressive relaxation is one technique that can help you reduce anxiety.

Start by finding a quiet place where you can be alone. Take a few deep breaths, and close your eyes. Concentrate on your toes, and imagine the muscles are as loose as rubber bands. See and feel all the tension disappear. Then move on slowly and methodically to your ankles, knees and upper legs, one leg at a time. Now focus on your stomach, lower and upper back, shoulders, and neck, always thinking about how the tension is disappearing. Then move to your cheeks, nose, eyelids, and the top of your head. When you feel your body completely relaxed, spend some time there and enjoy the sensation. When you're ready to return, slowly stretch and open your eyes. In addition to this progressive relaxation exercise, you can focus on muscles that are particularly tense, purposely make them as tight as you can, hold for ten seconds, and then completely release the muscles. Listen to a meditation CD or simply gaze into the flame of a lit candle and forget the day's worries. Regardless of the method, the fact is that when you're fully relaxed, you can think more clearly and feel better, both physically and emotionally.

You are Blessed with Gifts and Talents

Everyone has gifts and natural talents. But if your self-awareness or self-esteem is low, you can sometimes have difficulty identifying what they are. Think about what activities you enjoy or are good at. Once you have a gift or talent in mind, develop it through continued practice. A side benefit is an increasingly ascending self-confidence. It's clear that you're doing something well, maybe better than most people could and you're building on your strengths. This increased confidence can overflow into other areas of your life.

Small Groups Can Make a Big Difference

One of the most effective ways to increase your self-worth is by feeling the encouragement, acceptance and love of a support group. Verbalizing your feelings in a safe, confidential environment, where all other participants are present to receive the same benefits, can be wonderful.

"I thought I was the only one who felt ashamed of myself," said

William. "My insecurities and self-doubts were hard to share with other people - at first anyway. But in a group setting, everyone was supportive and attentive as they listened to what I said. I was able to reevaluate my belief system, and realized how I had blown my insecurities way out of proportion On top of that, I also saw how others entertained similar feelings about themselves. By talking about our feelings and beliefs, we were able to successfully work through them with unbelievable results. Emotionally, I've never felt better, and I have our group to thank."

When you're alone, shortcomings or unsuccessful events can be built to immense proportions. But feedback from a support group can help challenge those destructive perceptions and bring you back to reality. Suddenly you find that you're not alone in feeling the way you do, that you're not so bad after all, and that you are fully accepted, imperfections and all. You see that those individuals who you believed had everything going for them, in reality had their own demons and insecurities to battle with. In a support group, you see people for who they really are; the more everyone shares, the easier it is to be real and accepting. When you reveal yourself to others, your relationship with yourself and others will improve. Everyone is helped to grow and become more secure, living as perfectly imperfect human beings. Your self-awareness and confidence increases as you try, and succeed at, new skills or degrees of sharing. You're nurtured by other people and can work through issues that may have been holding you back for years.

You can find support groups in a variety of places. Some psychologists offer small groups, as do certain religious institutions or spiritual growth centers. They all operate under similar guidelines:

• Confidentiality
• Acceptance of different views
• Respect and consideration
• Being supportive
• Freedom to share (or not) one's feelings and concerns.

If at all possible participate in one, because that's where you can make great strides in confidence building and personal awareness, while working within a safe and confidential environment.

Helping Others Helps You

"He just started crying in the middle of a meeting," said Don about a 17-year-old who attended an ACOA meeting for the first time. "I'd been working on my recovery for a few years and feeling like I hadn't made much headway. But seeing this kid reminded me of where I'd come from. And I also realized that I could be helpful to him by sharing what I had learned by being in program. So I befriended the teen—he's come a long way since and so have I. He received my support and encouragement while I realized my considerable value as a friend and teacher."

Sometimes we can become too self-conscious. We get so concerned about our looks or every little thing we say or do that we end up doing nothing. Better to be hidden than ridiculed. But there's a win/win solution to this problem. People need your help. Perhaps a fellow student who can't understand a subject you do, or an elderly neighbor who needs assistance carrying groceries. Maybe someone you know is sick or lonely and would love a visit from you. There are opportunities everywhere to help others. You can make a significant difference in the lives of others with a little care and kindness. And, in the process, your self-consciousness diminishes just as your self-esteem rises. There's no more concern about what you're doing, or wearing, or saying. The focus is on other people and the realization comes to you that you have much to offer. Self-worth is bound to increase.

Out of Your Comfort Zone, Expanding Your Competencies.

When you exercise and stretch your muscles more than usual, there is a physical discomfort that indicates growth. This is also true when you expand your emotional or social muscles. You're in new, unfamiliar territory. But growing your self-confidence requires it. A complete transformation will not happen overnight, but a steady succession of little excursions into new territory will expand your skills, self-esteem and life experiences. One of the best ways to increase self-confidence is by experiencing a succession of small successes that build into undeniable evidence that you indeed are more capable than you had previously thought. A strong wall of confidence is constructed just as a brick building is: one piece at a time. Moving out of your comfort zone will become easier and you'll feel confident about handling any possible situation. Change can be a good thing; it brings opportunities.

Guess what? You're not perfect. So what? Nobody is. But you are lovable, competent, and becoming more so every day. You forgive those who hurt your self-esteem, and are aware that <u>you</u> now have the power to build it up. You're gaining self-knowledge and self-acceptance. You know what's necessary to achieve high self-confidence and you're putting forth the effort. You admire and reward yourself as you achieve goals, work through ideas, appreciate your own uniqueness and become your own best friend. And you eventually grow strong enough to help others, share love, and feel good about it. The five-day action plan that follows will help you become more aware of some of your good qualities. All of the exercises and affirmations are here to help you. Going forward, you'll be establishing goals and monitoring your progress. You'll think of some good rewards for yourself and enhance your social skills. Your future is bright. Possibilities are everywhere, now that you're taking charge of your self-confidence and proceeding with love.

Building Your Self-Confidence to New Heights

You can build self-confidence regardless of your experiences in childhood by addressing your belief systems, learning new skills and recognizing that you're not alone in this endeavor. It starts with altering your beliefs about yourself and others that have been carried over from your development years as a child of an alcoholic. Alter your self-talk so that you'll be your own cheerleader. If you falter, give yourself credit for trying, learn why this attempt didn't fully succeed, make adjustments and try again. Recognize that others are mostly interested in themselves—not finding fault with you. In fact, others can be quite supportive. And remember that no one is perfect— mistakes are natural and usually aren't very important. Expand your focus from being narrow (what if I say the wrong thing today) to the big picture of living your life ethically and fully. Note your God-given talents and attributes, don't dismiss them. Keep your attention on the doughnut rather than the hole. And recognize that Spirit is with you on your journey, ready to pick you up if you fall.

The next component is skill development. Start with small goals, such as greeting a new person each day for the next week. There are conversational techniques illustrated in a later chapter but, if you'd like to, skip forward and start using them. Expand your mind (and conversational topics) by reading books and newspapers, attending class, listening to inspirational speakers, etc. Practice the five-day action plan often. Practice, practice, practice each new skill and don't give up, because you will succeed. You can do this and accomplish wonderful things with your life.

Goal setting is also important to your self-confidence. By meeting or exceeding your targets, you will see your confidence naturally build. You can plan each needed step and monitor your confidence-building progress. Establishing goals is also important for other areas of your life, and that will be the topic of the next chapter.

Five-Day Action Plan for Growth & Success:
Place a checkmark in each box as you complete the associated action:

❏ Make a list of all your good qualities, successes and positive changes. Then write each on a small card, carry it with you, and read the list twice each day.

❏ Approach one new person each day and communicate. Ask a simple question (Do you know what time it is?) or make a simple comment (Nice day we're having.). Gradually extend the duration of your talk and reward yourself with a treat.

❏ Stop saying negative things to yourself! As soon as you begin, yell "No." to yourself until you can redirect your consciousness to <u>positive</u> statements.

❏ Using a mirror, look into your eyes and repeat these affirmations aloud in the morning and evening, as many times as it takes until you feel confident about what's being said:
   • I'm lovable, competent and secure.
   • My self-confidence grows each day.
   • I am blessed.

Summary:
✔ You may have been born an eagle and told you were a chicken. Learning the truth will let you soar to new heights.

✔ Taking a self-inventory can clarify if you're in need of a self-esteem boost.

✔ Forgiving those who hurt you takes their power away and gives it to you.

✔ Positive self-talk has an extraordinary impact on your self-confidence.

✔ Compare your progress, improvements, growth and development to how you were in the past. Pat yourself on the back for your progress.

✔ Surround yourself with positive people and thoughts.

✔ Be aware of your strengths, talents and blessings.

✔ Support groups, formal or informal, can generate growth and healing.

✔ Extending past your comfort zone helps you grow more confident.

Chapter 5

Fulfilling Destiny, Finding Your Path
Establish Goals, Celebrate Progress

"To this day, I remember how humiliated I was in 5th grade when I handed in a project that was totally screwed up," said Gail. "Everyone just laughed at me. My assignment was to construct a complex, three-dimensional model of a volcano and surrounding land. Paper-mâché would be used to construct the model, but I didn't even know where to start. I asked for help from my parents but they were so affected by alcohol abuse that they insisted I make my volcano look like dog shit, never showed me how to finish the project and I ended up a laughing stock in class. Throughout my childhood, my parents never showed me how to approach or follow through on complex tasks. I still have trouble completing them."

Automobile clubs offer a map service where they'll plot the best possible route to your driving destination. You can do the same for your life's journey. That's what goals are all about, providing direction that'll bring you from point to point until you arrive at wherever your destination might be. But it's a skill that a child in an alcoholic home seldom learns. This chapter goes into detail about how you can construct the framework, break large goals into smaller ones, take inventory to determine what's needed, and set up a reward system to encourage the pursuit of even more ambitious goals. High definition television promises to deliver a picture in a crystal clear format. In the same way, you're encouraged to vividly see your goals being achieved. With the knowledge of how to achieve goals and celebrating progress along the way, you'll also increase self-confidence, the subject of the previous chapter and an important ongoing developmental component.

We'll look at why goals are so important, determine what you'll need in order to succeed, and list the detailed steps. Then you'll establish a timetable and use various motivational techniques to ensure that your desire will come to fruition. Proceed incrementally and what seemed like an insurmountable goal suddenly becomes very attainable. You can also examine different areas of your life and prioritize what would be most desirable for your goal-setting.

Establishing goals focuses your energy and gives your life new meaning. It solidifies what it is you want to accomplish, identifies measurable steps on how to get there, builds self-confidence, and plans time to celebrate along the way.

Self-Interview Taping Exercise:
Use a tape recorder to record questions and answers to the following. Then rewind and carefully listen for the feelings along with meanings behind your responses. Summarize important insights into a notebook for reflection or action.
• What do you most want that you don't have?
• What is the one thing you want to accomplish with your life?
• Which goal do you want to aggressively pursue first? What would be needed to get it?
• If you achieved your goals, what would your life be like?
• How would this benefit your loved ones?
• When will you start working on your goals?
• What steps are necessary for your goal achievement?

Toss Out the Garbage

We can have such destructive and self-limiting thoughts at times. They need to be eliminated before goals can even be considered. The kind of "garbage thinking" I'm talking about includes:
I'm too old to try new things.
I'm not smart enough to figure this out.
Nothing ever works for me, so what's the sense in even trying?

Those self-defeating beliefs are wrong, so try your best to discard them. The truth is that if you have the desire, the will, and the perseverance to follow the necessary steps, you will successfully achieve your goal.

A Vehicle Needs Direction… How About You?

Without goals, you're like a ship without a rudder: you go nowhere, living life aimlessly; time passes by but nothing of substance gets accomplished. Behind every outstanding achievement, there's always a person behind something outstanding being done who started with an idea and passionate desire. Goals can get you motivated in all areas of your life and once you have your direction, the accomplishment of simple or great things is possible. There may be a more satisfying career for you to pursue. Or how does incredibly romantic love, spiritual connectedness or financial independence sound? Perhaps you just need to bring more fun and play time into your life. No matter what the goal, it brings new meaning, direction and motivation. What do you want for your life?

There are some common characteristics present in all types of successfully achievable goals. First there's a very strong desire to achieve it. The benefits are clearly discernable and highly valued. You can see how your life or the lives of your loved ones would very much be improved with its attainment. The goal could be a vision for you, a mission or a calling. However you want to describe it, you are definitely being drawn to it and there will be substantive benefits.

"Last year I decided to change my life and be happy," said Gloria. "I tried getting involved with different things but I'd always end up at square one. What am I doing wrong?"

Goals need to be very specific. For example, saying you want to be happy in twelve months is much too general. You need to precisely identify what would make you feel happier and then break it down further so you can develop a clearer plan on how to get there. Once you have identifiable steps, you can then place them into a time period. For instance, each week, maybe even each day, you may schedule a short-term goal or action that will bring you a step closer toward achieving your long-term target. You can measure your progress each week or each day. And finally, whatever your goal might be, you also have to see its relevance to your life. How important is it to you? Is it meaningful enough?

Taking Inventory

A store will go bankrupt if it doesn't have enough stock to fulfill the customers' needs. What resources, information or other assets are currently available to assist you in achieving your goal, internally and externally? Before you can move forward, you have to take inventory.

If something needed is missing, you'll have to determine how to obtain it. For example, with a goal of improving the appearance of where you live, you might need paint, time, physical abilities and help from friends. See what you've got and need. Do you have the time? Are you physically able to participate? If you have said yes so far, then you'll have to go to the store, purchase paint and ask for help from your friends. It's a very simple process once you have defined the starting point. When you get the needed resources or help, all that's left is to track your progress and celebrate incremental successes (one room painted, for example) along the way. When you achieve your long-range goal, have a super celebration.

How to Consummate Goals

Following are some of the necessary components to help you attain your goals:

Have a *passionate* desire and keep focused.
It bears repeating: your primary goal really has to mean everything to you. It should be dominating your thoughts and your conversation because then it will program your mind to succeed and solidify your direction. A mediocre destination is not going provide sufficient motivation and you may give up if things don't go perfectly. To bring the highest amount of passion into your goal, detail all the benefits that will come from it. Write them down on a card, and then post it on your refrigerator or mirror, so each day you will look at the benefits and be reminded of what you would give up, if you give up.

If you're intense about reaching your goal, you'll probably want to take the superhighway. A straight line will get you there and keep you away from distractions and roadblocks. When you keep your thoughts focused, your mind and actions will flow just like a river headed for the ocean. Scattered drops of rain just dissipate, but a continuously flowing stream makes a clear and direct path. Keep focused on your direction and you'll get there right on schedule. You can obviously increase passion by maximizing desirability. So, most definitely, detail every benefit, including those affecting your loved ones. Add new benefits as you think of them. The more benefits, the greater the desire and motivation. Your skills will also be developed while you work. As your short-term plans are increasingly met, you'll gain self-confidence, increase assurance that you can do it, and you'll be on your way to your long-term goal achievement.

<u>Details, details, details – don't forget them.</u>
One of the most important things necessary to achieve your long-term goal is to break it down into small steps. There may be quite a few of them, but try to include them all and make additions as needed. Determine which need to be accomplished first and act accordingly. The remaining items should then be prioritized. See where you can obtain the information needed and acquire general knowledge along the way. As long as the progression is logical, meaningful, and measurable, you'll reach your goal. Enlist the help of your friends, loved ones or anyone else who can assist you. If you come across certain obstacles, identify how you can overcome them. Determine the resources necessary and make a detailed plan on how to obtain them.

You may also awaken certain talents that have remained dormant. Certainly you'll gain confidence in yourself as you continually achieve progress in your journey. Writing your details on paper will solidify your master plan and further confirm every piece of the puzzle. Thorough preparation is essential. Although all these details can give you a temporary headache, in the end you'll be glad you devoted the time to establish them. They join together to make your goal achievable.

<u>Set up a timetable.</u>
Planes and trains have scheduled arrival times, so why not establish them for your goals? Once you set a detailed timetable, you'll be on track to arrive at your destination. Just like a train has many *stops* along the way, allocate time for each *step* toward your final goal or destination. You'll be motivated when you finish each step, and anxious to move on to the next. Build in a little extra time if you wish. Your focus will be clear and eventual completion pretty much guaranteed. But be reasonable and compassionate with yourself. If you're running a little late in your schedule, remember that the achievement of your long-term goal is most important, not the exact timing. Just revise your schedule, try not to deviate too much and keep your eye on the prize. Timetables can be monthly, weekly, daily or any other length of time that would be helpful to you in monitoring your progress.

<u>Be persistent regarding your once-in-a-lifetime opportunity.</u>
Did you ever sit in on a sales pitch for a time-share vacation or try to buy a used car? Those salespeople can be unrelenting at times, but that's their job. If you want to accomplish your goals, perseverance and commitment is also required of you. There are lots of distractions, a few roadblocks, and many other factors that can stop or slow your progress.

There's no question that you can achieve your goal by being persistent and never giving up. Dr. Robert Schuller has authored many books on possibility thinking. He sometimes uses short, catchy phrases because they make a point and are easy to remember. One is "inch by inch, anything's a cinch." All your little steps will add up.

Never give up on your goal and remember all the benefits that will be yours once you reach it. Great achievements never come easy. They take time and practice. Just like it takes practice and efforts to learn to drive a car, play a sport or build relationships. Unlike what some sales-people will tell you, opportunities are always present. However, we all have limited time on this earth, and as we get older, certain abilities begin to diminish. Obviously, time runs out for some opportunities, so it's best to be persistent and not put off what we'd like to accomplish. Success will be yours if you just persevere.

Seeing Your Goal Happen in HDTV

High definition TV delivers a picture in a crystal clear format. In the same way, you should vividly see your goal being achieved. Visualization is a proven technique that works. Your brain responds very strongly to pictures and emotions—fortunately, you are the programmer. If you clearly and enthusiastically visualize your goal already being accomplished, you will find it to be extremely helpful. If you repeatedly feel yourself enjoying the benefits associated with your goal, those emotions will filter down into your subconscious that, in turn, will act very much like a goal-seeking device. Whatever you want or concentrate on most will be brought to you. If you think of yourself as a failure, you'll be one. But if you think of yourself as a success, you will be one. This has been referred to in books and also organized religions. Visualize, prayerize (asking in prayer), and then see it materialize. What you can conceive of, believe in and vigorously proceed with, will become reality. Clearly visualize your goal, monitor your progress and reward yourself as each step is completed.

Your Just Rewards

Self-bribery is good. It's not against the law and it is a good motiva-tor. Define what rewards you'll give yourself for accomplishing steps that lead toward your goal. They should be proportionate to the degree of difficulty. For example, your reward for successfully completing each class should not be as grandiose as that for being awarded your degree;

that deserves a super celebration. The point is that rewards (particularly chocolate) along your journey provide consistent and sometimes needed motivation. They are well-deserved and can remind you of your progress. They serve an important purpose, so don't forget to be generous with yourself. Keep the motivation going.

The Return of Self-Talk

I know, I know, we have already visited this topic. But positive self-talk is vitally important to goal achievement. Be aware of what you're saying to yourself. Especially with long-term goals, you can get discouraged if you start using unproductive words about your progress or direction. Don't let a bad attitude sneak up on you.

What Goals Can Do for Your Life

Do you know what's important in your life, right now and looking ahead? What is the achievement that most needs to be accomplished? Some areas to consider include:
- Recovery: resolve childhood issues that still haunt you as an ACOA.
- Social competence: learn conversational skills, become comfortable and confident in your relationships.
- Career: improve so that you'll be promoted or change your profession to one that better fits you.
- Educational: seek that degree you've been wanting.
- Self-acceptance, self-confidence and self-love: live life joyfully.
- Spiritual development: get more in touch with God and your spirit and soul.
- Financial independence: increase your savings; learn to make money in stock investments, real estate or other areas.
- Relationships: improve the quality and intimacy of your relationships, bring a significant other into your life, and increase the number of your friends.
- Improve your everyday life, and any other personal improvement areas that come to mind.
- Have more fun and enjoyment; increase time for play and humor.
- Expand your capacity to love and to serve others.

Think carefully about what takes priority and what activates your strongest desires. Then set one or two goals, break down the components and monitor your scheduled progress. An example of a long-term goal might be to become more comfortable talking with people. Short-term might be saying "good morning" to four people each day for a week, with eye contact and a smile on your face. The more often you practice, the easier it gets and before you know it, your long-term goal is achieved. As you complete incremental tasks, reward yourself with ice cream, candy or whatever works for you. Bribing (or rewarding) yourself is a good motivator.

It's important to systematically continue setting goals and monitoring your progress. You'll not only experience a succession of achievements, but you will also develop a lighter spirit and build self-worth. All this strongly assists in your overall personal development.

You can establish extraordinarily high goals that will bring fame, wealth and power. Or you can ignore goals and drift through life. In fact, you can also do anything in between because you are the decisionmaker in charge; I suggest that you make it a life well-lived. But that is only my opinion. What's yours?

Fear and anxiety can paralyze. What's your greatest fear and how can you diminish it? What actions can you take that will help you manage and possibly overcome your fears? There are effective ways to take control and make your life more anxiety-free. The next chapter will address this.

Five-Day Action Plan for Growth & Success:
Place a checkmark in each box as you complete the associated action:
❑ Think about your life and identify your most important goal. At the top of a blank page, list one very desirable goal and underline it. Then take the following steps:
• See what resources you presently have and determine what you'll need. Think about where you can get those resources.
• Review how important this goal is to you. Write a list showing every benefit that would be derived.
• Then list the small steps/actions you can take on a daily basis that will eventually build your achievements to the point that your long-term goal will be yours to enjoy.
• Set a timetable for completion of each step. Use a calendar to mark projected dates of completion.
• Every time you complete a small step, place a checkmark next to its description and reward yourself with a treat.
• Commit to achieving this goal, bypassing any roadblocks that may try to slow you down.

- Visualize your goal as already achieved.
- Repeat this process for other goals but don't overwhelm yourself with too many too soon. Review your progress each week, take corrective action if necessary. Have fun and be sure to reward yourself generously for each success.

❑ Using a mirror, look into your eyes and repeat these affirmations aloud in the morning and evening, as many times as it takes until you feel confident about what you are saying:
- I'm reaching my goals.
- I love and accept myself today.
- My goal for today is to _____.
- My small steps will turn to big accomplishments.

Summary:
✔ Having goals provides direction and meaning for your life.
✔ Take inventory of what you have and determine what you'll need.
✔ Your primary goal should generate a passionate desire.
✔ Break down your goal into small steps; think of all the details and prioritize them.
✔ Establish a timetable, and write it in your calendar to ensure that your focus will be clear. Check off each item as it's completed and reward yourself.
✔ Commitment and perseverance are extremely important. Ignore the distractions and bypass the roadblocks.
✔ Visualize your goal as already being accomplished using highly charged emotions.
✔ You know what's important in your life right now. Set your # 1 goal based on that information, follow all the steps and have a super celebration when you accomplish everything you set out to accomplish.
✔ Then move on to goal # 2.

Chapter 6

Stopping Fears from Controlling You
Repel Anxiety and Unnecessary Worry

" '*Get out of my house, you jerk*,' my drunken father yelled as I lay in bed in the middle of the night," said Doug. "I was only 14 years old and had no place to go. Another time he crashed through a sliding glass door and fell at my feet, drunk, cut and bleeding. The police were no strangers to my house. On other occasions he came after me with fists and chased me with a baseball bat—but he was a normal father when sober. I never knew what to expect and, after a while, existed in a constant sense of anxiety, expecting bad things to happen. And even today as an adult, I'm on high alert at all times—waiting for something terrible to occur in my life. It's a habit that served me as a child, but do I have to be so fearful all the time? I can never stop worrying and have paralyzing anxiety attacks."

Fear and anxiety routinely fill the homes of tens of millions of Americans as a result of alcoholism. Children tremble when they see their parent coming home drunk and wonder what might happen next. Overnight they could be awakened by various types of assaults so they close their eyes but try to remain as vigilant as possible. And there are also anxiety-producing events outside the family for which they can't go to their parents for help. Chapter 6 helps you identify what types of anxiety you might be susceptible to, recognize where unnecessary worry is coming from and sort through three broad categories under which most anxiety-producing events fall. Techniques to aggressively fight fear are introduced as well as ways to respond when immediate relief is required. Actions are suggested that can serve as temporary antidotes and you're shown how anxiety can produce positive results, how to manage fear and how to eliminate unnecessary worry.

In general, anxiety isn't all bad. It can motivate and also warn you of a possible hurt or loss (real or imagined). Before you can respond effectively, you have to determine where the hurt or loss might occur, and if the threat is credible. By employing ways of coping, you'll be able to directly attack the sometimes-debilitating effects of anxiety. If anxiousness has been holding you back, even marginally, this chapter's for you. It employs a few techniques you're already familiar with and introduces several new ones.

More serious anxiety disorders, caused by a combination of environmental and biological factors, go beyond the scope of this chapter. Instead we will focus on the general anxiousness that many ACOAs occasionally struggle with.

Anxiety: Where It Comes From and What it Does to You

Changes over which we have no control produce significant discomfort for ACOAs. Just look at what happened during childhood and it's easy to understand. In the present, life-altering changes, time pressures and unexpected tragedies can generate fear and anxiety. Anticipated losses (of control, self-esteem, comfort, and love) can increase anxiety levels on top of everyday stressful experiences. Anxiousness may have been built into your belief system if you were taught that the world was a dangerous place and that you should fear others, or if you were made to feel inadequate by your alcoholic parent. While untrue and inaccurate, those beliefs perhaps were accepted as factual. They may have been incorporated into your basic self-talk, and expanded in scope and severity. If never challenged, these thoughts and beliefs can continue to live on. Regardless of its source, past or present, there are skills available to better deal with anxiety.

Self-Interview Taping Exercise:
Use a tape recorder to record questions and answers to the following. Then rewind and carefully listen for the feelings along with meanings behind your responses. Summarize important insights into a notebook for reflection or action.
- What beliefs about yourself and the world did you learn in childhood?
- What are your greatest fears at this time? What do you fear losing?
- Describe yourself when you're feeling anxious and when you're not. What's different?
- What limits do you need to establish?
- Which fears do you want to overcome first? What's your plan to do so?

Anxiety Can Be Your Friend and Lead to Transformation

Anxiety may not be a warm friend you welcome with a hug, but it can certainly be one that will help you grow. The discomfort of anxiousness or fear can be a strong motivator. Anxiety can prompt you to develop your coping skills and/or become emotionally stronger. And it can help you plan for eventualities.

"I was afraid of losing my job," said Jody. "There were layoffs in other departments so every day I came to work feeling anxious and expecting to be fired. This went on for months until I decided to prepare for the worst and while hoping for the best. I practiced meditation and breathing exercises to control my nervousness. Then I took control by generating a new and improved resume that made me sound like an excellent find for another company. I'm still hanging on to my job but am thinking of being proactive about finding another."

Are you going to let fear and anxiety overwhelm you? Or will you use it to become more successful, learn new skills and understand yourself? This chapter illustrates various ways to cope with anxiety. You can choose those that work best for you and further develop some of your own. As a result, you'll have more choices and better control over your life.

Identifying and Addressing your Fears

When you confront things you're afraid of, you can usually overcome them. When you don't, they tend to recur and increase in intensity. Do you actually know what you're afraid of? Some common fears include:

• an unknown future	• believing you're unlovable	• being a failure
• making a bad decision	• being out of control	• change
• insufficient money	• being alone	• being hurt

While you can be nervous about a variety of things, perhaps many of them can fit under these three broad categories: fear of losing control, fear of losing love and the fear of losing self-esteem.

Loss of control – "I've learned that I only have control of me and no one else," said Dominic. I've given up trying to make others do what I want because it only causes disappointment and trouble." You may be nervous about losing control of the *situation*, *yourself* or *someone else*. In reality, any control you believe you have over another person is largely temporary and, at best, somewhat illusionary. If people are solely dependent on you for survival, perhaps you may have great influence, but will still be unable to control their minds and feelings. From years in Nazi concentration camps, Victor Frankle learned that external possessions may be taken away, but one freedom that can never be stolen is the freedom to choose our thoughts and attitudes. Each one of us controls that. If you want someone in your life who genuinely cares about you, it has to be without duress. Accept the fact that <u>you can't control anyone but yourself</u> and there's no longer a reason to retain that related anxiety.

Losing control of a situation can certainly get you nervous. For instance, if you're a substitute teacher about to enter a classroom of kids from hell, you'll feel anxious. Or a police officer can feel quite anxious at a street demonstration, as she or he attempts to keep apart two groups that despise each other. To ease anxiety stemming from the possible <u>loss of situational control</u>, plan ahead as much as possible and consider how you might best react to various situations.

When you fear <u>losing control of yourself</u>, it usually means you've refrained from expressing your feelings, and that emotions are ready to go wild. When you do not express your emotions, they build up and eventually explode or implode. You can avoid this by being more open and expressive. There are techniques in various chapters of *Transformation for Life* that will help you more fully express yourself.

Loss of love – This includes losing the love another person had for you, or alternatively, losing your own belief that you are lovable.

"I keep my relationships fun-filled and light. We have a good time together but don't talk about anything personal. I just don't want to make myself vulnerable in case she decides to leave," said Charlie.

Everyone alive has experienced heartbreak. It's a part of life, to explore different relationships until you find one where both individuals are satisfied. You can invest a lot in a relationship and become quite transparent, so naturally there's concern about vulnerability and loss. But worrying excessively about whether or not someone will leave you will destine the relationship to failure. You'll be guarded, less open, and manipulative. That type of behavior keeps the other person at arms length and eliminates any chance of success. If she or he does leave the relationship, try to understand why *from their point of view*, accept that their reason is valid to them although you might disagree, and most importantly move on. *We, as ACOAs, often hold on when we should let go.* You will survive the pain and be loved again by someone who is more compatible. Bringing people into your life always involves some risks, but if you do not, you'll end up lonely and isolated.

When you no longer believe that you are lovable, hopelessness can drag you into depression. So it's important to challenge that destructive view before it takes hold. You're just human and bound to make mistakes, but that doesn't mean you're unlovable. A basic human need is to be loved: by yourself and by at least one other person. But if you're afraid that you're unlovable, you may tend to avoid any possible rejection by giving up and withdrawing. You'll be isolated; and when you don't learn how to cope with losses, they will most likely recur. Once you accept your imperfections, you can react differently. Accept yourself; continue positive self-talk and you'll soon develop enough self-love to sustain yourself, even through the rough times. You'll learn from mistakes, work things through and try again until you're successful. Throughout the process, you'll continue to love yourself, which also makes you more attractive to others.

Loss of self-esteem – Like the belief that you're not lovable, low self-esteem can also make you feel helpless and depressed. Remind yourself that you were not responsible for your parent's alcoholism and are just as valuable as the person next to you. You are a child of God and need to recognize that you're not lacking in any fundamental way.

You may fear the loss of self-esteem if it's improperly linked to performance. "If only I had gotten perfect grades, won the beauty contest, were the most valuable player in soccer...." In reality, you *are* valuable, no matter what. If you fail at a task, remember that your value as a person is not affected; it remains. *You are not simply what you do, but who you are in spirit and soul.* Recognize that you as a human being are continually growing, which naturally means you are inevitably going to make mistakes. If you fail at something, simply accept it as an indication of where you can improve. But if you're so anxious about making mistakes or feeling loss, you may not take the risks necessary to grow. When you become emotionally stagnant, part of you dies, so be careful not to go there.

Remember too, that if you don't confront your anxiety, it will continue to grow. Once confronted however, it will diminish or disappear. For example, speaking in public is frightening for most people. By practicing over and over again, that fear diminishes until you (almost) get to the point where you enjoy it. The ability to think clearly, to communicate well, to laugh, to be productive and to feel healthier along with other benefits, are yours once you can better control anxiety.

How to Aggressively Fight Anxiety and Score a *Knock-Out*

Carmen said, "I was so afraid of authority figures and then was placed in a situation where I was surrounded by them. At work, they needed someone to take notes in the Executive Boardroom. They looked to me and I found myself surrounded by top management in what turned out to be weekly meetings. During the first few times, my hands would be sweaty and I just wanted to hide. Deep breathing helped a little, but over time, I began to see that these authority figures were mortal too. They made mistakes, became embarrassed, were talented yet flawed. They weren't so much different from me. Eventually my anxiety disappeared and to this date I view authority figures differently."

Depending on the severity of your anxiety, you have several options. You can use one or a combination of several approaches:

• Relaxation techniques. They slow your body down, relax your muscles and bring your consciousness to a deeper level by alleviating physical aspects of anxiety.
• Behavior therapy. You learn how to better cope with anxiety-producing events through controlled exposure to difficult situations. For example, if you're shy, make a few phone calls to stores and ask about their products. You can always hang up if you feel overly nervous. Extend the duration of calls by a minute or so as you become more comfortable.
• Cognitive therapy. This approach is utilized to change harmful thought processes into productive ones. Analyze the situation and challenge unrealistic thoughts.
• Cognitive behavior therapy. It teaches behavioral skills to deal with anxiety-producing situations.
• Medication. It's often used to alleviate severe symptoms of anxiety so other types of therapy can proceed.

Depending on the degree of anxiety you're feeling and the effectiveness of various treatments or approaches, you may want to consider trying others.

   Not all anxiety is bad for you. You can use anxiety constructively to avoid actual danger, or as a motivator to help you improve and grow while concurrently avoiding the immobilization that can result from irrational fears. You can use your mind, body and spirit to provide yourself with immediate, although temporary, relief from anxiety. After identifying what you're most afraid of, there are actions you can take to control fears and minimize anxiousness. In the process, you'll understand yourself better and come to the comforting conclusion that you have many options available.

   Share one or two of your fears and a plan to overcome them with a trusted friend. Those anxiety-producing situations will no longer have the same impact, and you'll find new courage to move forward. Plan to be as stress-free as you can and you'll be better off emotionally, intellectually, physically and spiritually. But there can be instances when you can't wait. What about times when you need relief NOW?

When You Need Immediate Relief from Fear and Anxiety

   By using your mind and spirit, also taking action emotionally and physically, you can use skills/techniques that almost act as temporary antidotes. To quickly relieve common anxiety, try one or more of the following:

Using your emotions or mind
   • **focus elsewhere** - When you're in the dentist chair and about to hear that wonderful sound of the drill, focus on an environment where you've felt comfortable and at peace. Vividly see yourself enjoying the day, watching attractive people wave to you and smile. Monitor your thoughts and if you find your focus wavering, force it back as much as you can. Or concentrate on and repeat, one word. It could be *peace, calm, God*, or any other word that brings you serenity. Repeat it over and over, excluding all other thoughts.

   • **talk about it** - Share your anxious feelings with someone safe. Verbalizing helps you clarify and work through feelings. Sharing things that have happened during your day is also helpful in preventing stressful or negative energies from building up. You can also write about it in a journal. You'll feel relieved once you express yourself and let it out.

   • **think about what's really important** - When you prioritize your schedule, you'll have direction and know what has to be completed first.

And conversely, a plan that clearly identifies what is not as important. Should there not be enough time to complete the less important tasks, you know the world will not end. Prioritize: take one thing at a time and stress will be minimized. For example, clear your desk of everything that does not pertain to what you're doing. You'll avoid becoming scattered, distracted or overwhelmed.

• **internal messages** – James Russell Lowell observes, "misfortunes hardest to bear are those which never come." Become an emotional detective, analyze the situation and determine why you are feeling anxious. If it's connected to your past, recognize that the current situation may not warrant the degree of anxiety you're feeling. Once that's clear, you can respond more appropriately and relax. And by replacing negative observations about yourself with positive views, you can better care for yourself and minimize anxiety. For example, replacing "I'm going to make an idiot of myself" with "I can do this", you'll affirm yourself and feel less anxious. You can also add, "if it doesn't work out perfectly, it's no big deal." Avoid talking yourself into an anxiety-producing event that really doesn't exist.

• **consider worst case scenarios** - If everything that could go wrong did, would it be life-threatening? What's the worst possible outcome? Accept that even the worst outcome would not be catastrophic. Then all other possible results will seem mild and acceptable in comparison. The stress-inducing intensity of the situation will be minimized.

• **laughter is great medicine** - If you're about to make a presentation to a group, picture them in clown suits, with underwear belonging to the opposite sex or any other visually funny image. This will get your mind off of the stress-producing impression you have of them or the situation, and will let you sidetrack or defuse anxiety by using humor.

Using your body

"Why did I ever agree to lead next week's ACOA meeting?" asked Johnny. "I get so nervous when I'm the center of attention that I sometimes forget what I need to say. But I'll try some techniques that worked in the past and hope they do this time. The day before the meeting, I'm going to work out at the health spa, take a sauna and then get some quality sleep. Then right before the meeting starts, I'll loosen up my muscles by using progressive relaxation and take deep breaths. If I can calm my body, my mind will be free to communicate effectively."

There are several *physical* ways to reduce anxiety:

• **exercise** - The best way to relieve stress from your body is to physically exercise. The tension in your muscles will be released, you'll end
up healthier and your mind will be sharper because of the increased
oxygen supply.

• **physically remove yourself** from a stress-producing environment
- If you're in a group where several people are arguing, you may want to
leave the area. Go for a drink of water, the bathroom or just take a walk.
If you don't need to be in a negative or anxiety-producing environment,
why be there?

• **meditation or progressive relaxation** - Meditation can relax your
mind, body and spirit. It's helpful to visualize a soothing environment
surrounding you. As you've already learned, progressive relaxation has
you focus on one muscle area at a time, slowly relaxing each until your
entire body has released tension.

• **deep breathing** - Take long, deep breaths repeatedly until you feel
your body starting to relax. Hold each breath for at least six seconds.
When you're tense, breathing becomes shallow. In contrast, deep breathing calms you naturally.

• **pillow talk** - Repeatedly punch a pillow while verbalizing about the
event that's causing you to be anxious. It will relieve physical tension in
your muscles.

• **don't push yourself beyond reasonable limits** – Trying to do more
and more with fewer resources and in less time is the definition of ef-
ficiency. But there comes a point where anxiety and fatigue become so
excessive that the quality of your work and health deteriorate. If at all
possible, avoid pushing yourself excessively.

• **medication** - There are many different anti-anxiety medications
that can be prescribed after consultation with your doctor. There are also
herbal alternatives available without a prescription. If you're having
difficulty sleeping as a result of your anxiety, over-the-counter sleep
medications may also help.

• **food and rest** – When you avoid caffeine, nicotine and sugar, you'll
be less jittery. Eat healthy and get enough rest. Pamper yourself with a

hot bubble bath before you go to sleep and you can't go wrong.

Using your spirituality

• **prayer** - When praying, recognize that all-powerful, loving God is there for you. Give thanks for your many blessings. Any anxiety or difficulties can be placed in God's hands for resolution. Ask for His help—turn it over and be open to guidance or hearing answers.

• **help someone** - When you offer yourself to a person experiencing pain, you're making a difference in her or his life. You'll also feel better about yourself and in the process, redirect anxious thoughts to more constructive ones. Seeing difficulties other people have can sometimes put your own in proper perspective.

• **attend a religious / spiritual organization** - Knowing that you're not alone, that your spirit is being renewed, and that spiritual and emotional support is available in a group of like-minded people will help you feel less anxious. Hearing that a higher power loves and cares for you can be quite comforting.

• **join a small group** - When a properly supervised support group meets, safety is assured. You can talk freely about what's really going on in your life without worrying that others will disapprove or gossip. If it's an ACOA group it will be particularly appropriate for you. Regardless of what type of group, you'll certainly receive support, encouragement, and will be able to release difficult emotional and spiritual thoughts that might be holding you back.

Whether you use temporary but immediate antidotes to stress, develop more long-range solutions, or choose to pursue a medical doctor's advice, anxiety can be managed. Stop fears from controlling you and you'll no longer be afraid of success, change or speed bumps along the way. You will discover a new freedom filled with possibilities

In addition to immobilizing fears, shame, guilt and depression are all serious problems that need to be addressed and overcome. The next chapter will deal with all three, offer options to help you deal with them and move away from self-defeating conditions or feelings. You deserve a life filled with positives, and that's where you're headed.

Five-Day Action Plan for Growth & Success:
Place a checkmark in each box as you complete the associated action:
❑   Talk to a friend about what's causing your anxiety. Express your
      concerns and explore the worst that could come out of the situation.
      Then consider all the other outcomes.
❑   Identify your top three anxiety-producing fears. Develop a plan that
      includes facing each fear directly. Approach this in incremental steps.
❑   Make a list of techniques that would best help you to overcome anxi-
      ety. Use them the next time you're feeling anxious.
❑   Using a mirror, look into your eyes and repeat these affirmations
      aloud in the morning and evening, as many times as it takes until you
      feel confident about what's being said:
      • I feel calm and in control.
      • I deal with my fears and overcome them.
      • I'm a work-in-progress, getting better every day.

Summary:
✔   Everyone feels anxious at times. Anxiety can drain you, distract your
      thoughts, minimize effectiveness and take away the enjoyment of
      life.
✔   If you were taught that the world was a dangerous place or received
      negative messages about yourself, seeds of anxiousness were planted
      into your belief system.
✔   Anxiety can be your friend and warn you of possible losses.
✔   The possible loss of love, control and self-esteem can cause anxiety.
✔   By using your mind, spirit, taking action emotionally and physically,
      you can use skills/techniques that can provide some immediate relief.
✔   Face your fears and you can overcome them.
✔   There are many different ways to fight anxiety.
✔   The discomfort of anxiousness or fear can be a strong motivator. It
      can prompt you to develop your coping skills and become stronger.
✔   Plan to be mostly stress-free and you'll be better off emotionally,
      intellectually, physically and spiritually.

Chapter 7

You are God's Creation and Treasure
Beat Unwarranted Guilt and Shame

"My mother would be alive today had I only stayed home," said Brian. "Instead she's been gone for 12 years." His mom was a Christian Scientist who believed in spiritual healing for what she thought was the flu. Her health problems were more than that. In fact she died of congestive heart failure, aggravated by the stress of a verbal attack by Brian's drunken father as she was lying down in what turned out to be her deathbed. "If I had been home, I could have kept him away. I could have gotten her to the hospital if I saw how serious her condition was. All she needed was for me to protect her while in a helpless condition, but I wasn't there in her time of need and she lost her life because of it. I should have known that my father would get drunk and go after her. I just should have known."

The child of an alcoholic often believes his or her existence or behavior causes a parent to drink and therefore must be present 24 hours a day to eliminate possible consequences of the alcoholic's behavior. If something bad happens, the child takes the full blame. The guilt leads to shame, emotions are internalized and because they're often unexpressed, depression can develop. In chapter 7, you may consider your own feelings of guilt or shame. These emotions can originate from past or present events and often are not appropriate. We, as ACOAs, could be assuming guilt and shame that shouldn't be ours to bear, or perhaps we do indeed need to make amends for some behavior. In any event, these feelings must be expressed in a healthy way and released. The "shame cycle" is explained in this chapter and you will learn how to break it.

Guilt, shame and depression can be addressed in a variety of ways. Sooner or later, these conditions/feelings touch most of us. But the

question arises—is it such a good idea to overcome ALL guilt? After
all, when we do something bad, shouldn't we feel guilty about it?
In my opinion we should, but there are times when guilt is generated from unexpressed anger or is simply "inappropriate guilt." Why
inflict unnecessary self-injury? You are not a mistake and it's time to
set yourself free from unwarranted emotionally debilitating conditions. And what is "inappropriate guilt?" It's guilt NOT based on
anything we've done or neglected to do. Rather it is related to externally developed belief systems, rules or unrealistic expectations fixed
by someone who was in a position of authority—such as an alcoholic
parent. Assuming responsibility for your parent's drinking or not
performing "perfectly" may have roots in the past, so it's inappropriate to assume guilt under these circumstances. According to Janet
Woititz, author of *Adult Children of Alcoholics*, one of the common
characteristics among ACOAs is that they judge themselves without
mercy. They also assess blame to themselves for anything that goes
wrong; they feel inadequate and different from others. These characteristics combine to form a breeding ground for guilt or not being
"good enough."

Brian's story illustrates how guilt and shame can be derived from
the unrealistic expectation of controlling external events precipitated by the behavior of an alcoholic parent. He further believed that
his mother stayed in this bad marriage because she wanted a stable
environment for his childhood, therefore he felt guilty for causing
her suffering by his very existence. Brian also felt guilty about not
insisting that she see a doctor and not rescuing her from that environment, because, in his mind, either may have saved her life. But
Brian's mother wouldn't have left her husband because she still was
in love. Not only that, but being a member of a church that believed
in spiritual healing, she chose to reject medical treatment. Her religious belief system was solid and she had the freedom to make her
own choices. Brian was trying to do the right thing by staying home
to protect her, but there came a point where his responsibilities ended
and hers began. The point here is that his guilt was *inappropriate*; he
now needs to forgive himself and resolve the pain. He did the best at
the time and under those circumstances. Harboring unnecessary guilt,
shame and depression now only helps to emotionally destroy the very
child his mother loved so dearly. That's not the outcome she would
have wanted.

Are you feeling inappropriate guilt or shame?

How to Address These Conditions

There are no easy solutions to guilt, shame and depression, but this chapter will assist you in understanding why these conditions are present and offer you several approaches to healing. To get started, you have to activate the recovery process, because those feelings and conditions will not go away by themselves. Don't be hesitant to admit your woundedness, because that's when healing can begin. If you need help, certainly ask for it. This may include assistance from therapy, medications, religious institutions, friends, group support and others. However the roots of guilt, shame and depression are often hidden and complex. So are the solutions, therefore it's imperative to dig down and find these roots, facing each with a positive, solution-based approach. It's also important to recognize that actions suggested in this chapter can empower you to take control and address these conditions. But before we consider them, reflect on how you have been wounded. Consider your answers to the following self-interview exercise.

Self-Interview Taping Exercise:

Use a tape recorder to record questions and answers to the following. Then rewind and carefully listen for the feelings along with meanings behind your responses. Summarize important insights into a notebook for reflection or action.
• What do you feel guilty about? What are some ways to resolve this?
• How do you "feed" your guilty feelings?
• Were you fully responsible for what happened or did external circumstances or past events play a part?
• What are you ashamed of? Describe any shameful messages you received from your parents. Did you believe what was said about you? Do those messages still reside in your belief system?
• How do you "feed" your feelings of shame?
• Are you depressed? If so, when and where did it begin? What can you do about it?
• What have you learned from your guilt, depressed feelings and shame? What can you do to alleviate these conditions?

Innocent, but You're Undeservingly Found Guilty. Cry Foul!

Can you imagine watching *Law and Order* on TV and hearing the judge make the following verdict: "Because you were raised with an alcoholic parent, I sentence you to a lifetime of guilt and shame because you just didn't suffer enough as a child. You were responsible for every bad thing that happened and should be ashamed. I order you to feed your guilt and shame by continuously believing that you're despicable—the world will be a better place as a result of your self-condemnation." That's an extreme scenario, but is it so far off from what you've been doing to yourself with regard to guilt and shame? Consider this example:

"I should have known that my mother would drive drunk on her way home from last year's Christmas party. I asked her to call if she needed a ride. But she didn't. I should have picked her up anyway," Denise said. "She crashed her car and ended up in the hospital for a week and it was all my fault. No matter how much time goes by, I keep feeling terrible about it—that she wouldn't have been injured if I hadn't been so lazy and inconsiderate by not driving her home."

What are the sources of *your* guilty feelings? It's one thing to feel bad about something you've done to purposely hurt someone, quite another to feel immobilizing guilt over something you had little control over. Perhaps you need to accept that you did your best at the time and under those circumstances. Maybe you weren't your best or didn't think of everything, but that doesn't mean you were (or are) a bad person. You can accomplish much more and live a happier life if you simply forgive yourself for not being perfect. Recognize the goodness in you and in other people, and acknowledge that not everything that goes wrong is your fault.

Another origin of guilt can be unresolved hurt or anger turned inwardly against yourself. You can either choose to express anger or hurt or keep those feelings inside and risk having them develop into more severe issues. That's why it's so important to talk about your feelings as they occur, to determine if you should take ownership of guilt or not. In addition, if anger is held in until you explode, your outburst may be more severe than warranted. Then you will perhaps have hurt someone else and will feel even guiltier because of it. If you believe you're a bad person, there's a general tendency to withdraw and withhold anger even more. The cycle becomes self-perpetuating. But you may very well be the innocent party here. If so, protest your innocence and don't be so quick to assume guilt.

There are No Magic Words

When we feel that we've done something that hurts others or violates our core beliefs about what's right and wrong, we can feel guilty. When anger is held inside us and not expressed, it can evolve into guilt. In addition, when we were children, we often blamed *ourselves* for our parent's alcoholism or incompatibilities. The child thinks that "if only I wasn't there, if I had gotten better grades, if I were not as bad as I was, everything would be fine."

And as adults, we sometimes think, "if I had just said the right words, things would have turned out differently," so we feel guilty. But there are no magic words. To think otherwise can only result in anxiousness and being so careful about what you say that you're no longer authentic. There will be times when you purposely say unkind things—and other times when your choice of words or actions isn't perfect and the other person may feel injured. Is guilt appropriate for all times when someone feels discomfort as a result of having contact with you? No it isn't. Let go of guilty feelings coming from circumstances you had no control over. For those you did, initiate corrective actions. Perhaps your guilt can be a positive motivator to heal a relationship. It can prompt you to change your direction or to deepen a relationship with heartfelt communication by taking ownership of the pain you caused the other person and asking sincerely for forgiveness. Discuss the guilt-producing event if there was a misunderstanding and try for resolution. Admit your responsibility, learn from the experience and do better next time. You will, with practice.

Sometimes people who feel guilty don't think they're deserving of happiness. They withdraw from life believing that no one would want to be in a relationship with them. But accept that you acted the way you did because of your circumstances. Perhaps you weren't your best self, but you weren't a bad person either. Sometimes you're simply an innocent victim of the past, but it's now time to stop being a victim by releasing inappropriate guilt.

Do what works for you so that your guilt might be relieved. Seek a physical, emotional and spiritual release. Cry, scream into a pillow, talk to someone, pray about it. If you sincerely ask for forgiveness from God, you will be forgiven.

Ejection is the Best Option for Bad Tastes—and Emotions, Too

When something tastes bad, you spit it out. It's the same with emotional distaste. You have to deal with your pain and express your various feelings or that bad emotional taste can become a part of you. If you don't, you run the risk of being repeatedly drawn to same painful emotional situations without learning important interpersonal lessons. When you hold pain inside, it can taint what is good, weigh you down, and prevent you from enjoying life. The guilt-producing event needs to be evaluated and feelings expressed so positive solutions can be considered.

If you feel guilty, ask yourself what you might have done differently. If things you said or did were unethical and hurt others, take corrective actions. Always try to do the right thing for yourself and others. But if guilt is emanating from unresolved anger or hurt, or if it's being generated based on things over which you had little or no control, recognize that fact and have some compassion for yourself.

How to End Shame's Destructive Cycle

The difference between guilt and shame is that with guilt you feel bad about an event, whereas with shame you globally believe that you yourself are defective and worthless. And if you convince yourself that you should be ashamed of yourself, that condition runs your life. Believing you are unworthy, inadequate and essentially worthless can make you just want to hide, wallowing in self-deprecation. And if you're ashamed of yourself, you don't want anyone to get too close, so you hide behind a mask - resulting in isolation, loneliness, deception, suffering and self-rejection. That's no way to live.

"I always knew that I was born out of wedlock and that my parents later married because of me," remembered Jack. "My father was a Navy guy who felt trapped being a father. So he drank and became an alcoholic because of me. All the pain my mom had to go through was because of my being born. I was so ashamed for being alive and causing this. No one could ever love such a person. I put on a mask so I wouldn't be alone all my life, but people abandoned me anyway. I'm just a miserable person."

Shame can originate in verbal or non-verbal messages received from an alcoholic parent. In order to cope, sometimes you learn to retreat behind a false self. And in some cases, activities such as drinking or using drugs are employed to feel better. According to John Bradshaw, the cycle of shame goes something like this:

• I'm defective and unlovable.
• No one can love me so I need something to make me feel better.
• Distracting/deadening myself (by drinking, drugs, TV, sex, etc.)
• But I have to pay the price (hangover, hurting others by using them,
• I was right – I'm a miserable person.
Then the cycle starts over again.

Getting Assistance in Overcoming Shame

You are NOT defective, inadequate or a mistake. Created in the image of God and placed on this earth to accomplish certain works, you are not a person deserving of shame. Unfortunately, simply believing those spiritual and emotional facts will not automatically make your shameful feelings disappear. In fact, if you're feeling shame, it's likely that you'll find it difficult to accept those facts. So to supplement those spiritual truths and the help a self-help book can provide, the assistance of a mental health professional may be advisable. After all, you're working to overcome a condition with a hurting spirit that requires more than acquiring new skills or what other self-help methods can provide. Even in a therapeutic environment, it may *initially* be difficult to verbally express your shameful feelings. You may be afraid that acknowledging your shame might risk intensifying it, or might confirm in your mind that you deserve to live a shame-filled life. Repression, the avoidance of self-observation, denying or avoiding conflict may have historically been your way to get by. And, keeping people at a distance by talking only about superficial things, you have been able to avoid dealing with shame.

Even in the therapist's office, you might try to talk about a picture hanging on the wall, other people's activities, the weather or any subject other than yourself. And you may decide that therapy isn't doing anything for you and walk away. Using these distraction or avoidance techniques is a sure way to prevent healing from happening. Remaining hidden rather than dealing with your needs will short-circuit any recovery. So be aware of these resistance factors and ensure that they don't stop you from pursuing recovery. Therapy can help change your perceptions, beliefs and patterns in a way that will bring you success, intimacy and closeness in relationships.

As a supplement to therapy, determine where your feelings of shame originate. If unresolved or unexpressed guilt is the source, further analyze what it's based on:

• *Actions or words you have initiated that did harm or violated your moral beliefs.* If so, atone, apologize and try to resolve the issue. Ask for forgiveness from the person, but also from God. You can be assured He will forgive.

• *Inappropriate guilt.* If so, find the true source, whether it be false beliefs originating from an alcoholic parent, misconceptions or unrealistic expectations from others. Recognize that it is not your guilt to bear and that you do not deserve self-punishment, isolation or shame. If you can change your self-talk, you'll cut off the feeding supply to shameful feelings and they'll disintegrate.

• *Unexpressed anger that was redirected inwardly and turned into guilt.* If so, express the anger in appropriate ways and release.

Previous judgments that pronounced you to be "defective" or "inadequate" were incorrect. You are not perfect - along with everyone else in the world. But you do deserve to be free of shameful feelings.

Depression—Treatable or Not?

Guilt and shame, if not released, can develop into depression. Symptoms include:

• hopelessness	• sleeping problems	• despair	• eating disorders
• lack of energy	• suicidal thoughts	• isolation	• low sex drive

Depression is treatable, and a combination of medication, therapy and exercise is usually most effective. Since the problem could be psychological, emotional, a short-term reaction to an event or a combination of many cumulative factors, a professional must be consulted to obtain an accurate diagnosis and treatment plan.

If your depression is mostly chemical, psychological treatments are helpful but not completely effective and the reverse is also true. But if your depression is psychological, there are simple actions you can take as a supplement to therapy:

• Don't isolate yourself – join groups or talk to friends. Increase your social skills so you can easily reach out to others. Become more proficient at creating a social support system. You need people in your life to feel connected, cared for and accepted.

• Challenge depressing thoughts or belief systems and adopt a positive self-concept. Drs. Robert Schuller, Norman Vincent Peale and Pastor Joel Osteen have shown that positive thinking directly affects self-confidence and human potential. Focus on positive events rather than negative and increase the frequency of your pleasurable activities. Stay away from activities that are difficult for you.

• Stop holding your emotions in, deal with them and vent if necessary. Grieve your losses, cry, share your sadness with a friend and stay in the present. Depression is often brought on by keeping emotions such as grief or guilt bottled up inside. Share your sadness with a friend.

• Take credit for your successes and put in proper perspective any responsibility for failure. Ask yourself the following questions: How were others, luck or fate responsible for the outcome? How were *you* responsible as a result of your actions, skills, abilities, knowledge, and efforts? This evaluation assigns recognition for your abilities but also responsibility to external factors for some unsuccessful outcomes.

• Reduce negative thoughts and replace them with positive ones. Seek out the best possible resources to help you on your recovery. Try several different activities such as exercising and doing something good for yourself today. Above all, take action to overcome depression, because it will not go away by itself. And remember that a full diagnosis is necessary to determine the cause and proper treatment. You can overcome depression and live a happier life once a diagnosis is made and corrective actions are pursued.

Other Methods for Overcoming Guilt and Shame

One self-help approach involves sharing your perceived inadequacies within the context of a support group. Acceptance within a group has the potential to reduce feelings of shame. The safe and confidential nature of the support group provides a framework for healing.

Another exercise to address childhood shame involves writing a letter to your parents (delivering it is not necessary) explaining how you were hurt and what you needed but didn't get. You communicate with your inner child and can re-parent her or him in a loving and supportive manner. Being recognized and feeling accepted helps to heal the inner child.

In addition, other exercises in the five-day action plans can help you build self-esteem, accept yourself, and visualize success. Affirmations and cognitive methods to challenge irrational beliefs/false conclusions can all work together to reduce guilt, shame and depression. You need to feel love and acceptance – everyone does.

The choice is either to overcome guilt, shame and depression so you can live a life filled with love and acceptance, or to continue to wallow in those conditions. If you do nothing, there will be isolation, sadness and a lack of intimacy in your future. But take action and you'll find that guilt, shame and depression can be minimized or eliminated. Once that's done, they will be an increase in your self-acceptance and you'll be free to enjoy life. Work through the following five-day action plan to gain further insight and relief. You'll be taking control over conditions that previously seemed uncontrollable.

And finally—be yourself. If you try to be someone you're not, you will always lose because you can never take credit for successes. Be *yourself* and you'll always be ahead of the game:

• live a meaningful and honest life that rejects guilt and shame
• accept yourself fully and build a healthy self-esteem
• learn lessons from your past disappointments so they don't recur

Shyness and a lack of social abilities often accompany feeling bad about yourself. If that is a difficulty for you (and remember that most people report being shy at one time or another), there will be information and skills to show you what to do about it in Chapter 8.

Five-Day Action Plan for Growth & Success:

Place a checkmark in each box as you complete the associated action:

❑ Sit across from an empty chair and visualize the person you are seeking forgiveness from. Explain what happened from your perspective, ask for forgiveness and hear the other person forgiving you.

❑ Write a letter to someone whom you didn't help or do your best for. Don't mail it; just write it, feel the grief and fully forgive yourself because you did the best you could at the time. Admit regret or grief, say you're sorry about the pain you may have caused and offer to talk it over. Think about what you'd like to accomplish.

❑ Write a letter to yourself from the person (living or deceased) whom you feel guilty about and express her or his forgiveness to you. (You may want to save this letter to read again sometimes.)

❑ Make a list of all the people and things you're grateful for. Validate yourself by listing all of your good qualities and strengths.

❑ Look into your eyes in a mirror, and repeat these affirmations aloud in the morning and evening, as many times as it takes until you feel confident about what's being said:
   • I release my guilty feelings.   • I've proud of myself.

Summary:

✔ Guilt may result from a violation of your personal moral code.

✔ Inappropriate guilt is NOT based on anything we've done. Rather it is related to externally developed belief systems, rules or unrealistic expectations fixed by someone who was in a position of authority—such as an alcoholic parent.

✔ The difference between guilt and shame is that with guilt, you feel bad about an event whereas with shame, you globally believe that you yourself are defective and worthless.

✔ When shame runs your life, you can end up living a lifetime of deception, suffering and self-rejection.

✔ If you stop "feeding" guilt and shame, they will disintegrate.

✔ Depression is treatable by a combination of medication, therapy and self-help exercises. But the first thing to do is obtain a diagnosis from a professional.

✔ Therapy may significantly help you overcome guilt, shame and depression even though you might be reluctant at first to consider or cooperate with it.

Chapter 8

Never Be Alone Again
Conversational Magic, See Shyness Disappear

   Jennifer's father was a violent drunk. He would slam her against the wall and threaten to kill her, often without warning. She was terrified and learned an adaptive behavior to survive. When he became aggressive, she simply became more and more passive. " 'I'm sorry I upset you and will do anything you want,' was my usual routine," Jennifer said. "At the time, my thinking was that if I gave in to him, he would be less likely to attack. But my self-esteem disintegrated and today I've become a shy, passive and withdrawn adult. I'm not much of a talker, nobody wants to be with me and my thinking is that I'm better off alone. That way I don't waste anyone's time and I'm not hurt when someone leaves me."

   Human beings are social creatures; we need each other to be emotionally healthy. This chapter offers ways to minimize shyness and includes a significant number of conversational techniques that can build your social confidence. Various degrees of intimacy and their respective communication levels are illustrated. Each is explained in detail along with guidelines indicating when they would be most effectively used. Some of these techniques are taught in training classes for crisis intervention hotlines but also work in non-crisis situations. They can promote deep-level communications and instill conversational confidence. You will be introduced to free-flowing association and shown how to effortlessly keep conversations interesting. Active listening skills are explained as well as non-verbal ways to effectively communicate and attract friends.

   You may or may not think of yourself as shy—but almost everyone has felt that way at some point or within certain circumstances. You can become trapped in a small emotional box, unaware that you can break out any time you wish. Of course there are things to learn, skills to practice, and also beliefs you need to become more realistic about. But it's never too late to decrease shyness and become socially proficient. Even if you don't consider yourself shy, there are always improvements that can be made to your communication style. In fact, you can learn to take the most problematic, emotionally charged conversation and almost magically transform it into something positive. There are techniques to do so, and as you do, you'll better understand the other person, too.

If you grew up hiding your feelings as a child of an alcoholic, you may never have learned how to communicate effectively or to feel secure enough about yourself to take social risks. Growing up in an environment where you did not experience guidance or encouragement can make you more susceptible to shyness than a child who did because ACOAs generally feel insecure and different from other people, and lack conversational skills. Shy or not, you'll find important communication skills in this chapter. You'll also learn different techniques that can increase your social competency. With practice, you'll be more at ease in social gatherings and enjoy communicating with others. You will be venturing out of your somewhat protective comfort zone as you practice new skills and take a few risks. But instead of living a life of solitude or ineffectiveness, you'll be empowered to explore new opportunities, experience intimacy and love. The wonderful benefits far exceed any temporary discomfort you may feel. So let's first understand what shyness is and then see what to do about it.

Anatomy of Shyness – The Components

Basically, shyness is comprised of several different components, all of which can be altered. It has nothing to do with any inherent personal inadequacies – only with habits that can be changed and skills that can be improved.

1. Under-developed social skills
Social skills are like any other skills – they can be learned and practiced, and as a result, you can get very good at them. Circumstances from your past may have kept you from learning certain interpersonal skills earlier. But there's nothing but you holding you back now.

2. Fear of negative evaluation

Irrational beliefs about your imagined inadequacies may have been formed a long time ago, evolving into social anxiety. At that time and even now, you could somewhat avoid any possibility of being criticized, ridiculed or made to feel inferior as a result of other people's comments by simply staying away from people. When you have no choice but to interact with others, you may be so preoccupied with what you might say, how it could be perceived, and what to do next that your mind freezes up. When your mind goes blank, not knowing what to say, it can perpetuate the belief that you are socially inept. Compounding that, you may also be so sensitive that even constructive suggestions for improvement are blown out of proportion. In your perspective, they are direct attacks on your feelings of worth or competence, and simply reconfirm the incorrect belief that you just don't have what it takes. In reality, you have everything necessary within you.

"I know it was foolish to think that if I got perfect grades, always said the right things and dressed perfectly, my father would have no reason to drink," said Pritti. "But he would always put me down for my failings and drink heavily afterward. So I tried harder and harder to be perfect but could never be. The drinking and put-downs continued." The fear that you'll be made fun of or rejected has its origins in the unrealistic belief that everything you do must come out perfectly and that everyone else must think of you as being faultless. But these are irrational and untrue beliefs. Alcoholism can perpetuate behavior in a parent that can leave a child feeling inferior. The truth is that you and everyone else make mistakes. No one is perfect. Making an error doesn't mean that *you* are in any way a mistake. You can throw out your old critical belief system and replace it with a healthy and realistic one. And the more skills you learn and practice, the faster conversational proficiency becomes a reality for you.

3. Negative thinking stinks

We've already seen how important self-talk is. Shyness can increase tremendously if you say negative things to yourself. When you're so critical of yourself, you reinforce negative self-worth. Who wants that? Then you tend to give up easily and simply avoid the very social opportunities that can help you develop new skills and overcome shyness. Just as you can learn new skills, you can change your thinking process and belief system.

As soon as you begin thinking negative thoughts, remember the smell of a skunk, attach it to those words and get rid of what stinks. Instead, flood your mind and spirit with positive and affirming words. Give yourself credit for taking action.

A Bigger, Brighter and Expanded World Opens up for You

"I'm getting married next week to the girl of my dreams," said Mario. "I used to be so shy that I couldn't even talk to women my age for fear they'd reject me. But the loneliness was so painful that I decided to do something about it. There was a shyness clinic at a local hospital and it helped me look at myself differently and learn how to relate to others. It was the first time in my life that I started to like who I was. Previously my personality was hidden from others and me. But as I worked to overcome shyness, the veil was removed, the real me was revealed and my life began to change. Loving relationships were formed, new opportunities at work developed, I could handle temporary setbacks and I finally felt in control of my life."

Once you've minimized shyness in your life, you can say goodbye to isolation and loneliness. You'll interact with a greater number and variety of people, expanding your opportunities. The way you talk to yourself will change and you'll become more socially active, even though it will feel a little uncomfortable to do so at first. As you learn and practice new social skills, it's important to give yourself credit for your efforts, even if the results aren't perfect.

Expanding your world will change your life. Emotional well-being, success in your career, discovering that you can and should have high self-worth – those and so many other benefits far outweigh any temporary discomfort. It is a gradual process, so be patient with yourself. There's no doubt that you'll feel discomfort and apprehension as you move forward and out of your solitary confinement. That uneasiness is a good thing because it means you really are taking risks and not just going through the motions half-heartedly. Because of your efforts, your world and competencies will be expanding.

Self-Interview Taping Exercise:
Use a tape recorder to record questions and answers to the following. Then rewind and carefully listen for the feelings along with meanings behind your responses. Summarize important insights into a notebook for reflection or action.

• What happened to cause you to feel shy?
• What keeps you from increasing your social competencies?
• How will you practice your new skills?
• Talk about five things you like about yourself.
• How would you start a conversation with a stranger?
• What are some things you can talk about tomorrow?

Back-to-basics Conversation Techniques

Some of the following information about social skills will be basic to you. But a refresher never hurts. If you feel it's too elementary, simply skim through this section and move on. If not, begin now to learn the skills that will bring you social success.

Yada, yada, yada or blah, blah, blah – that's about the degree of communications we'll first be looking at. There are different levels and innumerable types of verbal interaction between people. The easiest but most meaningless is called a cliché. For example, "How's it going?" or "What's new?" You go a little deeper when you talk about facts or opinions about what's going on. For example, the weather, the physical location you're in or the activities that are happening. All are superficial yet common subjects that can be useful when initiating a conversation with a stranger because they are impersonal and easy subjects to talk about.

For a little more substance in your communication, you can move on to discuss what a person likes or dislikes, her or his interests, personal needs, values and, eventually, feelings. Sharing your feelings with someone adds depth and quality. In general, the more you share your feelings with others, the more they'll open up. But easy does it - not everyone will be receptive. Even when they are, make sure that the level of sharing is evenly balanced. And generally it's helpful if a foundation of friendship already exists. Monitor what's going on as you start sharing your emotions. Someone may back away from you if they interpret the interaction as being inappropriate or if your disclosure of feelings is premature. Conversely, if you don't share enough about yourself, others may find the communication too superficial. In that case, perhaps you aren't allowing others close enough to really know you. This is not to say that you should fixate on this balancing act, just be aware. If someone seems uncomfortable or distant when talking with you, simply ask yourself if you're revealing your emotional self appropriately. You can always easily adjust.

When asking questions, open-ended ones will almost always help the conversation flow more easily. That means any question except those that require a one- or two-word answer. Avoid questions that can be answered with "yes", "no" or "maybe." Start with "how, in what way, what" and so forth. This allows the other person to fully explain her or himself and conveys a message that you are really interested in finding out more. In addition, it takes some of the pressure off you. Become genuinely interested in the other person and appreciate the opportunity to share. Think about what she or he would enjoy talking about rather than just focusing on your agenda.

To keep the conversation going, you can relate what has already been said to something similar from your experience. You can also talk about related subjects or start an entirely new topic. If you think you'll be nervous in a particular interaction, coach yourself with a series of questions or topics in advance, but do not use it as a script. No matter what the subject, always be honest and authentic. It's usually not hard for others to pick up on insincerity. Ask questions only when you're sincerely interested in hearing what the other person has to say. And don't think about *impressing* – instead concentrate on *expressing*.

Branch Out:
Use Free-flowing Association for Creative Conversations

Relax and let your mind use free-flowing association – connecting your experiences or knowledge with whatever is being discussed. Your interactions will flow freely and easily, and you'll be more interesting. Relax. If your mind is frozen in terror, your social experiences will unfortunately be limited to brief interactions. Think of a main topic of discussion as a large maple tree and your mind as a squirrel running along the many different branches. No, you're not a nut if you do this - just a better conversationalist. First, practice when you're alone so that you see how it works without having to immediately respond to another person. Then try it out with a friend. It's a new skill that takes practice, but it is great fun after you master it.

People You'll Never See Again: a Perfect Practice Opportunity

If you're on a bus, plane, in line at the supermarket, or anywhere in public, try practicing your new communications skills. The more you rehearse, the more desensitized you become to social anxiety. Start a friendly conversation about your surroundings, the weather or anything of a casual nature. Test out how well certain questions, facial expressions or other techniques work. Some people will be more open than others to talking to a stranger. They may, in fact, be shy, so remember that not everyone will cooperate with your experiment. But many will. You have nothing to lose but your shyness. Consider it a game, keep track of how many new people you approach, and reward yourself lavishly (a massage, a decadent dessert, etc.) when you reach a certain number. Remember - these are people you'll never see again, so if it doesn't work out smoothly, it shouldn't be a big deal. Laugh about what happened and forget it. And cherish the times when you have a good experience. You're simply using their presence to practice skills, and at the same time offering what could be a pleasurable experience for both of you.

By taking more risks, fine-tuning a number of social skills through trial and error, and developing skills into habits, you'll learn poise and social confidence. It's also helpful to observe others who seem at ease in social situations and mimic what they do. Identify and copy their verbal skills and non-verbal actions. Use what would work for you and discard the rest. Your mental attitude will become more positive when you become more at ease talking to people, and you'll be increasingly comfortable talking about yourself. It'll probably be "two steps forward and one step back" for a while, but don't shy away from these new challenges. You're growing and breaking through barriers so you can enjoy social proficiency and live fully.

Active Listening Skills Can Get You Out of Hot Water

This is a more advanced technique taught at seminars. It is mandatory for CONTACT crisis intervention hotline volunteers but anyone can use it. It's especially effective when a subject is emotionally charged or when you want to completely understand what's being communicated. Here's how it works:

• Listen for Feelings
As you listen to a person speaking, watch for all non-verbal and verbal cues that might reveal what she or he is feeling. Listen to what they're *saying* but concentrate mostly on what they're *feeling*. For example, "My sister is moving out" could be responded to with "You're kind of worried about that?" or "That has really upset you?" or "How do you feel about that?" when you want to determine what's

really going on. If someone is yelling at you, calmly reply by say-ing, "you're feeling very angry at me." That will enable the person to clarify what's really going on and also vent what needs to be released.

• Acknowledge Feelings

If a person is annoyed, you might acknowledge her or his feeling by saying, "I can see you're annoyed." This validates their feelings and gives them an opportunity to further elaborate.

• Clarify the Feelings:

If you're unsure about what the person is trying to express, ask for clarification. Phrases like these are helpful:

You sound... (angry, sad, concerned, etc.)
Can you give me an example of...
Could you tell me more about this...
Are you saying...
Can you tell me what you meant when you said....

• Use Open-Ended Questions

Begin with *How,* or *Tell me more* and the person will more fully express thoughts, feelings and concerns. Never use the word "Why" since this tends to sound judgmental. If you do, he or she may shut down, effectively ending constructive communication.

• Adjust Your Tone of Voice

Decreasing your talking speed or increasing the tentativeness of your questioning differentiates constructive questions from inter-rogation. Also the tonal quality of your voice is important. Speaking slowly and quietly conveys more intimacy.

• Paraphrase - Check It Out

Make sure you're hearing the person correctly by paraphrasing - repeating what she or he has said, using your own words. After the speaker has fully expressed herself or himself, test your understand-ing by "feeding back" what you think you heard. This feedback technique also helps the speaker clarify what they're saying and feel-ing. And it shows whether or not you have really understood. You can lead into a paraphrase by saying something like:

Let me see if I heard you correctly. What you're saying is ...

And finally, always allow the other person to fully say what they need to say, without interruption or argument. Active listening generally isn't appropriate for everyday communications because of its intensity. But if the subject is sensitive or critical, and if you really need to understand what's being said, active listening is the way to go.

Appreciation – Nourishment for The Soul and Fat-Free

"He's always there for me," or "she makes me smile" or "I love the way he's so passionate to me." Are you expressive in your gratefulness to others? There's an old but true story about a teacher who noticed tension between her students. As an exercise to help them appreciate one another, she had everyone write their names on the top of a piece of paper and pass them to the next person. The classmate would then write one positive thing they liked about that person and pass it on until all students participated. Almost all the kids were nicer to each other after that but she didn't realize how powerful that exercise had been until years later. The teacher had retired and was attending the funeral of one of her previous students when the student's widow approached her. She handed her a crumpled piece of paper – the same one listing all the positive comments from that exercise. It seems he had carried that with him for years, always looking at it whenever life got tough. It brought him the self-confidence and courage to become very successful in life. And the teacher met some of her other past students at the wake, who told her that they also kept and cherished their pages filled with positive statements. To be appreciated is perhaps one of the most important feelings a person can have. It's nourishment for the soul. Each of the students can attest to that.

When there's something you honestly like or appreciate about another person, let them know about it. People crave appreciation – that was noted decades ago in Dale Carnegie's book, *How to Win Friends and Influence People*, and it's still true. It's just human nature. When you're delivering a compliment, be specific, call the person by her or his name, and you can even follow up with an immediate question to make the flow a bit easier. For example, follow "you're very talented - that's beautiful artwork you've created", with "how did you learn to do it?" That allows the other person to appreciate the compliment, release any embarrassment and feel good that you want to know more. And for obvious reasons, the best time to deliver words of praise or appreciation is when you aren't looking for anything in return. If you are the one receiving a compliment, say "thank you" and accept it rather than diminishing or ignoring it. Internalize the compliment.

Finally, ask yourself what you could do to make a conversation more enjoyable. Don't just talk about what interests you. Think about what the other person is involved with or might be interested in. You'll be well received. And remember that people are naturally drawn to pleasure and away from pain. You don't always have to be "up" and talk about wonderful subjects, but keep in mind that negativity breeds more negativity. Make yourself into a social pleasure magnet for positive and supportive people.

Non-verbal Communication:
A Secret to Being Fully Understood

Eye contact, smiling, facial expressions and body language can have much greater impact than words alone. The phrase *a picture is worth a thousand words* is true. Consider someone saying "you drive me crazy" with a smile, a warm hug, and loving eyes. The non-verbal cues override the words themselves. So keep that in mind when you're communicating, especially when you are expressing your emotions. Try to match your verbal and non-verbal messages. Have an open posture, use your arms and general body language, and even exaggerate your movements occasionally. Freeing your body can release stress. You'll certainly be more interesting when you verbally *and* physically (non-violent gestures) convey the message.

Refer to Your List - Vividly Experience Success

At any point, your self-esteem can be measured by comparing the number of positive things you feel about yourself versus the negative. You've made a list of your positive attributes in a previous chapter. Refer to it now or make a new one. Remember your good qualities by referring to the list as needed. Helplessness can be replaced with feelings of competency by continuously building a succession of positive social experiences.

In addition to focusing on your good qualities, it's important to clearly remember, and emotionally experience, your successes. The psychological impact will reinforce the belief that you can increasingly try to achieve more. It creates hope and increases self-worth. Of course, you will experience both success and disappointment. But people who are shy are inclined to blame themselves when they are unsuccessful. They also give the credit to something/someone external when goals are achieved. That's a no-win approach and the habit needs to be broken. Instead, take credit when you succeed and look for external reasons for failure. If things go wrong, you can also try harder next time, but don't automatically look for inadequacy in yourself. Be constructive in your journey. See where you can improve. Feel proud of yourself for trying, and look to succeed next time.

Definitely better late than never

No one comes into this world pre-equipped with verbal and non-verbal skills. In order to interact well with others, skills need to be learned - either sooner or later. It's no big deal if you master some skills later than someone else does. The important thing is that you are now learning, and the results will be the same. You are the catalyst behind your successful encounters. The attainment of skills, organization of information, mental rehearsal, revisions, and ongoing effort will bring you an increasing number of successes. Every time you apply the appropriate new skills and feel the success, you become more comfortable in social situations. If your mind is relaxed, free mental association can be utilized and you'll become more proficient in longer-lasting conversations. You'll develop a style that's more interesting and alive.

Reasonable goals

Your social goals must be realistic in nature – neither too hard nor too easy for best results. If you choose extremely simple goals, and the encounter is not difficult, there's little credit to take. Set your sights too high and success can be dismissed by saying you were just lucky. But if the level of difficulty of your social goals is reasonable, then the attainment of those goals is unquestionably attributable to your efforts. You can then take full and complete credit.

What if I crash and burn?

Look at the reasons why someone might have been unreceptive to your approach or why your invitation was turned down. Consider her or his interests and perspective; did you think about what the other person might enjoy talking about rather than just setting your own verbal agenda? If things weren't successful, maybe you didn't try hard enough. Just give it more effort next time.

On the other hand, many failures can be attributable to external factors, like bad timing or an unrealistically high goal in an unreceptive environment. An example of that would be going to an opposing political organization and trying to change their opinions. How successful would anyone be? Write it off to being a problematic and almost impossible endeavor.

In a personal encounter, there can be any number of reasons why someone might not favorably respond. Maybe the other person interprets your invitation as one that could lead to a romantic relationship. She or he may be involved with someone else and therefore unavailable. They may be recovering from a painful breakup, or may be preoccupied with other things. Their needs/interests may not be the same as yours at the present time. Or they may not be interested in pursuing a relationship with anyone. The other person may be shy, upset or simply not in a sociable mood.

Some external factors that can affect the outcome of your invitations are:
• Availability – there may be previous commitments or time constraints.
• How receptive the other person is – your invitation could be misinterpreted or she or he may simply not be interested in any new friendships or romantic relationships. Or perhaps they're just having a bad day.
• History – maybe you don't know each other long enough. Once the other person sees you over an extended period of time, there may a change of mind and a favorable response.
• Needs/desires – they change constantly and the other person's desires may or may not be the same as yours. A doctor doesn't feel rejected because you aren't sick. In the same way, you shouldn't feel rejected if another person has different needs than yours.
• Interests – you may not share common interests. Everyone is in different stages of growth and has varying tastes.

You don't know what's going on inside their world. So keep any rejection in proper perspective. No one ever gets 100% approval. Just learn from the experience and move on to someone who would appreciate the many things you have to offer.

Getting it All Together, Using Conversational Magic

You now understand what shyness is comprised of and you have learned various techniques to minimize it. You've also seen that there are progressively deepening levels of communication:

Small talk/cliches: What's up? How about this weather?
Facts: I work for _____. I'm taking a trip tomorrow.
Opinions: This is a good book. California is a beautiful state.
Feelings: I feel angry with you. I love you.

You can ask questions, show interest in people's responses, link the discussion to your own experiences and form a relationship. When you share your feelings, it enables others to really know you. Trust builds as the content of each other's sharing becomes deeper. Non-verbal techniques help to reinforce your verbal communications. When you regularly practice your skills, your proficiency increases. Add a realistic and positive belief system and you've got a recipe for maximizing your social competency. The walls that have kept you in solitary confinement (what we call "shyness") are disappearing, every day a little bit more. And you now know how to communicate even in emotionally charged situations. Your skills are definitely developing, so it's time to make new friends. If you were or are feeling lonely, that's going to change.

In the next chapter we'll look at anger. It's an interesting and potentially explosive emotion. You'll see the good, the bad and the ugly. But when anger is correctly managed, it can produce wonderful results. Relationships can be greatly enhanced and you can realize that it's okay to express, rather than repress it.

Five-Day Action Plan for Growth & Success:
Place a checkmark in each box as you complete the associated action:
❑ Observe how others communicate and try some of their techniques.
❑ Every day this week, start a friendly conversation with three strangers.
❑ Show your appreciation to a friend. Fully accept compliments from others.
❑ Monitor your self-talk very carefully, and if you start to say negative things about yourself, stop immediately. Either replace them with positive words or if necessary, silently yell, "Stop, Stop!" to yourself. Release the stinking thinking.
❑ Practice your non-verbal expressions and movements, first in front of a mirror, then in public. Also practice free-flow association each day.
❑ Share some of your feelings with a trusted friend.
❑ Make a list of all your successes during the week and reward yourself.
❑ Look in a mirror, into your eyes and repeat these affirmations aloud in the morning and evening, as many times as it takes until you feel confident about what's being said:
• I'm friendly and people like me. • I deserve happiness.
• I'm a good communicator.   • I feel great about my success.

Summary:
✔ Shyness is comprised of underdeveloped social skills, negative beliefs and a fear of being perceived as inadequate or deficient.
✔ Shyness is nothing more than a temporary condition that you can change.
✔ There are different levels of communication – small talk/cliches, facts, opinions, feelings.
✔ Free-flowing association connects your experiences with whatever is being discussed.
✔ With active listening, you listen carefully for feelings behind the words. You also paraphrase to confirm that what you heard was correct.
✔ Using verbal and non-verbal skills together is most effective.
✔ The fear of negative evaluation needs to be minimized.
✔ Set reasonable goals, be yourself, and you'll have fun with your new social skills.

Chapter 9

Expressing Anger Without Going to Jail
Release and Use Anger Constructively

"I'm a non-violent person but in that instance, I could have killed him," Ralph remembered. Thirty years later, he still remembers the intensity of his uncontrollable anger. "My mother tried to get the car keys from my drunken father who was leaving to go to a bar and she was violently thrown to the ground along with a glass table that shattered as a result of the impact. I heard the crash along with my mother crying hysterically and ran to see what happened. It just took one look, and I punched my father in the face who fell back into a television that also crashed to the ground. The next thing I remember was that my hands were around my father's throat, strangling him. Anger, to this day, still frightens me because I don't know if I'll end up out of control."

This chapter explains that anger must be released rather than stifled or ignored; otherwise it can grow in intensity and produce catastrophic results. You may explore why you might be holding it in, including reasons related to being raised in a household where alcoholism was present. Direct and indirect ways of expressing anger are illustrated and you're shown how to choose between the two. Alternative actions are presented for when you are feeling excessive anger that needs immediate relief. And finally an action plan is developed to use anger constructively.

Do you ever feel out of control? There are many ways to express anger, or you can choose to stuff it inside as you probably did as a child. If you don't release or vent the emotion, it has the potential to evolve into guilt or depression. And physically, you can end up with an upset stomach, stress and maybe even an ulcer. If you do release it and let it out in a massive explosion, relationships (or even bodies) may be irreparably damaged. Anger, depending on how you treat it, can be destructive or can help you feel better and make your relationships more authentic.

You'll also become aware of possible other culprits that may be making your anger much more explosive than the immediate circumstance would warrant. A reasonable degree of conflict can be quite productive and you'll understand how you can make it so. You'll see the difference between assertiveness and aggression, and also become empowered to make choices. Everybody can win.

Self-Interview Taping Exercise:

Use a tape recorder to record questions and answers to the following. Then rewind and carefully listen for the feelings along with meanings behind your responses. Summarize important insights into a notebook for reflection or action.

• How did people in your family deal with anger when you were a child? Think of a specific instance.
• What do you feel when people direct their anger at you? (victimized, angry, sad, embarrassed, worthless, etc.)
• What makes you angry?
• How do you now express anger? (explode, withdraw, feel sad, passive-aggressive, etc.)
• What have you learned from NOT dealing with anger?
• Think of a recent time when you felt angry. What secondary feelings were underneath it? (fear, rejection, guilt, loneliness, etc.)

Stuff the turkey, not your anger

"All of my relatives came for Thanksgiving dinner the year I turned 13 and it was a disaster," remembered Angela. "My mom hit the bottle a few hours before and was barely able to stand without falling over. She proceeded to tell everyone what a failure I was and then called me a slut because I was wearing nail polish. I was humiliated and enraged but could do little else but run from the table. The next time she was drunk, the unexpressed anger exploded. I screamed at her, shoved the dishes off the kitchen table and threw a glass at her. I just couldn't hold it in any longer."

Anger happens when there's an attack (verbal or physical), a threat, stress or possible loss to us, people we care about, property, or self-esteem. It also happens when we don't get what we want or experience an assault on our values. If you can outwardly express your anger, it will usually be dissipated. But when you hold it in, bad things happen. Anger can continue building up and easily turn into rage. Or it may transform into guilt. If these feelings remain chronically unexpressed, they can develop further into a sense of helplessness and depression.

Anger is a normal feeling that needs to be expressed; however, it is often stifled for various reasons. As a child, you were entirely dependent on your parents and the environment was volatile to begin with. Expressing yourself may have made matters worse, and in some cases precipitated violence. And you may have learned from various experiences that there's an unacceptable price to pay for being expressive. Perhaps you've lost a friend, were ridiculed or punched in the nose. Or maybe you simply felt remorseful after lashing out at someone. Every circumstance is different, and stuffing your anger *every time* because you may have received some negative responses is counterproductive. What's keeping you from expressing your anger today?

Do you stop yourself because you think you'll lose control?
If you vent anger before it builds, it'll never reach an explosive state. You can learn how to be in control of your anger. In fact, the better you become at expressing it, the more under control you'll be. When you *don't* express it, that's when it can go wild.

Do you keep quiet because you're afraid to hurt someone?
You may be concerned that the other person is too needy or fragile and will be unable to take the hurt. However, you can be sensitive and compassionate, taking her or his well-being into account while still expressing your anger and freeing those emotions. You're doing a disservice to others by not being real with them. If they're overly sensitive, simply be gentle; let them know why you're angry and that your friendship is still important to you.

Retaliation can be a serious concern.
When a motorcycle gang passes your car, you shouldn't try to run them off the road because the noise is making you angry. There could be some retaliation or worse: injury. In a safer environment, retaliation can take the form of a person's silence, withholding of favors, termination of the relationship, and so on. But the consequences could be manageable. Look at the situation and make a rational determination.

Do you refrain from expressing anger because someone is "buying" your friendship?
Sometimes people can be afraid of losing you so they try to lock in

your friendship through gifts or being excessively nice. Unbalanced generosity can cause you to feel resentful. This resentment can grow into anger, but you could be reluctant to express it. That's because you may feel a debt. But you are being manipulated and it's natural to be angry. Your friendship doesn't come with a price tag. Be open about your discomfort with the imbalance and make it better.

<u>Do you not express anger because you believe it to be destructive?</u>
Using anger constructively can actually help relationships become closer. When you're up front and disclose how and why you feel angry, it's possible to resolve difficulties. However, that's not possible if you keep your anger hidden inside. Your true friends want to be close to you and have the relationship be real. You're being open and honest with your feelings. There's nothing destructive about that.

There are many other emotional blocks that can keep you from expressing anger. But once you identify them, you can take a closer look and see if that actually is the best course of action or not. It's dependent on the situation, but keep in mind that if you always stuff your anger, the result can be physical and emotional problems.

Anger Dynamics and Progression

"My estranged father and I were to have dinner for the first time in years," said Kelly. "I thought he might like to resolve some of the difficulties brought on by his alcoholism during my childhood. But when I showed up at the restaurant he was with a business associate so we couldn't talk about anything of substance. I was fuming by the time I got home. How dare he waste my time and turn what could have been a time for healing into superficial nonsense! That son of a bitch never loved me and he continues to prove it. He probably had this all planned to continue abusing me. I'm never going to talk to him again and hope he drops dead."

A minor irritation can escalate into significant rage. How does this happen? That small annoyance left to fester in your mind, replays itself over and over. It grows with the accompanying self-talk that magnifies the perceived unfairness and sheer audacity of the other person's actions. The volcano is ready to explode. And what caused the anger in the first place holds little significance in comparison to the rage you're now experiencing.

Alternatively, you could blame your lack of assertiveness or self-worth for letting this event happen to you and become depressed. Those are two of the roads you can take, both bumpy ones that can cause you pain. Who needs that? Why not instead take a direction that can deepen your relationships and solve difficulties? You can do this by using anger skills. Before examining them, there are "anger dynamics" that should be understood. Underlying the current occurrences prompting you to feel angry may be experiences traced to past traumas or disappointments. Unresolved ACOA issues may be the cause of *unusually strong* emotional responses. That's because energy or words from a current situation may remind you of similar but more intense situation from your past. With that dynamic happening, sometimes we're not so intensely angry for the reasons we think.

Next time you feel angry, look to your past and see if there's something contributing to the intensity of your emotional upset. For example, if your girlfriend/boyfriend becomes overly affectionate in public after a glass of wine, you may be reminded of a time when your parent became promiscuous after drinking. You associate today's actions with the abuse or shame you once suffered and react similarly. Certainly if unresolved, what was done to you as a child can still cause you to react disproportionately to an occurrence today.

But when you recognize that most of the anger is coming from a past event, you can put things in proper perspective. You may still have reason to be angry, but the intensity is more reasonable.

How to *Directly* Express your Anger: Skills that Will Help

"I felt humiliated and angry when you told your friend Donna that I wasn't the greatest lover," said Hector. "That is a private, sensitive subject for me and by broadcasting my shame, I felt my manhood was being attacked."

If someone has done something that's made you angry, it's best to speak directly to her or him about it. Before expressing your anger, consider what part you may have contributed to the situation. For example, if you're too sensitive or misread their words, you may be blaming her or him for your misinterpretations or incorrect beliefs. You can quickly alienate others by incorrectly attacking them for *your* issues. When you're clear about where your anger should be directed and are ready to talk, find a non-threatening and neutral location. A walk outdoors can be an especially good place because of its openness. Ask the other person if you can meet with her or him to discuss something important. Then begin your conversation owning your anger. For example, "I felt mad when…" enables you to state your feelings without attacking the other person.

If you find it less intense to talk over the phone, take that approach. Make certain the other person has time to talk, and again set the mood by saying you have something important you'd like to discuss. I would recommend *against* writing a letter or e-mail. The written word has the greatest chance of being misinterpreted. That's because you can't observe body language or listen to the tone of a person's voice. When negative comments are put into writing, they can also be reread over and over again, long after the disagreement may have been otherwise resolved. After talking, give the other person an opportunity to respond and note their reactions. It may be a simple misunderstanding, so be ready to forgive. However if she or he does not respect your feelings, maybe it's time to find another friend who does.

Sooner is Better than Later – Anger Builds Exponentially

Live in the present. Deal with anger issues when you actually feel the feeling or shortly afterward, and don't allow them to accumulate. The most effective way to express your anger is to talk about your hurt to the person who you believe injured you – and as soon as possible. You should be honest, clear and direct while taking responsibility for your feelings. Don't attack or blame, but rather just report what you're feeling, using the word "I". If you attack or are blaming, she or he will likely become defensive and the argument may spiral out of control. The relationship could be damaged rather than improved. Take note that the other person may have done or said something you perceived as hurtful although it was not intended to be. Expressing yourself openly and without aggression allows for a clearer understanding of the problem and its possible resolution. Take responsibility for your anger by owning it. For example, say "I'm angry about…" rather than "You get me so mad." Using "I" enables you to also clarify exactly what you're feeling while avoiding a situation where the other person becomes defensive.

Following your expression of anger, let the other person know that you feel better and thank her or him for listening. Seeing that your pain has been relieved, the person can sense your forgiveness and relax. It's important to work through your anger and resolve it so that no residual feelings remain. By doing so, you'll likely experience increased intimacy and closeness. And to repeat: the sooner you do it, the better. Resentment will grow when the situation isn't resolved, and rage can be quite harmful. When anger is expressed constructively and in a timely manner, a resolution can often be attained.

Assertiveness versus Aggression – No Need for Boxing Gloves

"I'm feeling angry at you and would like to talk about it." "I'm going to smash my fist into your face." These two approaches are quite different. As previously mentioned, anger expressed appropriately can be helpful and productive. Certain hidden issues can rise to the surface and perhaps be resolved. Cleansing relationships of built-up emotional toxins reduces stress and makes for a more open exchange of feelings. When you verbalize, it also becomes possible to discover some of the feelings *underlying* your anger. For example, when someone is promoted at work instead of you, are you really angry or could you be feeling hurt, jealous or inadequate? Talk to someone about it. Look behind your anger and you might dramatically increase your self-knowledge.

Asserting yourself means being forceful but not attacking the other person. It does not require negativity or aggression. If you are unfamiliar with this skill, you might look to adult schools for a class – it's offered quite often. By using assertiveness techniques, you can address your needs and stand up for yourself. You'll be able to use anger constructively and become more empowered. You can also become assertive with your actions by being motivated and going after what you want.

Thinking that nothing can be done about how others treat you and that you're simply a helpless victim is wrong. Assertiveness can save the day. Anger is an opportunity for you to access your feelings and learn from them. Use it to stand up for yourself. You'll gain self-respect by empowering yourself and taking the initiative to use anger constructively

How to *Indirectly* Express Anger

Sometimes the person you're angry with is not available or may simply be too dangerous to talk to. You still need to vent, and there are ways to release your anger indirectly. While there's no opportunity to resolve the problem, this approach will probably unleash a good amount of pent-up anger. Some are a bit strange, but they might just work for you.

Empty chair exercise

This is a technique used by mental health professionals and some support groups. Place an empty chair across from you and imagine the person you are angry with seated there. Speak to her or him saying exactly how you feel. Fully express your anger. Then switch chairs/roles and make the ridiculous excuses you think they might to try and excuse their behavior. Stand up, scream at them and destroy her or his arguments. Deliver any residual anger and talk as long as you feel relief.

Scream or cry

Find a place where you can be alone, at home, in your car, or possibly even in nature. There's a lot of energy trapped inside and screaming or crying can help release it. If noise is an issue, muffle it with a pillow. The point is to release those angry feelings.

Write a letter but don't deliver or mail it

Start your letter with "I am so angry with you because…" and make it as long and nasty as you like. After you're done, put it aside for awhile. Think about it and eventually go back and review what you've written. Make any additions and include more feeling if you'd like. You can also write the person's name on the paper and scratch over it with a pen over and over again.

Step all over the person

On the sole of your shoes, write the person's name with chalk or a crayon. Every step you take, you can have fun symbolically stomping her or him. Jump up and down, walk through the mud, and just don't set fire to your shoes while wearing them.

Sweat it out

Go running, bike riding, or visit the health club. Exert as much energy as possible but don't hurt yourself. Just get it all out. And you'll have the additional benefit of becoming stronger and healthier.

Burn baby, burn

Gather any notes, cards or letters you may have received from the person. Then go outside to a safe place and put a match to them. Watch your anger go up in smoke.

When anger turns inward, it can become guilt or depression. Then you become hopeless, start delivering victim messages to yourself and withdraw. Once you get to that point, it becomes difficult to see the light at the end of the tunnel. That's why it's so important that you direct your anger outward. When it's vented, you'll feel better and possibly avoid becoming depressed. There are many different ways to directly and indirectly release your anger. Of course, expressing anger directly may produce the best results, but the indirect approach can also be quite useful and effective. Do what best works for you under the circumstance you find yourself in.

What to Do When Others are Mad at You

So far we've focused on *your* anger, but you can also say or do things that result in others feeling angry toward you.   They also need to vent. If you sense a reluctance on their part to talk, you might want to take the initiative and ask something like "have I done something to upset you?" Allow her or him to fully express their anger toward you and listen without interruption. Let them get it all out. If you did hurt them, admit it, apologize and ask for their forgiveness. Releasing pent-up anger and solving difficulties or misunderstandings naturally results in more intimate relationships.

Being on the receiving side of rage is another story. Some of the techniques are similar, but there are a few additional actions you can take. To begin with, listen *without interruption* as they express their highly charged anger toward you. Try not to be defensive, and after the person has finished speaking, *paraphrase* what you heard her or him say. Then ask if you heard the other person correctly, if you missed anything and whether there was anything else they'd like to say. Recognize and try to understand the other person's point of view, validate them and only then begin to think about explaining your position.

Dealing with Your Excessive Anger Without a Minute's Delay

If your anger seems uncontrollable or you have thoughts of violence toward yourself or others, speak with a professional immediately. If it's more moderate, there are other approaches you can try:
• Recognize that you are in control of your thinking and behaviors. You can choose to cool down, respond in a less intense manner or use a technique such as progressive relaxation to calm yourself.
• Check out how extreme your anger is. Ask yourself why it's so intense and if you're being too highly reactionary. Examine what other emotions are accompanying your anger (such as jealousy, insecurity, etc.).

• Identify irrational thoughts that magnify anger and replace them with less explosive ones.

• Walk away and remove yourself from the situation. Take some time to cool down. And avoid name-calling, sarcasm or physical intimidation.

• Monitor your thoughts and replace them with calming ones. Remember that it's okay to feel angry but it is not acceptable to hurt others. Treat others with respect and compassion. We are all God's children.

Getting Activated and Letting Anger Go... the Right Way

Being angry can be a great motivator. "I'm mad as hell and I'm not going to take it anymore" was a famous line from the movie "Network" a few years ago. If you're being under- or unappreciated and abused at your job, get mad as hell and decide to go back to school or get a better job. Work hard and show the other person how successful you can become.

Feeling angry is a normal and healthy thing to do. Learn as many positive ways to release it as possible. You can use direct or indirect approaches as needed. And while it's sometimes difficult to forgive, it's important to do so. When we hold on to negative feelings about anyone or anything, we are the ones who pay the price. Forgiveness is essentially a gift we give to ourselves. Try to let go after you've expressed your anger, and recognize that God is the final judge of the other person's bad actions or behavior.

Do you ever feel like you do so much for others and end up drained or unappreciated? As ACOAs, we often try incessantly to get approval from others. We'll look at this phenomenon in the next chapter. "People pleasing" can begin early in life. For example, a child may think "if I do everything to please my parent who _____ (drinks, is abusive, etc.), they will stop the bad behavior and _____ (pay more attention to me, love me). As an adult, if you get caught up in excessive people-pleasing, it's likely that you will be taken advantage of and have your energy drained. Your needs somehow become less important than the other person's. But your needs should not be secondary. In reality, they are very important and you're just the person to see that they're satisfied.

Five-Day Action Plan for Growth & Success:
Place a checkmark in each box as you complete the associated action:

❑ Try dissipating anger by doing one or more of the following: exercising vigorously, punching a pillow, screaming, crying, writing, talking with a friend.

❑ Recognize your anger when it happens and determine its origin.

❑ You can be assertive without being aggressive. Try it next time you're angry and remember that anger is a normal human feeling.

❑ Write a letter to the person you're angry with, but instead of mailing it, rip it up, burn it or step all over it with your shoes. Start by writing "I am angry at you because…"

❑ In a mirror, look into your eyes and say these affirmations aloud in the morning and evening until you feel confident about what's being said:
  • I'm in charge here – not my anger.
  • I deal with anger as soon as possible.
  • It's okay for me to express anger.

Summary:

✔ Anger happens when there's a threat; stress or possible loss to our person, people we care about, property, self-esteem; when we don't get what we want or an attack on our values. We may have learned to stuff our anger.

✔ We are often angry for reasons other than the current situation. The reaction to old violations or mistreatments can be triggered. These are unresolved issues that cause current reactions to be more volatile than warranted.

✔ Other emotions may be beneath your anger such as fear, confusion, envy, hate, feeling disrespected, etc.

✔ You can be free to express your anger once you identify certain barriers and circumvent them.

✔ There's a dynamic and progression that can escalate a minor irritation into rage or depression.

✔ The most effective way to express your anger is to talk about your hurt to the person who you believe injured you, and do it as soon as possible.

✔ Anger can be expressed in a direct or indirect manner depending on the circumstances.

✔ Anger can be a great and effective motivator for you to accomplish great things.

✔ Forgiveness is a gift you give yourself.

Chapter 10

When You're Much Too Giving
Balance People-Pleasing and Your Needs

"I've been dating this guy for a year and people say I'm crazy," said Tamia. "He doesn't work, I give him money that he spends at clubs where I know he's hooked up with at least one other woman. But I love him and want to make him happy. My therapist points out that, in general, I place my needs below those of others and I guess she's right. That tendency started early in life. My mother used to drink heavily and was unable to care for my younger sisters and brother. I did all the cooking, cleaning, and other necessary tasks. That was my role and how I derived value in life, but my needs went unmet. If I tried to take time for myself, I ended up feeling guilty. And I assumed that the only way I'd have value or wouldn't be abandoned was to earn it through performance. I've continued to ignore my needs by excessively catering to everyone else. But that's got to stop. I'm trying to believe that it's not what I do, but who I am that counts."

Words describing a "people-pleaser" are quite positive; however, you can end up feeling empty, isolated and sad on the inside because *your* needs are not being met. This chapter shows that the origins of this behavior are largely in an ACOA's childhood environment. You'll see how to keep your emotional bank account filled while concurrently considering the needs of others, how to balance relationships and also see how avoiding conflict or living in a frenzy of people-pleasing activities will not prevent someone from leaving—in fact in some cases it may precipitate separation. You can consider ways to change this behavior and have healthier relationships with others.

ACOAs will do almost anything to gain the approval of others. It stems back to childhood when they were emotionally malnourished and as a result developed a poor self-image. Being abandoned is frightening and they take extraordinary steps to avoid it by satisfying others to the nth degree. What a perfect breeding ground for *excessively* pleasing others rather than dealing with their own needs. But it feels great when people like you, right? And what's wrong with bringing happiness to others? The problem arises when you're jumping through hoops to please everyone but yourself. Not only do you lose sight of your own needs and desires, but you also bring your relationships to unbalanced places.

Self-Interview Taping Exercise:

Use a tape recorder to record questions and answers to the following. Then rewind and carefully listen for the feelings along with meanings behind your responses. Summarize important insights into a notebook for reflection or action.
- When growing up, whose needs came before your own? Why did they and how did you handle it?
- What needs are not being satisfied today? How can you change that?
- What are your feelings when someone doesn't like you?
- Who takes advantage of you and how do they? How can you change that?
- What would you do with your life if you didn't have to take care of everyone else?
- What do you expect from others when you are nice to them? Do they meet your expectations or is there something missing?
- What people-pleasing beliefs and behaviors are you ready to change?

Where Did It Begin? How Your Needs Were Ignored

"When my mother was drunk, the entire world revolved around her," remembered Ellen. "My father would have me and my sisters watch out for my mom. We'd take care of her every need. Nothing else mattered. Our homework, physical or emotional needs – everything was secondary to taking care of my alcoholic mother."

People-pleasing behavior originates early in life. It might start with a parent impaired by alcohol and/or one who was excessively demanding. In order to avoid being treated badly, the child found it necessary to cater to the abusive adult by trying to meet unrealistically high expectations. Naturally that caused her or him to focus on another person's needs or requests. In the process, you may have been disrespected, abused, undervalued and treated poorly. But you're in a different time and place now and it's more than okay to take care of yourself first without feeling guilty or being afraid of retribution.

When you place the needs and wants of other people above your own, it affects how successful, authentic and substantial your relationships are. And it inappropriately impacts important choices you make in life. Without reigning in this tendency, you can become emotionally drained, angry, frustrated and depressed.

There are common beliefs, characteristics and feelings associated with people pleasers. Negative consequences will be examined as well as ways to transform those tendencies into constructive behaviors. You'll learn specific skills that can enable you to change your excessive people-pleasing ways. And finally you'll be empowered to treat yourself in the manner you deserve – with kindness, attention to *your* needs, respect and love while being in healthy, balanced relationships.

You Look So Good...

The impression many people have of you is quite positive when you have a people-pleasing personality. And it may have served you well in your childhood. That's why it can be so tempting to act that way. Some descriptive words include:

• helpful	• supportive	• sensitive	• encouraging
• considerate	• cooperative	• loyal	• giving
• generous	• warm	• caring	• agreeable

... But Feel So Bad – The Cost of Overdoing Niceness

But because of the excessiveness that frequently develops, the self-evaluation and general feelings of a people-pleasing person can be quite critical and negative. These feelings include:

• insecurity, not being good enough, being undeserving, lacking in skills or abilities.

• anger and resentment at being used and abused.

• depressed because they avoid conflicts by stuffing anger, feelings of inferiority, embarrassed by themselves, self-critical, frustrated because of not being able to make everyone love them, lonely and isolated.

• fear of losing self-esteem or another person's approval, experiencing abandonment, letting others down, failure, and that people will recognize their inadequacies.

• feeling taken advantage of, unappreciated or victimized.

How others describe you and how you feel about yourself can be quite different. And when you become so involved with the needs/desires of others that you lose sight of your own - self-alienation is often the result. And these are some of the consequences:

- low self-esteem
- loneliness
- irrational beliefs that immobilize
- loss of personal rights, needs and identity
- guilt and shame develop from not being good enough or taken advantage of
- difficulties with problem-solving and leadership

Certainly, the excessiveness and self-alienation associated with people-pleasing can be problematic.

So Why are You Doing This?

What's the payback from excessively pleasing others? You may have become accustomed to taking care of others (such as your alcoholic parent, siblings or other parent) or placing their needs above your own and, if so, the role is one you are familiar with. It fits perfectly and gives you a sense of control, even though it may be false and temporary in nature. Maybe you're afraid that people will either not like you or be angry if you don't do what they want. Can you relate to any of these common beliefs that many people-pleasing individuals incorrectly accept?

- I'm responsible for the happiness of others.
- If I'm pleasant, nice, and not demanding, people will like me.
- Others will appreciate / care for me because of everything I do for them.
- My function in life is to serve other people.
- If someone doesn't like me, I must be deficient in some way.
- I can't do anything that might upset the other person.
- I can't let others know the truth about me or they'll abandon me.
- No matter how hard I try, it's never good enough but I'll just try harder.
- It's what I do that matters.
- People will never leave since I've made them need me.
- Others will think of me as lazy or selfish if I don't say yes to their request.
- They will abandon me unless I give them everything I have.

These statements are incorrect. And you can cognitively and emotionally reprogram your belief system to incorporate healthier attitudes. People pleasers often think their worth depends on what they do for others. They withhold their real thoughts, values and beliefs because they're afraid that someone will develop negative impressions about them. They often spend time with individuals who are self-centered and aren't considerate about their needs or feelings. In fact, she or he sometimes feels obligated to try to make insensitive or unhappy people happier. They do many things for others, but when it comes to their own needs, if they happen to consider them at all, they'll feel guilty for doing so. People pleasers often come from a defensive stance, acting nicely to proactively prevent another person from criticizing or expressing negative feelings toward them. It's not good for you, and often in a relationship that kind of manipulation doesn't have a very good result. You simply can't impose your wishes and beliefs on people. When anyone is manipulated or feels like they're in an unbalanced relationship, anger, resentment and abandonment will most likely follow.

Relationships have to be in equilibrium and they require time and effort from each person involved. However, while trying to be nice, people pleasers fixate on the needs of the other person while ignoring their own. Her or his attention is predominantly on others and away from themselves and as a result, they sometimes don't even know what their own feelings or needs are. Communication and effort becomes one-sided, and the relationship falls apart or remains superficial. In addition, if you're not expressing yourself in a balanced conversation, your growth and self-knowledge are minimized. Only where there's equality will there be growth - personally and in the relationship. And, by the way, it is who you are that matters, not what you do for a living and certainly not how much you excessively do for others.

Being Nice Doesn't Mean Everyone Will Like You: Never 100% Approval

In fact you can be the nicest person in the world but there is a guarantee that someone, somewhere won't like you. There'll be people who can't stand someone who is too nice. Or it could have nothing to do with you, but more about their past or external factors. Perhaps your eyes or mannerisms remind her or him of an abusive person from the past. Regardless of what it is, no one ever gets unanimous approval. That goal is simply unachievable and it's fruitless to attempt it. Accept that fact or you're headed for frustration and a belief system that labels you unworthy and defective. It can be demoralizing if you pursue an unachievable goal, and you may well be left feeling drained and unhappy. So the better alternative is to be realistic in your relationships and accept that even when you excessively cater to others, you'll still have detractors. Being real and balanced however, will always bring self-respect and good results.

Keeping Your Emotional Bank Account at Healthy Levels

Just as you can't continue writing checks on a bank account that only has outflows and becomes depleted of money (without being locked up), you can't continue giving without receiving. When you're "running on empty," you end up negatively affecting both your emotional and physical health. That's why it's so important to monitor your emotional deposits and withdrawals. Healthy balances have to be maintained. That's accomplished by having relationships that are reciprocal and also by not overextending yourself. If you need encouragement or hugs, don't hesitate to ask for them. At the same time, keep your outflows at healthy levels. Become aware of your needs, feelings and also what's happening around you. You can learn how to say no to requests that are too draining. And go after those emotional deposits.

Don't Be a Reactionary

"If my husband started drinking, I'd try to make him happy in other ways and distract him," said Carol. "If he wanted me to be a whore in the bedroom or join him in a display of hate towards a neighbor, I would. I'd do anything he wanted in an attempt to control his behavior."

Typical codependent behavior is tied to controlling other people by pleasing them, wearing a mask or being a chameleon – always reacting to external stimuli. This is a behavioral defense designed to protect you from being abandoned. But it's important to recognize your own value and avoid being dependent on the evaluations of others. Codependent people try hard to get people to like them by focusing on the other person in an attempt to gain favor. It sets them up to be victims and they end up not getting their needs met or even knowing what those needs are. ACOAs can often choose partners who duplicate their alcoholic parent's behavior because they're not aware of how the dynamics work. Before people in this codependent situation can grow, they must acknowledge what they're doing and consciously choose better ways.

Be patient with yourself, and if issues similar to the following surface, respond constructively:

• <u>Giving undeserved loyalty to someone</u>. When someone abuses or does not value you, it's time to leave. Use self-talk to support yourself and also ask for help from friends. In addition, you can speak with your minister or another professional, but the important thing is to stand up for yourself and refuse to let another person abuse you. Focus on your well-being and be loyal to yourself by taking care of your mind, spirit and physical self.

• <u>Being self-critical.</u> When you're hard on yourself, replace your self-criticisms with positive and supportive statements. Lighten up, relax, have fun and nurture your inner child.

• <u>Strongly needing approval from others.</u> Use self-affirmations more often and give them greater weight. They can reduce the need for outside approval. Be self-caring, accepting, and independent without becoming narcissistic.

Rather than excessively reacting to the needs or desires of others, get in touch with yourself, be authentic and thoughtful with your needs and wants.

If You Avoid Conflict, Do You Avoid Abandonment?

"My boyfriend was very excitable and volatile," said Jennifer. "So whenever we disagreed, I would give in immediately. I didn't want things to get out of hand. After a while, he had no clue who I was or what was important to me. I started losing sight of that also and became sad, and then depressed. We grew apart and would you believe it – after all I went through, he dumped me."

If you avoid conflict, do you avoid abandonment? No way! And it would be so much better to express negative feelings rather than stuff them and become depressed. You may believe that if you're nice it will save you from experiencing rejection, conflict and anger. That approach only keeps the relationship superficial and prevents the formation of bonds that come from sharing feelings. And it won't prevent anyone from leaving you. In fact, it may lead to exactly that.

It's only when you learn good communication skills that you'll be empowered to resolve problems and have depth in your relationships. You'll achieve a greater understanding of each another, and increase trust, intimacy, respect and happiness. Conflict is necessary for meaning-

ful growth. People-pleasing can keep you from acquiring the communication skills needed. When you avoid conflict, the opportunity is never
present to learn effective ways to talk and resolve difficulties. In addition,
no one ever gets to see the real you, so the relationship can get stagnant.
Real intimacy comes from mutual self-disclosure. And your partner may
be starved for intimacy that can come from discussing sometimes dis-
turbing problems and feelings. When you keep people at a distance, you
may be safer but you also can't feel love and closeness. Intimacy and
authenticity are sacrificed when you don't discuss negative (or positive)
feelings. Conflict avoidance is self-defeating at times.

Fear of difficult feelings and abandonment prompts you to do whatever is necessary to avoid them. But by refraining from any type of
conflict, overdoing generosity or placating another person, an important
opportunity is lost. And beyond that, your people-pleasing exuberance
could cause resentment and frustration. The other person may strike
back, withdraw from the relationship or even become physically aggressive. How can they be that way when all you want to do is please them?
Whether intended or not, they perceive your behavior as manipulation
and entrapment. This can prompt them to become angry and resentful, and decide to leave. A much better approach is to practice ways
to express anger, fear or whatever negative feelings you're having in a
constructive manner. Your relationships will be of a higher quality and
last longer.

No Longer a Doormat, and You're Still a Wonderful Person

A people pleaser would rather avoid or quickly end a disagreement.
But placating the other person by agreeing that *you* are entirely wrong
and the other person right, essentially helps you assume a victim role.
You're also, in effect, justifying the other person's bad behavior. That
in turn will most likely produce shame and diminish your self-esteem.
Resorting to passive aggressive behavior is not a good alternative
either. When you pout or refuse to talk, those negative feelings are left
to simmer inside you and get worse. In addition, the original problem
never gets solved. The more constructive alternative is to become less
dependent on the approval of others. By being assertive, standing up for
yourself and expressing your feelings, the relationship will become more
equal. You will solve problematic issues and can't help but win.

There are certain actions you can take to stop being mistreated or
taken advantage of. The most obvious action is to say "no" to excessive

requests or to pressure to act a certain way. One less direct technique is the *broken record* method. It's very simple but effective. Basically you repeat a short phrase over and over again until the other person gives up. For example, if you're in a car showroom being pressured to sign a sales contract, say, "I've never bought a car on the first visit and never will." Completely ignore their responses and simply repeat "I've never bought a car on the first visit and never will." Usually after four or five times, the salesperson will almost always see that convincing you to do what they want is hopeless and give up. It works in a variety of situations.

Another way to avoid being a doormat is to keep yourself out of problematic situations. Be proactive. For example, problems are inevitable when you enter into a dating relationship with someone who is recently wounded. It takes time to recover from a failed relationship. Your partner may not have healed enough to offer a healthy connection but is desperate for love and you unknowingly fall into the role of a white knight, princess or what is commonly referred to in this circumstance as a Band-Aid. You will probably feel that you're intensely needed and wanted - which you are. But just as when someone recovers from a cut, the Band-Aid (in this case *you*) gets discarded. It's not because the other person wants to be mean, is insensitive or has been lying to you. Her or his needs have changed. You were there at a time of need and they probably appreciate it. Regardless of how nice you were, they are in a transformation process; their needs are changing so they are drawn elsewhere. In effect, the relationship was doomed from the start. The lesson to be learned is not to place yourself in a position that will result in emotional pain. It's okay to say no to a romantic relationship or any other that begins with red flags. It simply means that you're taking control and *only* entering into healthy relationships that are more likely to turn out well for everyone concerned. You can sidestep being a Band-Aid or doormat by proactively avoiding problematic situations.

Don't Hurt Others or Yourself by Keeping Silent: Communicate Today

You've probably become highly sensitized to the feelings of others. In an alcoholic family, it was an acquired skill often needed to survive. And today there could be a tendency to keep quiet rather than say something that might hurt or upset another person. In one respect, that's a good thing because you don't want to purposely hurt or damage anyone. But sometimes keeping silent can cause serious problems.

In a dating relationship, there may be one person who desperately wants to have children. The other, a people-pleaser doesn't and may avoid such a discussion because she or he thinks it will cause an argument or even result in the termination of the relationship. They know they'll never commit. It might be because they find the relationship uninteresting, unfulfilling, or simply don't like kids or marriage. Or it could be related to their own issues. Whatever the reason, time goes by without any resolution. You don't want to hurt the other person, but also don't want to get yourself in a fight. So you keep quiet and in reality string the person along. It's rationalized by thinking that you don't want to upset your partner by saying something she or he doesn't want to hear. But by not talking honestly, you waste their time and prevent both of you from finding more appropriate relationships. Of course you don't want to hurt her or him by talking, but you end up doing damage by being quiet.

Adult children have a strong aversion to being the one who ends a relationship. Fear of abandonment, arguments, or dealing with negative feelings keeps that person from doing so. But opportunities and time are lost forever when you aren't direct with someone who needs to know where she or he stands. It's a much better approach to talk about each other's feelings, values and thoughts and about your future, even if it's uncomfortable to do so. You may both have similar expectations, but if not, you can at least come to an understanding. And you'll realize that by being direct, there's no longer a need to carry emotional baggage generated by being less than authentic.

Breaking the Cycle of People-pleasing... While Getting Your Needs Met

Cognitive <u>thinking</u>, open <u>feelings,</u> accurate <u>beliefs,</u> and your <u>actions</u> can alter people pleasing ways without fundamentally changing the nice person you are. There is nothing to fear. You will not become a grouch who'll never want to do anything for anyone again. People-pleasing is described as an *excessive* behavior, and all you'll be doing is shifting to a balanced and healthier approach to relationships. Consider the following:

Thinking
Eliminate self-defeating thoughts and replace them with affirming ones. You don't have to be liked by everyone or do everything requested by others to be valued and loved. True friends will like you unconditionally for who you are, not conditionally for what you do. And you may have friends who are very affirming of you. The best source of appreciation and praise, however, is from *yourself.* By actively identifying things

about yourself you're proud of and feeling those positive affirmations, you reduce the need for external applause. Your self-worth increases, as does your independence from the overwhelming need of approval from others. It may be preferable to be liked by others, but the most important thing is to feel good about and appreciate who you are.

Beliefs

Perhaps you believe that the more you give, the more people will want to be around you. But by overdoing it, the other person will likely feel uncomfortable, manipulated and even resentful, and subsequently be more likely to push you away. So there's no advantage to excessive people-pleasing. Change your belief system to incorporate that fact and adopt a positive and healthy way of thinking – one that values who you are and recognizes that equitable giving is best.

Feelings

When you are afraid about being honest with others about your feelings, you hold back and are someone you're not. You can never give yourself credit for your successes because you're just acting, not being real. So the cure is to learn and practice the communication skills necessary to openly express your feelings. This will require some courage because historically you may have been reluctant to show your feelings for fear of being rejected, abandoned, or left alone. But you can do it.

How about those negative feelings? Do you express them or should you? By wearing a happy face all the time, you can become a fake stick figure – unappealing at best. The relationship loses realness and vitality. Being too nice is usually not attractive because your desperation and manipulating behavior becomes obvious. It's always best to pursue authentic and balanced relationships. One of the best ways of doing so is to share feelings with one another.

Actions speak louder than words

Habits are formed early in life. In a household where alcoholism was present, a child frequently blames her- or himself for it. The child believes she or he is the cause and that if they act perfectly, the reason for the drinking would end. When that doesn't happen and the parent remains an alcoholic, these children often blame themselves for not trying harder or being good enough. But they try harder and harder to please. It was a coping skill that attempted to bring some control to an uncontrollable environment. But it also brought the belief that love is conditional with your behavior and that it has to be earned.

Do you only love your baby when she or he is not crying or your child when he or she gets As on a report card? Do you only love your dog or cat when he or she is not making noise? Of course not. Take action to break the cycle of excessive people-pleasing, confident in the fact that your true friends love you for who you are, not for what you do or do not do, and will remain your friends.

You can't please everybody, but how about yourself?

"Carol, Johnny, Phil and I wanted to go out the other night," said Beth. "Two of my friends wanted to check out a new club, one didn't care and I wanted to go to a movie. Usually I give in to whatever the group wants but this time stood up for myself and stated that the movie was *really* where I wanted to go. Not everyone was happy, but that's what we ended up doing. Sure I was pleased to see the movie, but I was very ecstatic with myself for being assertive and pleasing myself for a change rather than everyone else. My friends still love me and there's more balance in our relationships."

Your value is in who you are – not in the number of special favors you do for others in an attempt to impress them or make them indebted to you for your generosity and thoughtfulness. You can't make another person like you or want to spend time with you. People, depending on their personal history, values and need orientation, are attracted to specific individuals at certain times. Trying to manipulate or do all the right things to capture the heart or friendship of someone who's not interested can only end in disappointment. You can't control anyone but yourself. Self-empowerment is the key. So concentrate internally rather than looking for external approval by knowing, pleasing, and improving yourself.

You can control your own actions and belief systems. Focus on your needs, values and desires rather than desperately trying to please others and gain their approval. You'll be living with yourself for every moment until the day you die. So who better for you to make happy and fulfilled?

Be kind and considerate to others but be a little bit more so to yourself. Treat the woman or man in the mirror like someone you love. Focusing externally for self-validation only serves to relinquish your power and disconnect you from yourself. Learn how to say no when the request goes against your values or you may end up drained. Stand up for what you believe in, and ask for someone else's help when needed. Spend your energy and time to build and care about yourself. Look for what brings purpose to your life. And most importantly, become connected to and love the wonderful soul living in your body.

The next chapter will help you bring new friends into your life. You'll also learn how to build a new and improved support system. You've got a lot to offer and others will certainly be drawn to the healthier you.

Five-Day Action Plan for Growth & Success:
Place a checkmark in each box as you complete the associated action:

❑ Next time you want to say no, try the broken record technique. It entails ignoring the other person's arguments and repeating your same words each time the other person stops talking. For example, say "I'm not interested" over and over again to someone who's trying to talk you into doing something you'd rather not. Remember, never respond to their arguments. Ignore them and repeat "I'm not interested" over and over again. They'll give up trying when they see you're immovable and not even listening to what they're saying.

❑ Look in a mirror, into your eyes and repeat these affirmations aloud in the morning and evening, as many times as it takes until you feel confident about what's being said:
  • I deserve to have my needs taken care of.
  • It's okay for me to say "no."

Summary:
✔ The excessiveness related to people-pleasing is often problematic.
✔ Feelings and beliefs of a people-pleaser can be quite negative.
✔ No one ever receives universal approval.
✔ Relationships need to be balanced in order to succeed.
✔ Trying to control other people by pleasing them, wearing a mask, or being a chameleon can be counterproductive.
✔ Overdoing generosity can result in others perceiving you as manipulative. The other person may resent your actions and may strike back or withdraw.
✔ Conflict is sometimes necessary for meaningful growth.
✔ Victimization can be avoided by standing up for yourself.
✔ Being open and honest with your feelings can improve the quality of your relationships.
✔ Your thinking, feeling, beliefs, and actions can minimize your people-pleasing ways without changing the nice person you are. The excessiveness will be replaced with balance and authenticity.

Chapter 11

Overcoming Loneliness, Finding Friends
Build a Support System that Works

"I hung out with a few other kids in the neighborhood but always felt alone," said Julian. "We'd do stuff together—play games, rollerblade, throw the football around, but they never really knew me. There were times I wanted to tell them what was going on inside of me but never did because I was sure they'd run in the opposite direction. They'd never understand what it was like having an alcoholic father. But the truth eventually came out after classmates unexpectedly dropped by. My father was abusive toward them and they widely gossiped about their experience. Soon the whole neighborhood knew what my family was like and all of my so-called friends stayed away. To deal with it, I withdrew into myself and constructed emotional barriers. With new kids at school, I'd be superficial and distant, which didn't make for lasting friendships. I've continued that approach as an adult—with acquaintances, but no close friends. I'm not sure what I should do about it, but without exaggeration, I'm living a very lonely life."

Have you ever been surrounded by people but still were lonely? During childhood, you may have tried keeping secret the fact that you had an alcoholic parent. You devised masks and walls to hide behind. If so, you were left to deal with the events of a traumatic childhood alone and had a tough time forming close relationships. Even as an adult today, you may have difficulty connecting intimately with others. Deep inside, you may still feel unwanted, alone and different from others.

You're not so different. ACOAs feel it more acutely, but in a recent study 78% of respondents from the general population also reported feeling lonely within the last year. Loneliness is the #1 reason why people call crisis hotlines and, according to some therapists, it is an epidemic that affects all of us. Mother Teresa was quoted in *Leadership* magazine as saying, "The biggest disease today is not leprosy or cancer. It's the feeling of being uncared for, unwanted, of being deserted and alone." We need people, friends, self-acceptance and a connection to our spirit. Everyone needs to feel accepted, loved and included; when we don't, the isolation can be devastating.

There are several sources of and solutions to loneliness. This chapter will explore various connections that may be missing and help you take action to change that. You'll see new ways to bring people into your life and how to tune into yourself. There will be actions to minimize feeling disconnected in the short-term and others that will help you defeat chronic loneliness. This chapter can help you become aware of why you might feel lonely and show ways to respond. You'll increase self-awareness and also learn how relationships with current friends or acquaintances can be made more satisfying. There definitely are actions you can take to minimize or eliminate loneliness, but first you have to understand the root causes of your loneliness.

Self-Interview Taping Exercise:

Use a tape recorder to record questions and answers to the following. Then rewind and carefully listen for the feelings along with meanings behind your responses. Summarize important insights into a notebook for reflection or action.
- How do you think your loneliness is connected with your parent's alcoholism?
- Were you made to believe that you were unworthy of love? If yes, by whom? What were the messages and how can you change them today?
- Describe your need to escape a situation when you were a child. What similarities do you see with your need to currently have space/ an escape plan?
- How well do you know yourself? What makes you feel: angry...happy...hopeless...trapped...encouraged...afraid...wounded...sad...guilty?
- How have isolation and loneliness affected your life? What actions might you take to alleviate or minimize your discomfort?
- From maintaining defensive walls and keeping secrets, what have you learned?
- What do you disclose about yourself when developing a relationship? Are you comfortable being the center of attention? If not,

what needs to change?
- What makes you feel close to someone else?
- What groups (including family and friends) do you feel a part of? Do you feel fully accepted in each?
- How close can you be to a person before feeling uncomfortable or trapped?
- What triggers your need to run?
- What advise would you give another person about getting you to comfortably and gradually lower your walls? How do you feel about offering this advice?
- Describe your relationship with God and/or your spiritual side.
- How will you spend time and energy in building a relationship (with another person, with God) this week?
- What have you learned about yourself from this exercise?

The Positive Side of Loneliness

"I got into self-help books and meditation," said John. "Instead of sitting around feeling lonely, I tried to fully understand myself and find out what I was really about. I became stronger in my temporary solitude and more willing to share myself with others. At the same time, I know what types of individuals I don't want in my life. My newly found self-worth and confidence in my abilities empowered me to be choosy about my friends, and now I couldn't have better ones."

Don't despair over your loneliness because it actually is a valuable indicator showing that some important needs are not being met. It's gotten your attention like a bad toothache and is prompting you to do something about it. You can take action to ensure that your needs will be addressed by adopting some of the suggestions in this chapter. But you can do more than that.

Rather than run away from loneliness and try to forget or deny it, you can turn it into fruitful solitude. You can enter the desert of your loneliness and change it into a beautiful garden. That dry, desolate desert can yield endless varieties of flowers and reveal the previously unknown beauty of your soul. Use your aloneness as a strong motivator to learn about yourself and to do what's necessary to eliminate your isolation. Acquire new skills and reexamine your belief system. Certainly you'll move on to having meaningful relationships, but use your time now wisely and remember that this is simply a transitional phase that will lead to a great future. What's your story?   Take a moment to reflect on your attributes. Being created in the image of God, everyone has positive points, but sometimes we don't give ourselves credit or are too busy to make the effort. What does your best friend like about you? What do you like about yourself? If necessary, start with the basic fact that you are a good person, then make additions to your list each day.

Loneliness Cycles Need to be Broken

"I was so ashamed because I believed that my existence caused my mom to drink," said Craig. "I thought that God hated me too, and fell into a deep depression that's taken me years to overcome."

The cycle of loneliness works this way: emotional neglect, abuse or mistreatment leads to pain, shame and depression, which leads to withdrawal and isolation, which leads to negativity, mistrust and the maintenance of emotional barriers. Unless you take action to finally break this cycle, it just keeps repeating itself and reinforces a lonely way of living. To understand loneliness more fully, we need to realize its origin stems primarily from <u>missing</u> one or more of the following:

1. A connection to your inner self.
2. An intimate connection with at least one other person.
3. Acceptance as part of a group or organization.
4. A spiritual connection.
5. A belief that you are worthy of being connected and loved.

When you feel excluded from a group, isolated from loved ones, walled off from your true self or alienated from God/Spirit, you'll likely experience a certain degree of loneliness. But it doesn't have to be that way. Let's look at each condition and see how to turn things around.

1. Missing the connection to your inner self

"Throughout my childhood I'd constantly be in front of the TV in an attempt to block out what was happening in the real world," said Roberto. "If I heard my mom yelling in a drunken stupor, I'd simply turn the volume up. Today if I'm upset, I still go to the TV but as a result, I can't tell you what I'm feeling because I don't know. I've been numb so long that I'm a stranger to myself."

How numb are you to your feelings and how has that affected your relationships? Have you ever been angry with someone and refused to talk with him or her? What happens when you stop communicating with yourself? Do you contemplate what's important or what your values might be? Certainly it's important to do so because a healthy relationship with yourself is a prerequisite for any meaningful connection with another person, but automatically responding as you had as a child can prevent that. The amount of attention and respect you give to your needs and feelings is also proportional to how emotionally healthy you feel. Perhaps you're not even sure what you are feeling or needing. Self-alienation and disconnect can leave you, like Roberto, living with an emotional stranger residing in your body. And a poorly treated stranger at that, since your needs are ignored—just as they were in childhood. But you can decide to do what's necessary for your emotional well-being. Learn everything you can about your inner self and treat yourself well. Following are several constructive actions you can take.

How to develop a connection with your inner self

• **Reprogram your self-talk** – "Every morning I look at myself in the mirror and tell myself that I'm lovable, God is with me and others love me - and it makes such a difference, " said Christina. "Self-affirmation starts me off feeling assured and positive as I begin each day."

Self-talk has an incredibly strong impact on your competencies, self-worth and belief that you are worthy enough to experience a positive relationship with yourself. If you've previously been programmed to believe that you are unworthy or a bad person, there'd be little reason to try to get in touch with your soul. But in reality you are a child of God and He doesn't make defective products. With self-talk, you can create the kind of home for your spirit that you'd love to visit. Start by forgiving yourself for being human and making mistakes. Then create a list of your good qualities and attributes. If self-doubt tries to change your mind, refer to your "personal attributes" list. This will place the welcome mat for you to begin introspection and form a positive and loving relationship with your inner self.

• **Give your thoughts and feelings an audible outlet** – The tape recording of your thoughts and feelings is a centerpiece of *Transformation for Life*. The taping method is also useful in a free-flowing verbalization that captures whatever's on your mind. Spend some time talking and you'll often make enlightening discoveries about yourself and what's going on around you. Then you can avoid the "disconnect" from your inner self that generates lonely feelings. The times you've been closest to another person have probably been when she or he shared their deepest feelings. Consider your vocalization on the tape the same way—sharing what's really inside, trying to understand the feelings behind your words. This approach will most certainly bring you to a new, more intimate relationship with yourself. When you're ready, speak with a close friend about your thoughts; ask for feedback if you wish.

• **Write your life's story** - Keeping a journal or diary crystallizes your experiences. You can express feelings, desires and needs through writing. By thinking about your life, you have the opportunity to dig down and clarify what personal needs have to be addressed. But this is not simply a writing exercise. It's a method to get you in touch with yourself so while you're writing, look past the surface, examine your feelings and discover what's really important.

• **Meditate in a quiet and beautiful place** - Meditation forces you to retreat from your hectic pace, slows you down so that you can open your mind and soul. While it's helpful to be in an idyllic environment, if you're not, simply close your eyes and have your mind take you there. As you meditate, your body relaxes and you can often experience an inner peaceful feeling. While in this state, you're more receptive to ideas and thoughts that may have been blocked by your conscious mind. To meditate, find a quiet place where you won't be disturbed. Being outside in nature may also enhance the experience. Use the progressive relaxation techniques explained in a previous chapter and try to meditate as often as possible. Like dieting, you can't do it once and expect it to work. Keep at it.

• **Therapy can change the rest of your life** – If you're still having difficulty getting in touch with your inner self, you may need the help of a professional therapist - someone who is a well-trained expert in helping people to explore and heal emotional injuries. Do you want to live your life in loneliness and emotional pain? Do you want to limit your success and happiness in life? Of course not. Contact a therapist and work together with her or him to form a personal relationship with yourself. The warm sun is beyond the clouds of your life and all you have to do is push those clouds away with the empowerment that therapy often brings.

2. Not having an intimate connection with at least one person

There's a *Seinfeld* episode that includes the observation, "the ones that you like, don't like you, and the ones that do, you don't want." To have an intimate mutual connection is wonderful; you can feel like you've been joined together with your other half. The sex is pretty good, too. But it can be painfully lonely if you don't have that connection and feel like you desperately need it. Other times, you can be involved with someone and suddenly find him or her heading for the exit. People, for a myriad of reasons, sometimes feel they must end a relationship; everyone knows the pain of rejection. We also miss loved ones who may have passed away or moved to different areas of the country.

Some of us may have kept the walls so high and made them so impenetrable that we've never experienced true love or intimacy. Adult children of alcoholics are especially susceptible to feeling alone and different. That's because we learned at an early age to cope with situations by, among other things, escaping and withdrawing. We've built defensive walls to avoid rejection and abandonment.

Perhaps there's someone you can risk being open and authentic with today. There can be a tremendous improvement in your life when you have at least one close friend or lover. Your aloneness is diminished every time you disclose your feelings or secrets with someone you trust. You can share what's really going on inside, talk about your hopes, dreams and feelings. Not only will the relationship deepen, but also you'll become more self-aware and accepting. You can learn about yourself by listening to yourself talk, and your friend can also help you explore thoughts and emotions. If you verbalize your thoughts and feelings, misconceptions can be corrected, disagreements resolved and real growth pursued.

How to gain a special connection with someone

• **Develop your social competencies** – You've seen and practiced the conversational magic techniques in Chapter 8. Go back, review them and continue practicing. The more you do, the more comfortable you'll be in social situations. You've also become skillful in the same conversational approach used at crisis intervention hotlines and are aware of its application in everyday interactions. Use all of these learned verbal skills along with non-verbal information to maximize success. That's the road to eventually forming a personal and intimate connection.

• Reach out and you'll bring people in – "I made a pact with myself to invite one new person from work to lunch each week," said Sam. "It's been three months, I've made a dozen new friends and some have become close to me."

If you maintain the posture of an ostrich with its head in the sand, you won't meet new friends. You inevitably have to take a chance and approach someone before friendship is possible. Of course, that means you might be occasionally rebuffed. Everyone is at times, but if you don't try, that special person will never enter your life. The Conversational Magic chapter also explains in detail why an invitation may or may not be accepted and how to approach bringing new people into your life. Review the "branching out and free-flowing association" techniques that can have you skillfully maneuver conversations. Then call someone today, extend an invitation and explore the possibilities. When someone listens to your thoughts or feelings and is caring for you, express your appreciation and reciprocate.

• It pays to be persistent – Remember who won the race in the childhood story of the tortoise and the hare? The slow-moving turtle just kept plugging away until he finished the race first. If you're not successful right away in attempts to build a close relationship, don't give up. Be persistent in your quest for a meaningful relationship and you'll find one. You will eventually succeed, but only if you don't get discouraged and stop trying. Fill your mind with encouraging thoughts, knowing that you will succeed.

• Pursue mutual self-disclosure - When you'd like to change a current relationship to become more intimate, how do you go about it? Self-disclosure at incremental levels starts the process. The other person may also begin to disclose more personal information and if so, the relationship will deepen. You've already seen the "levels of conversation" in a previous chapter and have learned how to move from one to the next. Utilize your conversational skills to maximize the connection you have with another. But since superficiality was likely your previous way of relating, you'll have to monitor your conversations to ensure that you don't fall back into old habits. Some relationships will always be superficial but they have their value also. Sometimes you just want to have fun without much thinking or feeling. But the more intimate relationships will, of course, bring you connectedness.

3. Loneliness from not belonging to a group

"I belong to the Society to Prevent Paint from Peeling, and my group is spectacular." Whether it's being a member of a volunteer organization, church, family or any other group, it's important to feel that you're an accepted part of it. The physical proximity to other people doesn't matter so much. It's the connection you feel or sense of belonging that does. There's a sense of solidarity along with strength in numbers when you're with like-minded people. They affirm your beliefs and opinions, so being a member of such a support system can leave little room for lonely feelings.

<u>How to find and be accepted in a group</u>

• **Participate in a support group** – Rose joined a group at her church and said, " Since our congregation is large, I found it difficult to really connect with anyone. People were friendly but the conversations were superficial. However, small groups have changed all that. They replaced my loneliness with love, hope, intimacy and a new spiritual awakening."

I've led scores of support groups and later received thank-you letters from people who had attended. The consistent message was that they had never felt more loved and loving as when they were members of their respective support groups. For the most intimate connection other than a family, join one. You'll be in a confidential, safe environment where you can be transparent and fully accepted. Everyone is there to be part of a support system. You can receive feedback if you wish, test new skills, but most importantly you can share your inner feelings and know that you're intimately connected.

• **Join an organization that meets regularly** - Frequent contact enables you to build friendships. It could be a volunteer team, choir, adult school or another group related to something you enjoy. You'll automatically have things in common and since there's frequent contact, you'll likely make new friends.
• **Open up a dialogue** - If you have family members who are not emotionally close, try to improve those relationships. If you feel family bonds are important, tell them so and ask their opinions on

how the family can get closer. Open a dialogue that is productive and non-judgmental. Or look outside the family for opportunities to be with people—eating lunch at work or school. Gather members of your class or department together and make it a habit. Be an active listener, ask open-ended questions, and be genuinely interested in what others have to say. By frequently meeting, you'll become a member of an informal group of people joining together. Or gather several of your friends who don't know each other. You're the common thread that could bring them together to share group activities. It might grow into a solid support system for everyone concerned.

4. Loneliness from the lack of a spiritual connection

Like a battery in a disconnected laptop computer, you can become drained when detached from your Source. We are spiritual creatures in physical bodies but our spiritual connection can occasionally be blocked. How does your spirituality exist in relation to God? One analogy sees our individual spirits like lamps connected by invisible cords to the ultimate power plant—Spirit in Heaven. Whatever your belief, you do have the ability to tap into your spiritual source anytime you choose. But when disconnected, you can feel weak and lonely.

Marie's parents had a cedar chest that looked like a coffin and almost served as one. When her mother was drunk and out of control, she locked her young daughter inside it to repeatedly show who was in control. There was no light, only limited air and Marie never knew if she'd be released in time to survive or would die there. All she could do was cry, pray to a God who she felt had abandoned her and feel helpless. In a support group, she commented, "Looking back I think God was always with me. How else could I have survived, healthy enough to raise my own family in a loving way? An alcoholic caused my pain, but God helped me live through it."

There are times we feel alone, but God hasn't abandoned us. Sometimes we turn away and blame Him for evil things that human beings do. And sometimes the judgmental pronouncements that come from organized religion can make us angry. But there's no connection like your spiritual one with God or Spirit. Are you alienated from your spiritual side? Are you angry with God because of what happened in your childhood? Possibly you're struggling and hurting right now. God will be there to help. If you have faith, you can feel connected to the force that brought you into this world. Know that you're not alone. Your soul can be connected to a greater and limitless power. Your soul will not be left an orphan. Our Creator is always present, waiting for us with love, comfort and compassion.

How to get spiritually connected

• **Forgive God** - Remember that everyone has free will in this world, and that bad things happen. God is not the cause of those terrible childhood experiences. Sometimes we wonder why God doesn't intervene and stop the suffering. Asking "why" gets us nowhere in this existence. Maybe when we return to our Source, we'll understand fully, but not before then. God has forgiven us for turning away from Him, so have faith and forgive Him for your pain. Perhaps your difficult life experiences can be used in a larger plan. Talk to God in prayer about your hurts and forgive Him.

• **Get in touch with Spirit** - Meditation and prayer can initiate communication with God. Talk about how you're feeling. Express appreciation for the many blessings you have in your life; confess your love to Him. Ask for guidance or help if you'd like. Chapter 14 will offer other exciting options such as labyrinth walks and alternative approaches. An answer or message will always come, but it often will be in a whisper. Listen carefully; take note of what God is saying to you.

• **Commune with nature** - Seeing the sunrise and experiencing all the other wonders of nature can enliven your spirit. Consider that the same Creator of these magnificent wonders also created you.

• **Compassionately care** - Service to others recharges your emotional batteries. Sometimes the best place to see God is in the eyes of other people. When you're caring for others with compassion and love, you are doing His work. In their pain and yours, spirit emerges. Reconnect by doing good things for others and you'll feel the loving spirit in you.

• **Focus on your blessings** - You may be taking them for granted while exaggerating your losses. If you can't see your blessings, be grateful for simple things you might have, such as shoes or a bar of soap. Others in this world have to do without. Appreciate how these are God's gifts to you. Be grateful.

5. Loneliness from not feeling worthy

"She's out of my league so I'm not even going to try talking to her," said Robert. So a possible relationship ended even before it began.

Perhaps you don't try very hard to form relationships because feelings of inadequacy prevail. You have an internal tape player that recorded childhood messages and continues to replay them even now. When you feel the need to be with others but hesitate, what messages are you hearing? "They're probably busy. She or he has much better things to do than talk to me. They probably will reject me anyway, so why try? I'm unlovable. I'm not good enough; I don't know what to say." Convince yourself that you were born unlovable and it can have crippling consequences. For example: you may approach others expecting to be rejected and precipitate a poor outcome. Since you're always anxious and on guard during conversations, watching for signals that you're being judged as inadequate, there's little enjoyment. You'll be less likely to initiate social encounters that could bring you wonderful relationships. You won't let others get close if you believe self-disclosure only serves to make you vulnerable and leads to abandonment.

Many of these beliefs originated in childhood as survival techniques but are damaging today. These messages will prompt you to either not try at all or give up easily. As you work on skill development and increase your quality interactions with others, you'll feel more connected. But you first have to believe in your likeability and lovability. Successful relationships with others will prove this to you, but if you have any doubts in the interim, please take my word that you *are* lovable. It is the absolute truth. And the impact of positive self-talk has been explained in a previous chapter, but is worth repeating. With it, you can create a foundation of worthiness and self-esteem. Use positive self-talk today and every day.

How to feel like you deserve it

• **Out with the old tape, in with the new** – Programming from your childhood was tainted. You may have been left with a self-image and belief system that says you're not good enough. Lissette recently said, "In my alcoholic family, when I didn't get perfect grades or wasn't flawless in some other way, I felt inadequate. I had to be perfect, because I believed my shortcomings were the reasons behind my parent's continued alcoholism. In my mind, if I were perfect, they'd have no reason to drink. But then I made mistakes and continued to let everyone down. I felt defective, guilty and ashamed. I believed myself to be worthless and deserving of nothing, especially love."

If you recorded similar messages on your childhood tape, it's time to rerecord. The new message should be affirming, positive, loving and supportive. You can use affirmations, your personal list of positive qualities and self-talk to reprogram your internal messages. The most important fact to remember is that you are NOT <u>ina</u>dequate. If you start entertaining negative thoughts about yourself, stop immediately and yell at yourself, "No! I *am* lovable and competent," and replace the thoughts with positive and affirming ones. God doesn't make defective products, and don't forget that you are made in His image. Start loving yourself - others will be drawn to you.

• **Be your own cheerleader** - Everyone can use a cheerleader. Imagine being encouraged and cheered in everything you undertake. You don't have to rely on others for this but rather can flood yourself with positive and affirming messages. Encourage yourself at every opportunity and there will be no stopping you. Consider programming yourself for success by championing a strong belief in your ability to bring positive people into your life and to successfully build relationships.

Quick, Temporary Comforts when You're Feeling Alone

Occasionally you may need immediate, temporary relief from lonely feelings. Chocolate is a good idea for some people. Here are some less fattening options:

• Reach out to others, call a friend, visit someone, and make some kind of social contact. Laugh and express your humor, share jokes or funny stories.
• Cry, scream into a pillow - release your feelings.
• Visit a health club and exercise or take a long walk.
• Write in your journal or send an e-mail.

Avoid excessively sleeping, watching television, indulging in prescription drugs or alcohol, hiding from others, or just doing nothing.

Make a firm decision to take constructive action. You can connect with others who can help you on your life's journey as long as you don't surrender to passivity.

To summarize, you may feel lonely because you're missing one or more of the following:

• An intimate bonding with one special person
• Feeling worthy
• Being a member of a group
• A spiritual experience
• The connection with your inner self

Remedies have been suggested for each and now it's up to you to take action. You can almost eliminate loneliness from your life. It may sneak in occasionally but you'll know how to react. As you proceed, you'll be creating intimate and meaningful connections with others. You'll understand how to get in touch with your inner self and feel more comfortable when meeting new people. You'll be free to relax and have an enjoyable time knowing that other people are not measuring all your strengths and weakness to determine if you're worthwhile. People just want to get to know you and if there's enough in common, will want to expand the relationship.

You'll recognize a few important truths: Simple acts of kindness (like a smile to a stranger) make a difference. Self-disclosure deepens relationships and creating positive self-talk empowers you to take charge of your life. With your improved social skills, you'll bring up interesting topics while focusing on others and their interests. And spiritually, you are never separate from God. We never stop learning lessons and becoming better persons. As you work on loneliness issues and practice new skills or approaches, be easy on yourself. Setbacks will happen, but keep at it and you'll be successful and fully connected.

Transition to a more self-actualized person is the subject of the next chapter. You've already completed a great deal of work. Your full recovery and development will bring a tremendous transformation along with a realization that you're much more than your past.

Five-Day Action Plan for Growth & Success:
Place a checkmark in each box as you complete the associated action:
❑ Invite two new people for coffee or lunch this week.
❑ Share some of your significant feelings with a trusted friend.
❑ Say "good morning" to four people each day for the next week, with eye contact and a smile on your face.
❑ Meditate and pray 20 minutes each day.
❑ Look in a mirror, into your eyes and repeat these affirmations aloud in the morning and evening, as many times as it takes until you feel confident about what's being said:
  • I love and respect the real me.
  • I'm fully accepted by others.
  • I am never separated from God.

Summary:
✔ There are several types of loneliness brought on by different unfulfilled needs.
✔ Many millions of people have lonely periods, but ACOAs can be particularly susceptible because of their history.
✔ The cycle of loneliness can be broken.
✔ View loneliness as an indicator showing that some of your important needs are not being met. Use your time alone constructively.
✔ When missing *a connection with your inner self*, reprogram your self-talk, give your thoughts / feelings an audible outlet, write your life's story, or meditate.
✔ When missing *a connection with another*, develop social competencies, reach out to others, be persistent and pursue mutual disclosure.
✔ When missing *a spiritual connection*, forgive God, get in touch with Spirit through prayer or meditation, and compassionately care for others.
✔ When missing *inclusion in a group*, look for an appropriate support group or other organization. Perhaps you can also develop your own.
✔ Your loneliness can definitely be defeated.

Chapter 12

Building Trust and Safety
Behaviors, Beliefs and Attitudes that Bring Intimacy

"Men are just out for one thing - you can't believe anything they say," observed Terry. "In fact you can't trust anyone. I once had faith in my parents to take care of me—until my father raped me for the first time. He turned into a sexual predator when drunk and used the alcohol as an excuse for violating boundaries and scarring me for life. The next day he tearfully apologized and said it would never happen again. But it did over and over again until social services intervened. I'm sure my mother knew what was happening but she did nothing to protect me. If you can't feel safe around your own parents, you just can't trust anyone."

Trust is an important issue for all adult children. Since it was often violated in childhood, distrusting likely carried over as a natural approach to life as an adult. But global distrust makes it impossible to have anything but superficial interactions. This chapter acknowledges that trust is a prerequisite for a healthy relationship and explains how you can establish reasonable safety without the need for tall barriers. Trust-building actions, beliefs and attitudes are all explained in detail.

Whom do you feel safe around and why do you feel that way? Sometimes it's another person's behavior or an intuitive feeling. At times it's your programming. What did you hear? "I love you go away, don't talk to strangers, guys are just out for one thing, do it to them before they do it to you." Or was it more like, "people generally try to do the right thing, trust others and they usually won't disappoint you, or people are basically good." What's your global belief about people? Certainly as a child raised with an alcoholic caretaker, trust was an important issue. It was often violated. But past programming isn't necessarily applicable today.

You've learned new skills, adopted a healthier belief system and are probably more receptive to taking risks in order to bring new people into your life or deepen current relationships. Going forward, you'll have to make judgment calls, understand what trust means to you, and be aware of risks or rewards of trusting. This chapter will focus on those areas so you can develop an action plan that will enrich your life with intimacy, something that can only be achieved when safety and trust are present.

Alter Your Programming

"At a young age, I always believed my dad loved me," remembered Alan. "He just acted strange at times. During my early years in school, he promised to spend time with me but instead he chose to hang out with his drinking buddies. My father kept insisting that he was going to stop and live a sober life, but never did. And it seemed like every holiday began with celebration but was spoiled because of his alcoholism. As a teen, I could never bring my friends home because I wouldn't know if he'd be drunk and abusive or not. So I learned to never trust that things would just be okay in my home—or my life."

You weren't born distrusting. That's a learned response originating in childhood when you discovered that your needs were not met, promises were broken or boundaries violated. With that realization, you may have concluded that trust only sets yourself up to be hurt or disappointed. A parent's alcoholism and subsequent bad behavior has fed those beliefs. And if you misjudge another individual today, self-blame and feelings of incompetence or inadequacy can be result. Overall, a child's beliefs about trust and safety are formed as a result of experiences, observations and parental influences.

In Janet Woititz's book, *Struggle for Intimacy*, she stated, "trust is a necessary prerequisite for a healthy relationship." The poisoned messages you received as a child must be challenged and replaced by reality-based ones if you're to have successful relationships. A level of self-trust also has to be established. You're not perfect – no one is, so you're bound to make mistakes. But throughout this book, you are learning new skills and developing healthier beliefs while re-parenting yourself. You have more control over your life now, and can trust yourself to be loving, caring and considerate – to the inner child and other people. You're able to depend on yourself to make correct judgments most of the time, but when external factors misdirect, you can forgive yourself and move forward. You may feel like it's "two steps forward, one step back."

Sometimes it is, but you're always learning, even when you stumble, and it will become increasingly easier to rebound and flourish.

Safety, risk management and trust all have to be balanced. But when you consider the big picture, when trust *isn't* a part of your life you can end up living in a dead zone – a kind of voluntary solitary confinement. That's not a healthy thing for you to do; you'll miss what makes life wonderful—love, joy and feeling connected. Perhaps you can act as a caring parent would—protecting yourself, from hurtful people, but at the same time understanding that you still need to risk being open in order to have a truly intimate relationship.

What does safety mean to you? Have you established boundaries that are honored? Do you consider both the physical and emotional realms of safety? What do you have to give up to be completely safe – or is absolute safety ever attainable? How do you know someone is trustworthy? Risking doesn't mean putting yourself in dangerous situations where it's likely you'll be hurt. Trusting doesn't mean being naïve either. Use your intuition and review the components of trustworthiness to guide your decisions on who might be worthy of your trust or how to have others trust you. They are listed in this chapter. And you're probably stronger now than you've been in the past; are now able to deal with some disappointments, if and when they occur.

Self-Interview Taping Exercise:
Use a tape recorder to record questions and answers to the following. Then rewind and carefully listen for the feelings along with meanings behind your responses. Summarize important insights into a notebook for reflection or action.
• How can you feel more comfortable about trusting your feelings?
• What needs to be present before you start trusting others? How do you know when you can't trust another person?
• Describe some of your irrational beliefs regarding safety and trust.
• What new beliefs, skills and approaches are need developing in order to increase your willingness to trust?
• What can you do that will help yourself trust and love?
• What are you doing to build trustworthy relationships?

Meaningful and Loving Relationships Involve Trust

"Tom's always been there for me – a friend for life," said Henry. "Sure we disagree at times, but there's a continuity in our friendship along with mutual respect. We both know that we can count on each other no matter what."

Trust means that you have little or no fear about how another person will treat you. There's an underlying agreement that your friend will not abuse you or discount your feelings. You also hold the belief that the other person will not want to purposely hurt you but will rather work to resolve issues. With the knowledge that she or he is predictable, consistent and reliable, a deeper sense of trust is likely to develop.

Developing trust is an important part of any relationship. It's a risk but can bring worthwhile rewards. It may occasionally be unsuccessful, but usually you'll develop loving relationships with intimacy and closeness. However, if you project a *lack of trust* to others, people who *can't be trusted* are often drawn to you. And remember that you can't maintain an emotional wall and expect trust to develop. Several <u>behaviors, beliefs, and attitudes</u> are essential to build trust in yourself and others. If they're present, they'll be no need for walls.

Trust-building *BEHAVIORS*

Marcy recently said about her friend Karen, "We have a real balanced friendship. We both talk about our feelings and risk being vulnerable and authentic. There's no hiding being masks in our relationship. What you see is what you get. And it feels good being fully honest and open knowing that it will continue to grow, no matter what."

1. Be authentic and vulnerable. No one can love or trust a mask. Being superficial or acting like someone you're not comes with a high price. You can't take credit for your success, learn about yourself, or develop meaningful relationships. All you can do is temporarily deceive yourself and others, creating further isolation. Be yourself and you can feel that connection with others that diminishes lonely feelings. Rather than trying to <u>im</u>press, <u>ex</u>press yourself as you honestly are. You'll like and accept yourself more when you're genuine, and others will also. They'll welcome the opportunity to spend more time with you and a mutual bond of affection and trust will develop as sharing of each other's lives deepens over time. When you don't have to hide your blemishes or act a certain way to gain approval, you're free to be yourself. This is a place where you can truly be transparent. You learn about yourself and your partner by sharing while being authentic. Acceptance can transform abandonment to inclusion, and inadequacy to completeness.

2. Deliver adequate self-disclosure in a balanced relationship.
You have to let the other person know who you are or the relationship
will remain a superficial one - or just disintegrate. Explain your feelings to others and they will be more inclined do the same. But mutual
disclosure has to be just that – mutual and disclosed at the same time
and at similar levels. When it is, each person becomes more transparent
about her or his beliefs, feelings and experiences. Trust builds through
a balanced expression of who each person really is. Share a little about
yourself—if it's reciprocated, progressively share more.

3. Be honest. Lies have the potential to irreparably damage any relationship. Instead, build up your emotional bank account by always being
truthful. Say what you mean, and mean what you say. Credibility builds
trust. It's essential!

Trust-building *BELIEFS*

"My mom used to tell me that you can't trust anyone—that they're all
SOBs," said Lisa. "That was mostly the booze talking, but after hearing it throughout my childhood, it became part of my belief system. I
also felt that I couldn't trust myself because I'd screw up and make
mistakes about people. For one thing, I'd always choose the wrong guys.
And where was God to let all this happen, I wondered? I didn't trust
in others, my abilities or even God until the realization sunk in that my
negativity was only getting worse. Things began to change when I attended an AL-ANON meeting. I learned to let go of the beliefs that were
instilled by my alcoholic parent, to focus on improving my belief system,
self-esteem and relationship with God. As a result, I'm finally trusting
more and attracting wonderfully supportive people into my life."

1. Believe that people are generally good. If you believe that people
are mostly bad, why risk trusting anyone? But if you take note of the
good and unselfish things that so many people do for others, your belief
will change. Random acts of kindness can be witnessed everywhere if
you simply take notice. People volunteer to help the less fortunate, assist
someone stranded on a freeway, or display many other examples of being
a good citizen of the world. Focus on the good deeds of people and believe that if you risk trusting, you'll surely bring some of the best people
into your life.

2. Believe in yourself. When you accept and respect yourself, you're
empowered to take more risks. Your value is internally based, rather

than dependant on the opinions of others. Then you're not desperate for confirmation that you are worthwhile, but are simply connecting with another person because you like him or her. Therefore there's no pressure to run after others like a puppy, and no devastation if you risk and don't succeed. You can take greater risks when you feel less dependent on others and more self-accepting and secure. You know you're okay, and are confident that many people will want you in their lives.

3. Believe in a higher power. Many people find that faith in God tremendously affects their lives. Faith that a higher power has a plan and purpose for your time on earth can perhaps more than anything else does, provide encouragement to trust that things will work out for the best. This belief is extremely important. It can be a relief to know that an all powerful, loving God is available to help you on life's journey. But some cringe at the idea that they're not 100% in control of their lives. They point to the fact that bad things happen to good people and wonder why. Perhaps those things are attributable to simply living in a world where people can choose to do evil deeds – I don't know. But I do believe God has a plan to help us even through the worst times, so that we might live through sadness and disappointment – and metamorphosize/change as a butterfly does from its cocoon. Even in the darkest night, a new dawn is coming, and He helps us through. You've been blessed with friends, talents and a calling to use what you've been given. But you have free will to use your gifts or not. Knowing that there's a plan for your life, and that your spiritual self learns from every experience can free you to risk and pursue your potential. Let go, and let God lead you. Follow the path that will enable you make a significant difference in this world. Live constructively and leave a legacy of love, hope and honor for others to follow.

Trust-building *ATTITUDES*

"I was tired of being alone," said Jeff. "My friends said I had a bad attitude about relationships so I made a decision to change. I started dating Dawn with a feeling that it would be a positive experience. We were open, caring and stayed away from intolerance or ridicule. And it turned into a loving relationship. Beginning it with the right attitude made all the difference."

1. Make a conscious decision to risk and trust. One approach is to simply make a decision to trust more, and if someone violates that trust, take appropriate action. By not trusting, perhaps you can actually attract people who are untrustworthy and expend negative energy in the process. On the other hand, you have the option of bringing people into a relationship that's based on caring, consideration, mutual respect and freedom. When you know that you can talk about anything without worry of condemnation or ridicule, the door opens to an emotionally intimate relationship. You can make the decision to do so. And it also will help put your childhood traumas behind you by sharing and receiving support.

2. Have good intentions for your relationships. When you sense that the time spent together will usually leave everyone feeling good, the relationship will likely continue. But when you're "walking on eggshells" and afraid of what's going to happen next, there's no reason to attempt a more intimate connection. In fact, why have a connection at all if you leave feeling hurt or angry most of the time? Relationships should be there for the greater good of all concerned. Having a positive feeling about the other person brings all the more reason to trust her or him. Every enjoyable, caring experience you share together builds up your emotional bank account and lays the foundation for deepening trust.

3. Be a friend during good and bad times. When everything is "coming up roses" and everyone's just having fun, you'll likely have all kinds of people around. But who's there when you're going through a tough time and are sad or depressed? Those are the people whom you can trust to be there for you no matter what. Even when you feel unlovable, they're present to support and love you. These are friends you can feel safe with and trust completely. They are not just out to get something from you or waste your time with superficial nonsense, but rather are there to share the good times and bad. They are true blessings. Take notice of them, be grateful and *be that type of friend yourself.*

What If I'm Not Ready for Intimacy Yet?

"Yikes—I just came off of a bad relationship and don't want to jump into another one," said Kerry. "It'll take time before I'm willing to let my guard down again."

So go slowly. The term "relationship" doesn't always mean a dating one. Be friends – even with someone who has the potential to be more. Since there's less pressure, you can sit back and let the trust, along with the level of intimacy, develop naturally over time. If your reluctance to experience emotional intimacy is because you still don't <u>want</u> to trust, understand the price you'll pay. Loneliness, alienation, abandonment

– and self-induced solitary confinement are usually reserved for the worst offenders in prison.

Getting What's Needed to Feel Safe

"It's taken a while but I truly feel that I can trust my boyfriend," said Cathie. "In my family background, promises were always broken, so it was hard to establish trust as an adult. But I've been seeing my boyfriend Jim for over a year and he never lets me down. In fact, he's consistently building me up, emotionally and spiritually. We've shared what's going on inside and he loves me, even with my faults. Finally I know that I can trust another person and look forward to taking it to the next level."

There are many components of relationships that when combined, build feelings of safety and security. They include:
• fairness   • feelings of safety   • secrets kept   • harmlessness
• reciprocity   • commitment   • stability   • being non-judgmental

• The basic understanding that you will not intentionally hurt each other. This not only means emotional safety but also causing no physical or spiritual harm. Any hurt that is unintentionally caused can be addressed through methods such as active listening. Boundaries should be well respected, especially those of the ACOA partner.

• Stability. Consistency and stability build trust and feelings of safety because you don't have to worry that she or he will be wonderful one day and a terror the next. That's not to say the other person will not have a bad day here and there. We all do, but if overall behavior is consistent, trust and feelings of safety are more likely to follow. This is especially important for an adult child since it was missing in childhood. That's where a false conclusion that trust only brings disappointment was probably born.

• Keeping secrets. Intimate details of your life are reserved for special people you feel safe with because private details expose you to the core, making you vulnerable. And other confidential information that you've asked someone to keep secret may be less personal, but is also sensitive. When you share something in confidence, it's a demonstration of faith. By never violating someone's confidence, it demonstrates that you care about the other person's feelings. It shows respect and honor.

• Fairness and reciprocity. Karma, what goes around comes around, or a general belief that what you give out (kindness, trust, etc.) will come back to you is a comforting view of life. We may not see the results of our good deeds immediately. Sometimes they become crystal clear in the future, or we may simply be blessed in other areas of our lives. While we shouldn't be looking for rewards, they often follow. Caring feelings and behavior should, however, be balanced along with the level of intimacy. Lowering your protective walls equally demonstrates a desire by each person to maintain a meaningful and progressively deepening relationship. It'll also increase the probability that trust will be honored.

• **An ongoing relationship commitment.** When you both find the relationship worthwhile, it's in everyone's best interests to have it continue and flourish. With that verbal or perceived commitment, you can relax, knowing that it's worthwhile to expend time, effort and involvement. The potential is to have a friend or lover for life.

• **Being non-judgmental.** You may have made choices that the other person wouldn't have made. If she or he can love you anyway, you know you've got a partner you can trust who may disagree, but refrain from passing judgment. This helps demonstrate that you're safe and can share more of yourself.

• **Being safe.** Physical attacks and traumatic verbal exchanges are incalculably damaging. And emotional arguments can leave scars that last as long as physical ones. These cannot be tolerated. Creating an environment where no harm will come is a prerequisite for the foundation of trust. So everything possible should be done by everyone to ensure that safety takes top priority.

Fears can immobilize you if you choose to let them. There's always the possibility of having your trust violated, being abandoned or abused. But if you're able to understand that you are not a failure if things don't go perfectly, it reduces the pressure. You can understand what may have not worked under these particular circumstances and not be afraid to risk again. As a result, your emotional development will continue and success will eventually be yours. As the feelings of safety and trust increase, you're freed to show more of yourself. That's when you can really have a relationship that is trusting and intimate.

What Are the Rewards?

"For me, trust has formed a foundation to support quality relationships, and also allowed me an increased degree of self-esteem," said Mario. "I'm no longer consumed with safety issues and am able to trust myself along with other key people in my life. Sharing and caring has also brought me self-awareness, confidence and personal growth. As a result, I have new support systems that can help me weather any storm. And the reduced stress level in my life has me physically feeling better. The rewards of ensuring safety and living with trust include intimacy, quality relationships and personal growth."

It's been said that you can love and lose, but never really fail because the process of loving turns you into a wonderful person. Just expressing love transforms you. And it's acceptable to take a long-range approach. Knowing that you don't have to build your level of trust to a very high level at first lessens the pressure. Take your time, but always strive to move in that direction. Your emotional health and the quality of your relationships depend on it. It's certainly worth the risk of a possible rejection or misunderstanding. We were not created to be alone but rather to be in close, supportive relationships with others.

Is some distrust appropriate? There are times when it is. The absence of safety and trust issues or traits shown in this chapter should raise red flags and warn you to exercise caution. But overall, people who are trusting tend to be happier. They are not naïve. They simply can detect trustful or distrustful cues and act accordingly. But overall, they begin with the belief that people are basically good and proceed on that assumption.

There's an old story about twin brothers who grew up in a midwestern town. They went off to college but returned to run the family store upon the death of their father. The brothers were quite close; they married, had families, and their families also became close. Then one day something happened. A customer entered the store, made a small purchase and handed one of the brothers a $10 bill. While in conversation, the brother laid the money on the cash register and walked out the door with the customer. When he came back to put the $10 in the cash register, it was gone. He asked his brother if he had taken the cash, and he replied that he had not. All day, he kept asking he brother – "Are you sure you didn't take that $10 bill?" The brother kept responding that he had not. Rather than forgetting about it, distrust grew and they eventually stopped talking to each other. The relationship between the two families disintegrated and even the town ended up divided. The store was split into two with each brother owning half. They were in a very unhealthy competition with, and strongly distrusted, each other. Many years later a stranger came to town, parked his BMW in front of one of the stores and looked puzzled as he got out. He walked into one of them and explained the following to this brother who was now an old man: "I'm looking for a store that was once here but now I don't see it. I was in this town years ago, down on my luck and had been riding the rails. I got off a train and was walking behind this store when I saw the screen door open and a $10 bill on the register, and I sneaked in and took it. I vowed to myself that someday I would return it with interest, and that's why I'm here today. I want to find the owner of the store and pay my debt." With that the old man broke down in tears and took him next door to his brother and they were once again able to be together. But what about all those years lost?

Excluding trust from your life comes with a hefty price, while including it can have extraordinary rewards. In this chapter, you've seen what conditions are necessary for trust building. Use them to transform your life and you'll likely be extremely pleased with the results.

Transition to a more self-actualized person is the subject of the next chapter. You've already completed a great deal of work. Your full recovery and development will bring a tremendous transformation along with a realization that you're much more than your past. As you welcome transition, you'll be happy to move beyond your history knowing that a wonderful life is just around the corner.

Five-Day Action Plan for Growth & Success:
Place a checkmark in each box as you complete the associated action:

❑ Write a letter to the person who has violated your trust. Explain what happened as a result, and be specific about your feelings. Consider if you would be willing to trust her or him again. If yes, what would be necessary to regain confidence in the other person and a feeling of safety? If not, forgive her or him and devote your time and energy to those people who will enrich and have a positive impact on your life. (Do not mail the letter.)

❑ Ask someone you care about if there are any remaining obstacles to developing a deep trust between the two of you. Talk about them through a meaningful dialogue using active listening techniques. Then agree how you'll continue to develop a sense of safety and trust in the relationship.

❑ Look into your eyes in a mirror, and repeat these affirmations aloud in the morning and evening, as many times as it takes until you feel confident about what's being said:
  • I trust myself and am myself trustworthy.
  • I'm ensuring my safety and trusting when I should.
  • I'm open to new and positive relationships.

Summary:

✔ Beliefs about safety and trust are largely formed as a result of experiences, observations and parental influences.

✔ Trust is necessary for healthy relationships to occur.

✔ To feel safe, you have to believe the other person won't intentionally hurt you. There also has to be stability, security and a mutual sharing.

✔ When you can see the other person is predictable, consistent and reliable, a deeper sense of trust is likely to develop.

✔ To increase trust, several beliefs, attitudes and behavioral traits are needed about yourself and others.

✔ Trust-building *behaviors* include self-disclosure, being authentic and honest.

✔ Trust-building *beliefs* include believing in yourself, that people are generally good, and that God has a grand plan and purpose for your life.

✔ Trust-building *attitudes* include a good feeling about the relationship, a positive open environment, a decision to trust and an understanding that the relationship will be sustained through good or bad times.

✔ The rewards of trusting are great. Intimacy and closeness in a quality relationship enable you to grow, experience life and all it has to offer.

Chapter 13

Welcoming Your Life's Transition
The Positive Effects of Change

"I hate change—especially when I have no influence over it," said Patty. "As a child, I had no control over my dad's drinking or behavior. One minute everything was cool: he hugged me, we talked about my dreams, cute boys and how beautiful life could be. The next minute alcohol turned him into a hostile and distant stranger. He gave me the silent treatment and if I'd try to hug him, he'd scream at me to leave him alone. And his drinking resulted in a succession of lost jobs, so we'd go from being financially comfortable to poor, many times. I'd experience new financial conditions, places to live, acquaintances, schools and, most of all, a revolving door of behaviors from my father. Stability was what I needed, but change that brought feelings of insecurity and abandonment was what I got. That's why even today I want to keep everything the same, even if it means that I miss out on growth or opportunities."

This chapter illustrates how change is essential for a healthy and productive life. It recognizes that you've worked on many ACOA issues to this point, and that you have entered a new stage of life, largely unencumbered by past experiences or habits. Opportunities are developing, your self-concept has become positive, and the reluctance to change has been minimized. The "intimacy scale" will be introduced so you can clearly see what's needed for a meaningful connection. And "the neutral zone" is explored as part of the transition process. Ways to move past resistance are presented so you can become fully engaged in a revolutionary life transition.

Pat yourself on the back! You, just like Patty, are actually doing it. And as you become more loving toward yourself and others, things are changing. The ways you relate to others are different now. You no longer connect with people by acting as a doormat or their personal therapist. You're able to stand up for yourself and have the skills to build and sustain quality and balanced relationships. These are very good things. You're moving into new territory and it can be unsettling, but it's still wonderful and necessary for you to do.

The balance in your relationships is altered and so are your roles. But a few people will not be pleased with the new, healthier you. Change is not always welcomed – even if it's for the better. And your way of relating to others will further be altered as you gain additional confidence. You may find relating to your family and friends different. Many relationships will become more intimate but with some people, there'll be resistance. You probably will also find new, more supportive and emotionally healthier friends.

Whatever the present and future bring in your relationships, it's time to utilize your new skills and reality-based belief system. As a result, you'll feel connected at deeper levels and also have more choices regarding the people you invite into your life. This chapter will make you aware of a few bumps you might experience along the way to self-actualization and fulfilling relationships. It will help you understand the transformation process, to make it easier. At the same time it can increase your awareness of when relationships are truly high quality. It's natural to have self-doubts at certain times, but the fact remains that you are as wonderful a person as anyone else on this earth, and the time has arrived when you will emerge from your ACOA cocoon and become a butterfly. Your present and future begin now, unencumbered by the past.

Self-Interview Taping Exercise:
Use a tape recorder to record questions and answers to the following. Then rewind and carefully listen for the feelings along with meanings behind your responses. Summarize important insights into a notebook for reflection or action.
- Who are the people resistant to your growth and why? What's the best way to communicate with them about your development and changes?
- What marked the point when your life really changed?
- How have your turned a minus into a plus? For instance, how have you used your heightened sensitivity (that was developed during childhood and used to cause pain) to enhance a current relationship?
- Which parts of your life do you most want to alter?
- What have you already changed that has proven to be most meaningful?
- Where would you like to be, personally and professionally, in one, five and ten years?

Transformation Time - Self-actualization and Success

Every day is a new adventure that brings with it opportunities to learn, to do good works, and also times to play. Some of the happiest people are those with work that is nurturing and fulfilling. They feel enriched when using their gifts and making their best efforts. They have relationships where a true connection is felt and their spiritual existence is one without fear or other encumbrances. They interact with people, God and His other creations with love, openness and self-acceptance. Of course, it's a fallacy to think that you, or anyone else, can control the thoughts and emotions of anyone else. You can only be responsible for how you respond to others who will, or will not, welcome the emotionally healthier, stronger and more secure you. Why wouldn't others want you to be a complete and grounded person? Here are a few possible reasons:

• By adopting the caretaker role as a child, you previously had ranked your needs below those of your alcoholic parent or other family members. People you have relationships with today have perhaps become comfortable in always coming to you for comfort without considering whether your emotional bucket was full or empty.

• They've historically, consciously or unconsciously, taken advantage of you and are now not happy about losing the control they thought they had over you.

• Some people are so emotionally turbulent or negative themselves that they only feel comfortable being with similarly unhealthy people. Others are rigid because they didn't have control over anything when they were growing up. So when you start taking more risks or exhibiting increased self-love or anything beyond the scope of their blinders, they are not pleased.

For these and many other reasons, there may be resistance from others regarding your transformation. While some destructive relationships should be ended, others will evolve into more (or less) meaningful ones. And you'll attract new people into your life – people who are positive and loving. This is important: it's okay to have all different types of relationships. If one's superficial, that's fine as long as you and the other person accept it as such and don't have any other expectations.

The *Intimacy Scale* and How to have a Meaningful Connection

As you move forward, full of potential and open to new people, you'll experience different levels of relationships, but each has a purpose in your life. You can *weigh* how much intimacy you have in a relationship by considering levels of closeness, and their progression is in this order:

• **Minimal contact or acquaintance** – when you make a purchase in a store, for example you'll have contact with the cashier. She or he serves a purpose in performing a transaction, but has no connection to you in an interaction.

• **Companion** – someone to hang out with. An example would be a few people on an extended business trip. They may have dinner or see some sights and have fun together. But they are not forming any long-term bond.

• **Friend** – someone with whom you have developed a meaningful relationship. You know and care about each other in love, but without sexual contact. Friendships can last a lifetime.

• **Romantic** – someone who you are more deeply involved with - sharing each other emotionally, spiritually, physically and possibly sexually.

• **Committed** – someone whom you love deeply and have promised your devotion to. This relationship excludes all other romantic partners.

Healthy relationships include, among other things: respect, commitment, trust, openness, time spent together, mutually beneficial attributes, positive expectations, tenderness, consideration, forgiveness and freedom. *Healthy* is what you should be looking for. Some of your previous and current relationships have not been. Now that you're better able to choose whom you want in your life, you're able to make changes that better reflect a positive support system. What levels of involvement work best for you right now? What attributes fit with your value system? What type of people would you like to be close to? As you move from the old way of relating to the new, the answers to these questions will be instrumental in achieving what you want. "Win-win" relationships can be yours. You have more choices now than ever before.

One Door Closes... But Many Others Spring Wide Open

The saying - when one door closes another one opens can be true. But perhaps it's more accurate to say that your new opportunities will not become available to you until you're willing to end, in this case, your unhealthy emotional self. In William Bridges's book *Transitions*, he recognizes three distinct time periods, one where we experience an ending, then a time of adjustment, and finally the time when we begin our new lives. Since we often define ourselves by our roles and relationships, we're sometimes hesitant to leave our old familiar styles because indeed they are familiar and comfortable. But quite often we greatly benefit when we do. Ways to move past resistance and encourage yourself to continue on your transformation include:

• recognizing the specific positive and meaningful benefits that will be yours as a result of your transformation;

• looking back at your childhood and determining how you learned to respond to endings (a friend moving away, a pet dying, etc.). As an ACOA, abandonment has always been an issue. Realize that your current reactions may be triggering old emotional responses that of course, belong in the past and certainly not the present;

• understanding that you must evolve through the various stages of ending, adjusting and beginning anew, but you will reap significant benefits;

• continuing to develop your new skills, support systems and healthy belief system;

We go through a lifelong cycle of birth, death and rebirth. And in each phase there's something we need to learn. If we don't, we then move dangerously forward with unresolved issues that can haunt us and/ or unnecessarily create all kinds of problems. Each phase progressively prepares you for the next life experience or new period of growth. By resisting change and hibernating, you can stifle your own development. So even though it may be tempting at times to revert to old ways of relating and thinking, it's actually a very unattractive alternative. When you're ready and open to the next transition, a growth experience will be there for you to expand your world.

The Neutral Zone

"My boyfriend treated me just like my father had," remembered Nancy. "Nice when sober, horrible after a few drinks. Eventually I couldn't take it anymore and left him. However, I have all these conflicting feelings. I miss my x-boyfriend but at the same time don't want a romantic relationship—with him or anyone. I just feel like I'm adrift, not knowing where I'll end up. I don't even know who I am anymore but think I should take some time to find out so I can have better relationships in the future."

You're no longer here, but you're not there either. Your old identity is past history and may be getting in the way. There's resistance to change because perhaps you're afraid of the emptiness you might feel. The old fears of abandonment may begin kicking in. But you can move past them by becoming aware of where these feelings are coming from, knowing that you're just in a transitory zone, and that the rewards will greatly exceed any temporary discomfort. Remind yourself that you're not alone and that most people have discomfort associated with change. But you will prevail.

Maximizing the Successfulness of Your Transition

To help get the most out of your transition:
• remember the discomfort or lack of growth stemming from your past that prompted you to seek a better way of living, to escape from destructive thoughts and to leave an unproductive lifestyle;
• talk to your friends about the transformation you're experiencing and ask for their support;
• keep your eye on the prize: vividly keep the benefits of your transition in sight;
• take one day at a time, and when resistance occurs, examine where it's coming from. Don't rush it – take all the time necessary to move through the neutral zone, to enjoy and own the changes.

We have limited time on this earth. To quote Napoleon Hill, "Life is a checkerboard, and the player opposing you is time. If you hesitate before moving, or neglect to move promptly, you'll be wiped off the board… by time. You are playing against a partner who will not tolerate indecision!"

Time is always moving forward – we have to make moves or will simply lose opportunities to make our lives more meaningful. Take the opportunity whenever you can and run with it.

New Beginnings and Positive Possibilities

"I hated my corporate job but didn't know where else to go," said Albert. "Management was heartless to employees, even those who had been loyal to the company. It was *push, push, push – step up to the plate*, and then *get lost* when someone was no longer essential. I was afraid to leave whatever security I had there because after all, it paid the bills, but I was miserable. I thought and prayed about what else I could do with my life and eventually took the Myers Briggs test, which identified my personality type, and what occupations I'd be best at. I've just earned the additional credits necessary to become a school counselor and will start my new job in the fall. I want to help children become the best they can be. This new profession may be challenging but will bring new meaning to my life."

This may be a good time to get more in touch with your needs, what direction you want to pursue, and to reaffirm your new skills and value as a person. What you really want can be somewhat unclear, especially if one of your adaptive behaviors in the past had been to avoid self-aware-ness. There are several ways of expanding your scope. For example, there are seminars/workshops that can identify your strengths, inter-ests, and offer suggestions regarding what areas you might most enjoy. *Lifekeys* is a program offered nationwide in religious institutions that does just that. It takes a global approach and helps you focus on your gifts and interests within major aspects of your life (emotional, spiritual, vocational, personality tendencies, etc.). Then you have a clearer picture of what direction is best for you. In addition, many colleges and univer-sities have more intensive vocational testing, personality temperament sorters, etc. that can increase your self-awareness. But you are in charge of your future. These are simply tools that you can use if you want to, or discard if you don't. Identifying what personality type you are can pro-vide insight and guidance for your life's direction. It's helpful, but never definitive since each of us is unique. We should not be willing to simply be lumped into any form of generalization but rather we should take this new knowledge and use it as a tool.

Finally, think about how you would act if your birth certificate had an expiration date on it. What if you knew you only had a year to do what-ever you've always wanted. What would that be? What would you re-ally want to experience? Maybe that's what is now calling you. Perhaps you should listen and take action.

"I always wanted to become a pastor," said Jonathan. "But being an ACOA, my confidence level was always too low to even consider speak-ing in front of a group. I worked on that issue and today I'm fulfilling my life's calling. I can positively influence and minister to the 800 mem-bers of my congregation. Every day I'm excited to get up in the morning and do what I've been born to do. I love it."

It's time to stop preparing and start doing. Vividly picture yourself be-ing the new and improved you. You're successful and becoming a self-actualized person, unencumbered by your past. Be gentle with yourself but be diligent, taking one day at a time.

In the next chapter, we'll take a look at spirituality. The discussion about spirituality and God affects people in varied ways – all over the spectrum. People are distinct, come from diverse experiences and can feel differently at varying points in their lives. Regardless of your view, we are all spiritual beings. We'll look at that and more.

Five-Day Action Plan for Growth & Success:
Place a checkmark in each box as you complete the associated action:
❏ Talk to a friend about the greatest changes you've seen in yourself. Tell her or him how you've been able to accomplish this, and also about your goals for the future.
❏ Write how you'll eventually talk to a friend/lover who may be resistant to your evolution. Think of how to best approach the subject to minimize hurtful feelings. Be as gentle as possible yet also assertive in order to continue moving in a positive direction.
❏ Start a journal where you'll record the differences in your relationships with key people in your life. Note any new friendships that are beginning to develop.
❏ Look into your eyes in a mirror, and repeat these affirmations aloud in the morning and evening, as many times as it takes until you feel confident about what's being said:
   • I'm a positive force in the world.
   • I welcome new experiences and love the person I've become.

Summary:
✔ You can only be responsible for how you respond to others who will, or will not, welcome the new and improved you.
✔ There are levels of closeness: from acquaintance to companion to friend, to romantic partner and finally to a committed relationship.
✔ Three distinct time periods mark transitions – first where we experience an ending, then a time of adjustment, and finally when we begin our new lives.
✔ You can move past the discomfort of the neutral zone by becoming aware of where the resistance is coming from, knowing that it's just a temporary condition, and that the rewards will greatly exceed any transitory discomfort.
✔ New beginnings sometimes have unclear direction, and this is a time for you to reexamine your needs, wants and interests.
✔ There are various tools you can use to further develop an idea of what you want to do with your life.

Chapter 14

Experiencing Positive Spirituality, Nourishing Your Soul
A Spirit-guided Life

Marie's mother had a cedar chest that looked like a coffin and one day almost served as one. "My mom was drunk and forced me inside the chest and then locked it shut to show who was in control," remembered Marie. "There was no light, limited air and I didn't know if I'd be released in time to survive. All I could do was cry, feel helpless and pray to a God who I felt had abandoned me. What did I ever do, I wondered, to have God hate me so much that He'd let this happen? I also thought that there might not be a God at all—certainly not one who had any power. However my perspective has changed and looking back I think He was always with me. How else could I have survived, healthy enough to today raise my own family in a loving way? Perhaps God doesn't have control over the free will of people who can choose to do horrible things to their children. But He can be there to help us survive and heal if we let Him in. I've come to realize that an alcoholic caused my pain, but God helped me live through it."

Having faith allows us to see the miracles God does and also be open to expect and receive them. The miracles can include a full recovery from the damaging effects of being raised by an alcoholic parent. This chapter focuses on your soul and how it can be connected to the source of all Spirit. It doesn't preach but rather offers diverse ways of tapping into the limitless Source. It suggests that Divine Love can lead ACOAs to the recovery, personal development and commitment that empowers them to fulfill God's plan for their lives. Organized religion, metaphysical and independent approaches to spirituality are all considered. You may explore the best ways to effectively strengthen or awaken your spirit.

Believing in Spirit can strengthen us and we can become rivers of hope, streams of care, fountains of joy and oceans of love. It's impossible for you to be separated from your spiritual being since it's living in your material body. And we are never disconnected from the Source of Spirit unless we choose to be. There are times we feel like we are alone, but God hasn't abandoned us. If God seems far away, who moved? We've just temporarily blocked our experience of spiritual connection as a result of our anger, fears or doubts. How does our spirituality exist in relation to God? One analogy sees our individual spirits like cups of water taken from the ocean (which represents the greater Spirit or God). Another sees each of us as a light bulb that's connected to the ultimate power plant. Some envision invisible cords connecting each of us to the source of all Spirit in Heaven. Whatever your belief, you do have the ability to tap into your spiritual source anytime you choose. This chapter will explore various ways to do so.

How to Bring Nourishment to Your Soul

There are many different ways to experience spirituality: meditation, attending services at religious/spiritual institutions, nature, prayer, yoga and others. You are free to try as many or as few as you want in order to find what resonates with you. But I urge you not to stop until you discover a mechanism that will enable you to have a personal relation-ship with God. Without it, an enormous part of your existence is denied. The need for spiritual growth and connection is recognized in innumer-able books, including Stephen R. Covey's *7 Habits of Highly Effective People.* Covey suggests several self-dimensions requiring regular renew-al. They include the physical, mental, social/emotional and *spiritual.* He states that daily spiritual renewal can bring meaning to our lives, and that we can access our spiritual sides by, among other things, reading inspira-tional literature, meditating, spending time in nature and praying. I don't presume to know what will work best for you, and will simply provide you with some options throughout this chapter. Whichever way you choose, communing with Spirit can bring essential nourishment to your soul. Having faith can bring you positive opportunities. You may have questions answered about your experience of growing up with an alco-holic parent. And listening to your own spirit can renew your strength, lead you to the plan for your life, and allow you to plug into the Source that makes all things possible.

Self-Interview Taping Exercise:
Use a tape recorder to record questions and answers to the following.

Then rewind and carefully listen for the feelings along with meanings behind your responses. Summarize important insights into a notebook for reflection or action.
• As a child, what did you think about God or a Higher Power?
• How do you feel now about God? Account for the change, if any.
• How connected or unconnected do you feel with your spiritual side?
• What is your history regarding organized religion and how has it affected you?
• How can you best nourish yourself spiritually? What specifically will you do this week to accomplish that?
• What's the best way for you to enrich your spirit?
• What's your spiritual goal and how will you get there?

God is Love

I believe God is the essence of love and that He universally loves us all unconditionally. The love is simply offered and it's up to you whether to accept it or not. You can use it to build up your own "love bank account" so that you can, in turn, spread it to those around you. You can plant seeds of love in those you come into contact and watch them grow. Or you can ignore, deny or try to live without it. Some may be afraid of being loved so completely. But when you choose to be a spiritual person delivering God's love through your words and actions, you change lives including your own. When you use your human form to heal a hurting world through Love, it can be like providing a flowing stream of water to souls who are dying of thirst.

Divine Love can lead you to the personal development and commitment that enables you to fulfill God's plan for your life. That Love is unconditional and available to us all. Should it be given to people who act badly? Coming from my human perspective, I have mixed feelings. But one can look to nature and see that restrictions can't be applied. For example, it is impossible for a rose to offer its fragrance only to people who always do good things and withhold it from people who don't. How about a tree only offering its shade to selected individuals? In the same way, it appears that God offers His love unconditionally to all and relies on their free will and good judgment to accept it.

Are you allowing your spirit to feel the love and acceptance that only God can provide? Are you nourishing your inner child with love? Do you protect her or him from harm while providing opportunities for spiritual growth? What are you doing with your life and how can you better focus it on the plan God has for you? There's an old saying: "your life is God's gift to you, but what you do with it is your gift back to Him." Living with an emotional and spiritual bank account overflowing with love seems to be a win-win situation for all. Love from God is there for you, anytime, anywhere.

Spirit Calls You in Different Ways and Times

When I was elected as the Senior Elder at my church, I had serious doubts. After all, who was I, a person with lots of flaws, to sit on a governing board guiding spiritually-based decisions? I prayed about it repeatedly and it became clear that God called me to serve at that time, with whatever qualities or skills I could gather in order to achieve specific goals. I eventually served several three-year terms as an Elder and, while it required much work and effort, it transformed my life. The more I became involved with visitation to the elderly and sick, the more love and compassion I felt. When conducting discussions with other board members, some of whom were progressive and others conservative, I began to see that everyone, regardless of their political or personal persuasions, were all God's children and needed to be respected and fully heard. He uses us all, if we're willing, to accomplish great things that we never would have thought possible.

Serving others without expectations or hidden agendas touches your soul. Befriending someone, offering an extended hand, a hug, or simply listening can mean so much. Try doing these things for people in need with no expectations of receiving anything in return, and see what happens to your spirit. Heartwarming feelings will change your life and perception of yourself. It will reduce your loneliness and diminish the overwhelming dimension of your problems. There will be times when you may feel hurt, resentful or angry when you do nice things but get no thanks. You may approach it thinking you have no expectations but the old hurts may still resurface. Perhaps you've worked through some of these issues already, but if not, try and reexamine them. Revisit the concept of karma and remember that God is a loving God. And that the more you reach out to others, the more you'll be open to receive love and acceptance. Touching the spirits of others fulfills your destiny of acting as a child of God in human form to heal others. But you are also healed in the process.

How about organized religion and metaphysical approaches in your spiritual quest? What can you do independently?

Organized Religion can offer Tremendous Opportunities

The good news is that when you meet with others to expand your spiritual being, to pray or to worship, it can bring you to a place you cannot reach by yourself. "When two or more are gathered" is a phrase understood through the years as meaning that God is present. No matter what your spiritual background is, joining with other people in that environment expands your experience. This happens through discussion, support, hugs, smiles, group prayer, etc. And overwhelming numbers of religious groups do some very good things. To find out more, you might schedule a meeting with a leader or join a spiritual enrichment group. When spiritually-minded people gather to share their lives and experiences meaningfully, significant growth can occur. You may hear different ways people have overcome obstacles, successfully expanded their spirits, and adopt what's worked for them. And the spiritual leader may provide you with an inspiring sermon, idea or dream.

As with any type of organization, resources may be combined to provide various functions not available otherwise. Some examples are the televising of a church service such as that from the Crystal Cathedral or Lakewood Church reaching millions, the visiting of shut-ins or people who are lonely, food kitchens to feed the hungry, groups involved with religious or self-help topics, inspiring concerts, social gatherings, and plays, among many others. There can also be a feeling of belonging. Church leaders can serve as role models for children. And light can be sent out into the world when organized religion keeps focused on God's goodness and direction.

But Some Individuals Give Organized Religion a Bad Name

Like any organization, a religious group is comprised of people, most of whom do good works. But there will always be a few do serious harm to others. There are unfortunately a number of examples: the priest who sexually abuses children, the deacon who preaches on Sunday but cheats his clients out of money Monday through Friday, or the well-dressed congregational member who beats his wife. You can fill in the list...

Even though people who commit these damaging acts are members of a religious organization, they are *not* representative of it – or of God. And God is *not* perpetrating the evil; it is the person with free will who chooses to do evil, and she or he must take full responsibility.

In addition, the governing bodies of religious groups should always be supportive to the person abused and hold the guilty party fully account-able. It takes courage and fortitude to stop the wrongs that are going on, and sometimes there's a price to be paid. But if leaders/members of these organizations don't act properly (although they usually do), people will be turned off and simply disappear, injured and disheartened. We are all spiritual sisters and brothers; when one or more of us is abused, we all are. Intervention is imperative when one of God's children is hurt.

Some groups that were formed with the best of intentions, to wor-ship God in an organized manner and to provide support to people, have in some cases, been seemingly hijacked by a few people who end up discrediting the entire organization by association. Whenever people wit-ness or hear about such abuse, they automatically try to assess blame, of-ten placing it on God and religion, rather than where it should be. Again, the blame is attributable to individuals – humans who fail to consider the damage they're doing to others. The synagogue, mosque, church or any religious organization or gathering place has its strength and weakness in its people. Be the best spiritual person you can be if you're currently a member and see something hurtful occur. Ask for strength to do what's right when things go wrong. God is a loving God who, I believe, can only cry along with, and offer support to, those individuals who may have been damaged by the choices and actions of other people.

How Can You Nourish Your Spirituality Independently?

"My mother went to church when she was sober, and even though it should be a good memory for me, it brings up the times she was drunk on Sunday mornings," remembered Jessica. "So going to a church service as an adult triggers some bad memories for me. That's not to say that I'm a non-spiritual person. I simply choose to commune with God in my own way, through meditation. And I feel personally connected."

There are innumerable ways of nourishing your spirit without being involved in a formal group, and I'll list some that people have found especially meaningful.

• **Be with nature.** Find a calm and quiet place. Use as many of your senses as possible. Smell the fresh air, hear the birds singing, and see the beauty of this world that God has created. Spend time getting in touch with your spiritual self. Recognize that the Creator of all the beauty you're experiencing is also *your* Creator. This realization can replenish your spirit with the knowledge that the beauty in this world is not only great, but it also includes you. You are created in the image of God.

• **Meditation.** By excluding all the noise and interruptions around us, we're able to hear messages and guidance transmitted to our spiritual selves. Meditation can be accomplished in many different ways. Sometimes progressive relaxation is helpful to relax us. Candles, calming music, or even a massage can also assist. The point is to slow down, get in touch with your spiritual self and be open to hearing, seeing, feeling and knowing guidance from God.

• **Prayer.** We can pray differently - anywhere and at any time - the time or place we do doesn't matter. The important thing is that we communicate with God by opening a dialogue. Sometimes we can feel disconnected, but it is not that He is rejecting us – quite the opposite. Think of yourself on a boat in the ocean, while God is a nearby island. God remains fixed while you row all over the place, sometimes even away from Him. All you ever have to do is row in the right direction to be connected with His Spirit. He loves us, and is always there, waiting for us to come to him in prayer. Thank Him for all your blessings and ask for forgiveness and guidance in your life. Listen carefully and look for the direction that He will provide. You can make prayer a priority each day by scheduling it always at the same time, or you can choose to communicate with God anytime you so desire. His love and attention are open 24 hours every day.

• **Walking a labyrinth.** Visually, a labyrinth is a circular object (a construction of a maze-like pattern usually 20 to 40 feet in diameter) placed on the ground or floor with a meandering path leading to the center of the circle. Labyrinths can be found in places of worship and hospitals throughout the world. In the Middle Ages, walking a labyrinth was representative of a holy pilgrimage for people who could not travel far from home. A labyrinth walk is done independently, at your own pace: you simply have to follow the path. Usually contemplative music or candles add to the calming environment. Combining the imagery of a circle and spiral into a purposeful path, a labyrinth is an ancient symbol related to wholeness. It represents a journey to our spiritual center and has long been used as a prayer and meditation tool. Once you reach the center, you have the option of sitting, standing or simply continuing by following the path back outward. It is intended to simulate walking through your life with God. Religious and other institutions around the world host labyrinth walks that can be located through a search on the Internet (specify labyrinth and your location). These times of quiet meditation along with the spiritual connection you may feel when in the center, have been meaningful to many people who have tried walking a labyrinth.

• **Converse with others.** Share your blessings and struggles. Did you ever intuitively call someone you hadn't recently been in touch with, only to find they were thinking of you or were in need of support? Spirit often works through other people, as we are all connected. By sharing your spiritual side, you'll be more able to clarify and expound upon that aspect of yourself. In addition, other people can provide support and, sometimes, helpful interpretation. Just be sure to surround yourself with positive people.

• **Create a mission statement** for yourself and include where you'd like to go on your spiritual journey. Include the steps you plan to take, and your commitment to a life of personal integrity and service to others. How will your spirit affect people and events during your physical time on earth, and even afterward? What would you like your legacy to be? You may care to journal your thoughts, experiences and progress each day.

• **Experience different religions and writings**, including the Bible. You will best be able to make a decision about what touches you most by learning as much as you can. Read about the accomplishments of others who have recognized the impact of spirituality in their lives, and you'll witness Spirit in action. Consider all information that you come in contact with and use what truly talks to your spirit with love. There's an old saying: "Your mind is like an umbrella – it only functions when open," so don't box yourself in, or prematurely exclude certain approaches.

• **Listen to your dreams.** That's often how you can receive creative ideas, direction, solutions and positive opportunities. They can be messages sent from God. Suddenly what seemed hopeless becomes solvable. Opportunities open up and a clearer direction established. Spirit can connect you to God through dreams by letting you see mental pictures or hearing messages at a time when your defenses and emotional static are not interfering. Your life will have direction when you allow His thoughts to reach you through your dreams and may even inspire you to reach your destiny.

• **Live with an attitude of gratitude**. Even when you've lost something or someone precious, you always have so much left to be thankful for. Look around at your life and take notice. Do you have a friend? Can you find something to eat? Are you free? Many people would be so grateful for what you have. But there can be a tendency to take things for granted. Stop and take inventory of everyone and everything you've been blessed with, and thank God for them. Keep your eye on the doughnut – not the hole. Be thankful. Stay positive, retain a grateful attitude, and your spirit will flourish.

These are just some of the actions you can take independently to increase your spirituality. God/Spirit is all around us – in nature, other people, in our very souls.

Metaphysics and Spirituality

What is metaphysics? If you break down the word, "meta" means to transcend or see the situation behind something. "Physics" is the study of matter and energy. Metaphysics basically includes Eastern and Western philosophies along with "ancient truth teachings." It's another way of approaching spirituality that includes certain principles and premises:

- Everyone has free will to make her or his own choices.
- There is a higher self (God) and lower self (personality). God (sometimes referred to as the superconscious mind) lives inside of each of us and is accessible through meditation.
- Thoughts have the power to create.
- Life experiences occur to teach us lessons.

Certain universal laws apply within metaphysics, including the following:

• **Law of love.** Every soul is brought forth to experience love, which is the essence of existence. Self-condemnation works against your divine nature.

• **Law of karma.** Cause and effect, there is a reaction following every action. Good comes to us when we do something kind, but the opposite is also true. We reap what we sow. Religions that believe in reincarnation are tied to karma with the belief that we might go through several lifetimes to learn necessary lessons. Karma originates from our thoughts, deeds, what we think and do.

• **Law of attraction**. Your thoughts attract whatever you project – in a positive or negative manner. If you're regularly projecting fear about something, you may run the risk of attracting what you're afraid of. Project successful thoughts and you'll be more likely to succeed. This law states that we create more of whatever we focus on. To achieve our desire, it suggests that we feel very excited/happy, thank God for already providing what we wish, and allow it to come to fruition.

• **Law of return.** If you can't give compliments or love to others, you won't receive them. That's because you haven't unconditionally sent energy or opened a channel to receive. You always have to give in order to receive – emotionally, mentally and physically. This law is similar to the law of attraction in that respect.

• **Law of one**. You can never be separated from the Eternal Spirit/ God; you are a part of Him.

• **Law of mind.** There exists universal intelligence – the mind of God. This law says we can co-create what we need or desire.

• **Law of duality**. Everything has positive and negative energy. Feminine and masculine energies are present in each body and they need to be balanced in order to experience wholeness.

Metaphysical studies are another option that you can explore on your spiritual journey. There are many roads you can take, and you are in charge of choosing what's right for you.

Discovering the Divine Design – Let Spirit Guide You

"Never borrow sorrow, never step into tomorrow, just take care of today, and let God lead the way," suggested Helen Steiner Rice. God has a wonderful plan for you. And as you meditate or pray or do whatever brings you to the spiritual realm, listen for guidance. I know this might be radical because it seems to take away power that you thought you had over your life. But when you're worshiping merely money or power or anything on the material plane, it can disappear in a heartbeat, leaving your life apparently meaningless. "Not my will but Thine be done," is the only approach that will bring true lasting happiness and content-ment. There'll be a warm, beautiful glow around you and your life will have meaning. Everything could be yours if you put God first. He is the source of all good things including prosperity, peace and goodness.

Let Go and Let God

"Some days I think I'm on the road to recovery and then something bad happens to bring me back to the days when I was a frightened child," said Patricia. "As much as I try to act as an adult, my inner child still reacts to setbacks. Last night my boyfriend told me he didn't want to commit and I am feeling abandoned and sad. I've given everything I had to this relationship and it's falling apart. I give up trying and have to just leave it in the hands of God. If it is meant to be, it'll happen, but I trust Him to lead me elsewhere if it isn't."

In AA, there is a recognition that we are powerless and must turn to God for direction and recovery. No matter how hard we try, there are some circumstances for which we have no control. That's when we need to pray and trust that God loves us and will guide us to the best outcome for our current circumstances. But what about our past childhood experiences? Having alcoholic parents has in may cases devastated our lives; but there comes a time to release resentments, anger and self-limiting beliefs to God. Just let everything go and ask God for help. The super-generator of all things and people in this universe and beyond, can help you with your burdens and give you direction. With God, all things are possible. When we focus on God's unlimited power, we don't have to face the trials and challenges of life by ourselves. That doesn't always mean an easy path. Your spirit is sculpted by all your good and bad experiences. Something beautiful will eventually emerge but sometimes you may not get exactly what you want for several reasons. Maybe it's not for the greater good, or perhaps the timing isn't right. But He will be there for you if you have the faith to turn your life over to Him. Even in the darkest night, a new dawn is coming, and so is God's blessing for your life. You may feel devastated and think that things will never get better. But God will carry you forward, rebuild and strengthen you. You will be blessed. Let go and let God, and you'll experience the love and support only our spiritual Parent can provide.

Why Do We Have So Many Struggles?

Obstacles and challenges experienced in life may be perceived as barriers, but God has a plan for you to overcome them or find the direction where you should be headed. Some of the most challenging things we experience in life end up giving us the greatest gifts and/or knowledge. For example, you have a unique perspective because of your ACOA past that enables you to help others who may have had similar experiences.

Your sensitivity may have been enhanced to a degree that facilitates deeper connections with others. Your abilities are unique, and God has a perfect plan to use you in a wondrous way. Listen to your spirit and you'll be able to maneuver around or through the struggles. A mountain road, like life, is rarely a straight path. It will wind, it will curve, and it can detour for miles before you can move in the correct direction. But after making the right alterations in course, you will reach your destination. Spirit can and will show you your life's direction and purpose. Listen carefully through meditation, prayer, and the application of methods described in this chapter.

Keep your eye on the goal

Your spirit can be enriched, but it's up to you to start making it happen. Because it is easy to be distracted at times, it is important that you never waver. Your spiritual connection with God is essential for your well-being. So center your life on the will of God by communicating through prayer or meditation and keeping your eye on the goal. It's essential that you continue – always moving forward – to grow spiritually, emotionally, and intellectually. When growth is stifled, atrophy sets in as it does with muscles that are not exercised—this means that decay and decline can take place. But growth is always possible when Spirit guides you. And you can welcome each new day as a new opportunity for growth whether it includes pain or pleasure. Positive things happen when you follow this path. You can do it, because with God, everything and anything is possible.

As you can see, there are different ways of experiencing God and Spirit, and only you can best determine what works. Keep in mind that God is usually not heard in thunder and lightning, but rather in a still and quiet voice, so listen carefully. The loving Spirit is all around you, blessing your soul. Feel it in the warmth of the sun and hear it in the singing of birds. Nourish your spirituality at every opportunity.

The next chapter will bring some fun ideas. Your inner child needs to play and be taken care of. From building sandcastles and a little village on the beach to dancing to some music, smiles and laughter are on the agenda.

Five-Day Action Plan for Growth & Success:
Place a checkmark in each box as you complete the associated action:
❏ Pray and/or meditate every day.
❏ Keep a pen and paper in close proximity to where you sleep, and the next time you dream, immediately write down what message you received.
❏ Locate a labyrinth walk near you and try it out. If one is not available, take a slow and quiet stroll, preferably in a natural setting. Open your mind and spirit. Feel the Love and listen for a direction and purpose for your life. Follow through with action, and continue to nourish your soul at every opportunity.
❏ Look in a mirror, into your eyes and repeat these affirmations aloud in the morning and evening, as many times as it takes until you feel confident about what's being said:
• I'm blessed beyond my wildest dreams in miraculous ways.
• I've renewed spirit. I'm perfectly created in God's image. I am divinely loved.
• I have a strong spiritual connection and am supported by God.
• God/Spirit comes first in my life so my spirituality and life's purpose is fulfilled.
• I bless others as I let Love and peace flow through me.

Summary:

✔ It's impossible to be disconnected from your own spirit, but you have free will to choose if you do (or do not) want to be connected to the Source of Spirit, or God.

✔ You can bring nourishment to your soul and experience spirituality in many different ways.

✔ God is love and He offers it unconditionally to you, 24 hours each day.

✔ Touching the spirits of others fulfills your destiny of acting as a child of God in human form. You are also healed in the process.

✔ You can nourish your spirit independent of a formal group by doing such things as being with nature, meditating, praying, and listening to your dreams.

✔ There are many opportunities within an organized group of spiritual people that would not otherwise be available.

✔ Metaphysical approaches to spirituality incorporate many universal laws and principles.

✔ Follow guidance from the spiritual realm and your life will have meaning and purpose.

✔ You can overcome obstacles. Spirit will help and support you.

✔ God is usually not heard in thunder and lightning, but rather in a still and quiet voice, so listen carefully. The loving Spirit is all around you, blessing your soul. Feel it in the warmth of the sun and hear it in the singing of birds. Nourish your spirituality at every opportunity.

Chapter 15

Re-parenting with Love
Have Fun, Enjoy Humor, Nurture Your inner Child

"I experienced much emotional pain in my childhood," stated Kathy. "Hopes were dashed, promises broken, boundaries violated and nurturing or support non-existent. My mom loved her booze more than me. In fifth grade I fell down a flight of stairs and was rushed to the hospital with a severely broken leg. My dad left work to be my side but my mother stopped for a drink and never made it beyond the bar. I was terrified, in pain and felt abandoned. As a little girl, that experience was very traumatic. Twenty years have past but I still haven't forgotten—and abandonment continues to be an issue. If my boyfriend doesn't call when I expect him to, my inner child kicks in and turns it into a catastrophic event. I know certain events can trigger my tendency to overreact because of childhood issues, but how can I ever leave the reality of my past behind me?"

This chapter helps you identify, regress to, interact with, grieve over, and finally alleviate childhood pain. You're shown how to satisfy the needs of the inner child including safety, nurturing and fun. Several ways to access him or her are examined at different critical ages. Since ACOAs are generally serious people, many suggestions are made on how to find and have fun experiences. You are shown how to develop a smile mentality – an approach that universally creates positive feelings. In addition, you are shown how to nurture and deliver what was missing in childhood. The "laughter medicine" approach is explained and results in a new, improved way of living incorporating humor and fun. Life becomes less solemn and disappointments easier to bear.

Almost all the fun things you may have missed as a child you can enjoy today. In fact it's easier in some respects since you have more resources and freedom to make things happen, just as in bringing your inner child to an amusement park or on vacation. Also with technological improvements, some of the toys have been much improved. Your inner child wants to come out and play, hoping to leave the seriousness of the past behind her or him. But first you have to briefly revisit your child-hood years when your alcoholic parent influenced your life and resolve unresolved issues. That's actually what you've been doing throughout *Transformation for Life* and this chapter will simply go a little bit fur-ther. By working through the previous information and exercises, you've probably already grown a great deal. Much of that process is related to "inner child work." So while this chapter will look at and explain the general concept and process of healing your inner child, it will also ex-amine ways of getting in touch with what's good in your life and explore ways to have some new pleasurable experiences that your inner child will enjoy.

Humor is all around you if you allow yourself to identify and enjoy it. Suggestions are included in this chapter on how to bring more humor and fun into your life. Lightening up can improve your view of the world and put your problems into perspective.

Self-Interview Taping Exercise:
Use a tape recorder to record questions and answers to the following. Then rewind and carefully listen for the feelings along with meanings behind your responses. Summarize important insights into a notebook for reflection or action.
• What did you need as a child that you never received? Why didn't you?
• What does your inner child need from you?
• How does your inner child feel about you?
• Talk about a recent time when you needed to be accepted in a group. How did your feelings relate to when you were a child?
• When were you bullied? How will you comfort that inner child today?
• How have you rebelled? When did it work, and when didn't it?
• What are your dreams and how do you plan on achieving them?

Healing and Nurturing Your Inner Child

In Cathryn Taylor's *The Inner Child Workbook*, she suggests a six-step formula that includes identifying, researching, regressing to, inter-acting with, grieving, and finally healing your pain. In the process, your adult self would be instrumental in re-parenting the inner child. It may be somewhat intense to revisit your past in key stages of development but it can bring significant understanding and healing.

The process involves revisiting memories and beliefs acquired at various ages and addressing any distorted view of yourself and the world around you that can limit your potential and contribute to unhappiness. The key ages include the toddler years, the young child, grade school, young teen, adolescent and young adult. Some childhood periods included experiences that had a greater impact than others. Those are the years you may have learned to become adaptive at the cost of your nurturing, which may be the origin of difficulties you experience today.

For example, if an alcoholic parent was incapable of taking care of her- or himself, you may have adopted a caretaker role. Perhaps you think you're only good enough to continue in that role for the rest of life and don't deserve outside friends. Maybe you've even blamed yourself for causing a parent's problems. Undeserved shame may have planted negative beliefs about yourself that were, and are, totally inaccurate. As a result, someone may compliment you by saying what a nice person you are, but that little voice in your head responds by thinking "if they only knew what I was really like, they'd think I was a jerk." Those incorrect beliefs continue into adulthood unless, and until, you confront the issues and re-parent the inner child who suffered back then and may still be suffering. You can be the most wonderful person in the world but not believe it because those old self-critical tapes keep playing.

Picture yourself listening to your favorite band performing live, but the bass guitar is so loud that you can't hear anything else. That's what can happen when childhood traumatic events filter out the fun and joy around you. Your "let's be serious" voice can be yelling counterproductive messages so loudly that you can't hear or feel all the things that can bring smiles. Doing inner child work frees you to hear and enjoy the entire concert.

Life May Have Been Very Serious

"My family was very poor," remembered Louis. "Since my father would repeatedly get fired for showing up drunk at his jobs and my mom was too ill to work, money was tight. I got a part-time job with a cleaning service when I was fourteen. It changed to full-time after high school and I became the breadwinner of the family. They all relied on me. I was always more the adult in the family than the adults were and missed out on all the fun a child should have."

Being raised in a family where alcoholism was present required you to grow up much more rapidly than your age would warrant. Often it meant being more serious and parent-like than your parent(s). Play was bypassed and a way of living established that is hard to change. Therefore it may still be difficult even today to let yourself go in order to have fun. Whatever your history, inner child work can be tough because it entails re-parenting and requires introspection about key years of development—but it can produce substantial benefits. Some of the experiences you'll be recalling may have been sobering. But enough is enough. Too much seriousness can overwhelm happy feelings. Think of tourists riding on a train through magnificent scenery in the Rocky Mountains, but the blinds are down so they don't have a clue about what beauty lies beyond the windows. "What a boring, tedious trip," they say to each other, oblivious to the phenomenal show God and nature are presenting to those who choose to look. So it is if you *exclusively* focus on the seriousness of recovery while being blind to laughter and beauty all around you. As you work though your inner child issues, remember to keep a balance; take time to smell the roses that crown the thorns.

Getting in touch and communicating with your inner child may seem unnatural at first. But he or she is a part of you and deserves to be heard, to be given the love and nurturing that was missing in childhood.

"When I started to confront childhood issues, I just couldn't imagine myself as a little boy," said Jacob. "My friend suggested going to the park, watching children play and seeing my inner child participate. Another friend proposed that I make believe I'm an actor playing a child's role. Both approaches helped me to experience some insight, wonder and joy that I missed in the past. The more I went through these exercises in different childhood ages, the greater I experienced having childhood needs met such as being free to talk, trust, feel, forgive, hope, play and celebrate life. And when painful issues came up, I made certain to talk about them with my counselor. So whether the communication with my 'little boy inside' involves joy or pain, I am loving and considerate to him because he is worthy of feeling positive about himself. He's become fully aware of what's good in life, is given time to play, protection from hurt and has been set free from his troubled past. And I, the adult Jacob, have become truly happy as a result."

In spite of any pain you may have experienced in the past, you can now address the needs that were left unfulfilled as a child. You can take disappointments and transform them into possibilities.

Your Inner Child Wants Your Attention

She or he may not have gotten the nurturing or attention needed at the time, but today's a different story. As an adult, you have the ability, power and compassion needed to be a loving parent to yourself. And she or he needs to be heard and paid attention to - by you - especially concerning certain key issues:

- safety and security
- fun, fun, fun
- anger
- touching – both bad and good

- love and nurturing
- self-esteem and confidence
- loneliness

All these issues are important throughout life, but during different child development stages, certain ones become paramount. They are especially important during times of change. Let's look at some key needs in different age groupings as illustrated by questions or comments shown in the next section.

"Big You" nurtures "Little You"

It's time to open a dialogue between your adult and child selves. Within each age group, certain developmental issues come up more frequently than others do. So the sample questions are somewhat representative of concerns at various times of a child's life.

For this exercise, please locate a small mirror and look into your eyes with love and acceptance as you proceed in speaking with your adult and child selves. You might call yourself "little _____" *(use your first name)* when addressing your inner child. You don't have to be all-serious as you approach this. It is a loving and friendly dialogue - not an interrogation. Visualize yourself at the various ages described below. Ask if you, as the adult, could talk with the child. If she or he seems receptive, *start with some of the sample questions*. Then use these examples as a catalyst to think of a discussion that *more specifically* addresses what your inner child wants to talk about or explore.

Ages 2 – 6, (dependency and fear of abandonment can be prevalent)
Little you: Can you hold and cuddle me? I need to be loved and touched by you. Will you leave me if I'm mad?
Adult you: Yes, of course I can embrace you, any time you'd like. You're safe with me and I will protect you. I will never abandon you.

It's okay to express your feelings, in fact you have a right to be angry. And it's not your fault that mom/dad acted the way they did - you didn't cause their problems. I'll always be here for you with love and support.

Ages 7 – 12, (the foundation of self-esteem is often formed during these years)
Grade school you: I'm causing my father/mother to drink and am ruining everything. I feel ashamed because I'm not any good. Nobody loves me. They just make fun of me, I'm worthless and nobody wants to be with me.
Adult you: Your parent has a problem but it's not caused by you. Alcoholism is a disease and nothing you could ever do or say could be responsible for it. You know, little _____, those beliefs about yourself are wrong. Sometimes other kids can be cruel and parents not supportive. I'm here to tell you the truth. You are very lovable. And it's important that you know that things are not just black and white. If someone teases you, they may still like you. It's possible that they might just be acting foolishly or be jealous, which is their problem, not yours. Tell me what you need from me or whatever you'd like to say. After that, I'm going to tell you all the things that I love about you.

Ages 13 – 15, (fitting into social groups, mastering socials skills is important)
Early teenage you: My body's changing and I feel like a dork. I just don't seem to fit in and am tired of looking stupid. I want to have friends and to date, but nobody seems to want me.
Adult you: You're starting to grow up and are going through big changes. And it may not seem that way, but almost everyone your age experiences the same self-doubts. You have my friendship always, and you also have many other people who accept you just as you are. If you feel clumsy at times, I guarantee that it will pass quickly. I love you anyway. And you will have the love of others in friendship and intimate relationships. In fact, friends who want very much to have you in their lives will surround you. Please be patient with yourself, because you have grown, and continue to grow, into a wonderful human being.

Ages 16 – 18, (rebellion, beginning the transition to adulthood)
Adolescent you: It's not fair that I had to grow up in those circumstances. I'm not going to take it anymore.
Adult you: You're right – it wasn't fair. When your rights are violated, it's okay to be angry and do something to stand up for yourself. You're growing into an adult and sometimes need to rebel against what's kept you down. If you'd like, I can help you focus on what can be construc-

tive rather than destructive as you move into new territory with your life. Tell me about your struggles and how you're coming to discover yourself.

Ages 19 – 21, (learning to be responsible and planning for her or his life goals)

Young adult you: Where do I go from here? What do I want to do with my life? Will I be able to succeed?

Adult you: You're capable of doing whatever you choose. I'm here to support you. If you're unsure of your direction, let's talk about it. My guidance and experience are always yours for the asking. Regardless, you are a capable adult who will succeed in life and share yourself with people who will love you.

There are many memories and much information to gather and confront if you choose to delve more seriously into inner child work. All this goes beyond the realm of this chapter and might best be explored with a qualified professional. But if you feel the work you've already done is sufficient, simply concentrate on nurturing your inner child as your life evolves. She or he will always be a part of you and deserves your love and attention. The "big" and "little" you are parts of one soul and need each other to live a balanced life.

The Little Girl or Guy Has Rights... but What Are They?

Your inner child has the right to be treated with respect and compassion, and to have the adult you pay attention. She or he should be loved, nurtured and provided with fun times, has the right to feel safe about expressing feelings, and needs to know you're there for protection from others who might do harm. Your inner child now expects to receive from you, the adult self, all the rights unjustly denied as a child in an alcoholic home. It's up to you to insure that those rights are upheld: you have the power and abilities to do so. Be patient with and compassionate to your inner child for then she or he will feel safe enough to come out from hiding and bring insight about you as an adult. Learn from your inner child. Take all the time necessary to connect. It is effort well spent and will help you on the journey to become a happier, more balanced person.

Discover the Fun That's All Around You

"My whole ACOA group decided to put aside our serious discussions and go out and play," said Melanie. "Last Saturday we went to the Santa

Monica Pier where we lost our inhibitions on the bumper cars, Ferris wheel and half of the game booths. Then we traveled to Venice Beach where a man on skates sang to us accompanying himself on a guitar and harmonica. He was wearing moose ears on his head, a tail on his behind but even so, a few of us joined him in song. We ended the night with a game of volleyball on the beach. Most of us had lived no more than 15 minutes away but never taken advantage of the fun to be had. It was a great experience and one that my inner child will never forget."

Having good times is vitally important for an adult child. Life is serous enough without compounding it by retaining unhappiness from the past. Sometimes it is simply a matter of seeing what's out there and making the effort to experience different activities. Other times it's a frame of mind, or looking for the humor in everyday experiences.

For the next week, take a small pad with you and write down all the funny things you see, hear about, or experience. Then share the stories with others. They may have had or heard about similar experiences. It could become a fun-filled habit to share humorous situations and stories on a regular basis. That can make someone's day, especially if they were starting out depressed or sad. The whole environment can change and the dark cloud that was hanging over you can often dissipate as a result. Who knows? If you write everything down, you could end up with a sitcom and become a millionaire. Anything's possible.

But how about fun events – where do you find them? One answer is to observe where children go. The park is a good place to start. Try the swing for awhile. Or are there other things you'd like to play on? The point is to enjoy yourself and have some fun. Who cares if there are other people around? They may be noticing you with the most envious of eyes. After all, you are having a great time, possess a fun-loving spirit, and are able to leave the problems of the day someplace else. Try riding a bike or rollerblading; you can have fun and get some exercise at the same time. Join a team to play baseball, soccer or another sport. Groups are always looking for new members, and it's also an excellent opportunity to find new friends.

You can take the initiative to get people together to play a board game. Video games are also an option, but being with people rather than your computer is always a better choice. Joining with a group of friends can lead to telling funny stories, learning more about each other, and exchanging hugs, which is always nice. And there's no question that humor brings everyone together. As Victor Borge once said, "laughter is the shortest distance between two people."

Another way of locating entertaining activities is the newspaper. Usually there's a calendar or listing of the events that are scheduled for your area. Concerts, carnivals, comedy clubs and so many other opportunities for laughter. Then there's miniature golf, volleyball swimming, arcades, and even window-shopping. All you have to do is look for ways to get your butt off the chair. When you bring humor into your life on a regular basis, life itself becomes lighter and more manageable. Humor can serve as an outlet and release some of your pent-up emotions. Since it takes fewer facial muscles to smile than frown, you'll not only feel better but also look younger.

How to Develop a *Smile Mentality*

Nike said it best: just do it. The more often you purposely smile, the more natural it will become. You'll also receive many smiles in return. It's the international language no matter where you travel. Smiles are contagious and create a positive feeling where a negative one may have previously existed.

You can bring on the smile by thinking of funny experiences that happened recently. Do you remember the joke you were told or the practical joke that produced so much laughter? Your smile will be natural when you remember funny occurrences, and others will certainly welcome that grin.

Life's trials and tribulations can sometimes make you not want to smile. Certainly there are occurrences when it is inappropriate. But other times, a sense of humor allows you to step back from the situation and detach from the disappointment or sadness. By acknowledging the absurdity of it all and seeing the humor, you can disengage from the seriousness and look at it from a different perspective. Dr. Raymond Moody discusses the clinical evidence supporting the therapeutic benefits of laughter in his book, *Laugh after Laugh: The Healing Power of Humor.* In it, he suggests that doctors help their patients adopt a more mirthful perspective whenever possible. The bottom line is that laughter and humor can be beneficial even in the most serious environments. If it can make bad times better, it can certainly make good times great. So utilize some of the methods mentioned in this chapter and adopt your own. You'll find more instances of happiness and better health if you do.

Enjoying openness, love and sensuality is the subject of the next chapter. As you've worked on yourself with the five-day actions plan, self-interviews and affirmations in *Transformation for Life*, you've become better prepared to enter into a healthy and loving relationship. It's time for you to think about improving your current connections or sharing your life with someone new. Previously, there were messages from your past about yourself—self-talk that would end up sabotaging relationships. Those counterproductive messages are mostly gone now, replaced with more realistic and positive ones. So move on to enjoying healthy, enriching, and lasting relationships. You fully deserve them.

Five-Day Action Plan for Growth & Success:

Place a checkmark in each box as you complete the associated action:

❑ Find 30 minutes where you can be alone and have a conversation with your inner child. Choose an age range (you as a child) when you believe she or he particularly needs to talk with you (as the adult). Ask about her or his needs, wants, feelings and how you can help fill them.

❑ Start to compile a list of funny stories, and share them with others every day for the next 10 days. Have fun doing it and monitor how your mood changes.

❑ Look into your eyes in a mirror, and repeat these affirmations aloud in the morning and evening, as many times as it takes until you feel confident about what's being said:

• I relax and listen to my inner child. • I let myself go and have fun.
• Great things are happening in my life.
• I stand up for the rights of my inner child.

Summary:

✔ To fully address what happened to your inner child will involve revisiting many memories and beliefs acquired at various ages.

✔ Life may have been very serious and it may still be difficult to really let yourself go and have fun, but it's important to learn how to do so.

✔ You, as an adult, have the ability, power, and resources needed to be a loving parent to yourself.

✔ Your inner child has the right to be treated with respect and compassion, to receive your full attention and love.

✔ Humor is all around you. There are many ways to bring fun-filled experiences into your life.

✔ By adopting a smile mentality, you'll revitalize your emotional and physical being.

Chapter 16

Satisfying Your Emotional Being
Openness, Love, Sensuality and True Intimacy

"I once told Aunt Mary about how my father drank too much and how he'd yell at me for no reason when in that condition," said Charlie. "I was hoping she could get him to give up alcohol. All I wanted was a normal childhood and for him to act like the great dad I knew he could be. But the only thing that happened was that I got the shit beaten out of me and told that if I didn't shut up about private matters, the same beating would happen again. So I learned to keep everything to myself—including my feelings, needs and desires. The last thing I could do as a child was be open. I've also remained closed as an adult and it's gotten me into big relationship trouble. I'm starting to think that I should let my guard down before my girlfriend leaves me."

This chapter reveals the progression of openness that leads to love, sensuality and intimacy. You'll explore levels of accessibility and whether being open and intimate always works. Through guided exercises, it becomes clear that the alcoholism and behavior of your alcoholic parent no longer is relevant to current beliefs about openness and trust. Various levels of love are considered as well as tangible ways to attract a soulmate. These include verbal, visual, feeling and other ways of bonding with a special person. You'll see the difference between sensuality and sexuality, become aware that you are lovable whether in a relationship or not, and move toward emotional completeness.

What does being open mean to you? Should you be open 24 hours a day to everyone? Does being open make it more likely that someone will love you? Or is it more prudent to keep people at arm's length? Those old ACOA masks that served their purpose during childhood may protect you to a limited extent today—but no one can love a mask. Masks and facades only distance you from others and prevent the formation of meaningful relationships. Your capacity to love and be loved increases symmetrically with your willingness to be transparent. In what follows, you'll see some ways to safely increase the quantity and quality of love in your life at the times and with the people you choose.

Sensuality is that wonderful physical and emotional joining of two spirits. When and if you choose to share yourself in this manner with someone you deeply care about is up to you. But authenticity, responsibility, honesty, various moral standards and most of all love should be present and respected by both. This is the ultimate sharing of body and soul. If abused, it can seriously hurt. If shared with love and caring, it can be wondrous.

When you choose to be open, embrace love and sensuality, you'll discover true intimacy. Emotional distance and pain will disappear. Sounds like a good deal. What do you think?

Self-Interview Taping Exercise:
Use a tape recorder to record questions and answers to the following. Then rewind and carefully listen for the feelings along with meanings behind your responses. Summarize important insights into a notebook for reflection or action.
• Who is the person you've been most open with? What is it about her or him that encourages you to be that way?
• How open are you with your friends and lovers?
• How can you grow to trust members of the opposite sex?
• What can you do to help love yourself and others?
• How do you know you're lovable?
• Are you afraid of being completely loved, and if so, how could you change that?
• What is love to you, and do you live your life sharing it?
• In what ways do you express love? How do the special people in your life really know your feelings about them?
• What are your beliefs about sex?
• How can you bring more sensuality into your life?
• What have you learned about openness, love and sensuality?

Openness Brings Enrichment and Excitement to your Life

"I finally told Jodie what I had been thinking about for the last month—that I'd like more than a friendship with her," said Kenny. "She's my best friend and I cherish the time we spend together but was afraid of how she'd react. After all, I didn't want to ruin a wonderful friendship that we both cherished. But if she were open to dating, there'd be no limit to where it could go. I truly loved her. So when I told her, the initial reaction was surprise, then we decided to go for it. We've been dating for a few weeks now and we've never felt such a connection based on unconditional love. Since we already knew a great deal about each other, had established trust and simply liked each other, the transition was very easy. When I think that had I not worked up the nerve to ask her, we would have missed out on these blissful feelings, I cringe. This risk was one worth taking."

There's risk in everything, including doing nothing. If you remain closed off from people, there's a danger of depression, alienation, and much worse. Living as a hermit is much worse than having an occasional poor result from being candid and honest. There are innumerable benefits derived from being open. Intimacy is one of them. Other important benefits include your ability to verbalize and understand your own thoughts and feelings more clearly, increase your self-esteem, and meet a vast array of people who can enrich your life through friendship or more. Your support system can expand and perhaps you'll find many new opportunities for personal growth. This can all result in a personal, professional or spiritual expansion of your spirit.

"My attitude at work is that we're there to do a job, but we also interact with people who deserve to be treated with the Golden Rule in mind," said Loida. "So I ask about their personal lives if I think someone wants to share and offer support when needed. Because Audrey saw me as a caring person rather than a corporate figure, she clued me in on some backstabbing that was going on. A newly hired employee trying to get ahead was spreading lies about me that could have resulted in my termination. If I hadn't confronted him in time, this false information may have reached top management. The allegations would have been proven untrue after an investigation, but my reputation may have been tainted forever. It pays to have good relations and communications at work."

The benefit of having good relations with people is not restricted to non-work environments. Loida's experience demonstrates what might happen when you are left out of the loop. You could end up with little control over your professional future or be blind-sided. Open communication is important in almost every situation.

So what's the best way to open a dialogue? We can look to the great master in this field for guidance – the late Dale Carnegie. In his book, *How to Win Friends and Influence People,* he offers some advice. When starting from scratch or when you'd like to get to know someone better, try these approaches:

- be genuinely interested in the other person • smile
- talk about the other person's interests
- be a good listener
- sincerely make her or him feel important• use his or her name

This can form the foundation of a solid relationship, or you may discover that this particular person is not someone you'd like to know better. If you do like the person and she or he feels the same way, gradual and mutually balanced self-disclosure can follow. Then you've got something to build on.

Trust is *Increasing*, a Difference from Your Childhood Experience

"I don't make friends easily," stated Regina. "I couldn't bring myself to trust anyone after the pattern that my alcoholic father demonstrated during my childhood. Whenever he promised something, it wouldn't happen and I'd end up devastated. So I distrusted everything he said along with promises from everyone else. But over the last year, I met a friend in an AL-ANON meeting and we've gradually been sharing more about each other's lives. I've told her secrets that I've kept inside for years, and I have to admit, it feels good to talk about them. We genuinely care about each other and have come to the realization that the global distrust formed in both our childhoods can be now released."

As a relationship grows and a sense of safety builds, so does trust in each other. Once it has been established, it becomes appropriate to expand the depth of your openness. This is the stage where significant relationship growth and development can occur. You and your friend can experience the feeling of being completely accepted as you are, no matter what. You can talk about anything and everything without fear. And in the process, you learn things about yourself. Quite a difference from your experience as a child with an alcoholic parent! You can now face your imperfections. You can form alliances in the workplace or at school, resulting in a cooperative and supportive environment. Your beliefs about spirituality can be discussed with like-minded people, but just like politics, you have to be careful to ensure that you don't step on someone's sensitive toes. In general, when you leave the masks behind, openness with others brings new understanding and increased intimacy. Be sure to never abuse it, otherwise all the benefits can easily disappear. Respect others and always make sharing each other's lives into a win-win experience.

Openness for All? Appropriateness is the Key

There are still people who operate from a "do it to her or him before they do it to me" belief system. There are some people in business or personal life who will stab anyone in the back for either their own per-verse pleasure or to get something for themselves. That's why in the real world, you can't be naive. I'm not saying that people can't be trusted. In fact to approach people believing that they *can* be trusted is perhaps the best way to live your life. But realism and the duality of existence suggests we test the waters before diving in headfirst. Trust is built up gradually. So should your level of openness. If you are completely transparent with a stranger, they likely will not be ready for that level of intimacy and run in the opposite direction. Or they may take advantage or harm you, possibly prompting you not to be open with anyone, any-time soon. So appropriateness is the key to if and when you should be completely open with a specific individual in your life.

No More… "I love You go away" Routines

As mentioned in a previous chapter, there's a progression involved with the depth of conversations. When you get to the feeling level, you're beginning to get emotionally intimate. Being raised in a family where alcoholism was present, "I love you, go away" may feel strangely familiar. If a parent promised something and then alcohol got in the way, mixed messages were given. And if this scenario is still attractive to you now, think about it. This is how trust can be destroyed and the willing-ness to be open terminated. Instead, healthy openness and love that can lead to sensuality is much more preferable.

Love Levels can be Measured and Adjusted

"Once I moved on from my past and started loving myself, the whole world changed," said Ron. "I felt as many levels of love as there are colors in a rainbow. I looked at everything around me in a new way, appreciated the blue sky above me, the smell of clover in the field, the unconditional love from my children and wife. I was a new person, and continue to be as love has changed my life."

Just as there are different levels of communication and openness, so there are different variations of love. "I love chocolate" is quite different from "I love God", "I love you" or "I love my children." In fact if you love chocolate, you're thinking in terms of loving an object. You can replace the word chocolate with "my work or childhood home, the music of a certain singer and so on." Certain triggers may subconsciously recall a wonderful memory from your past, or you might simply find them pleasurable in the present. This variation of love can encompass something more abstract, such as poetry, traveling or meeting new people. It serves to lift you out of your normal day's existence and move you to an object or experience you fully and completely enjoy.

Another level of love is where you love another person such as a significant other, family member, or someone who has made a difference in your life. Whoever it is, your feelings for someone outside of yourself are elevated to such an extent that perhaps their well-being becomes as important as your own. Possibly you would even give up your own life to save the other person. Parents can feel this way about their children, as can individuals about their significant other. When you experience the soul of another so intimately, you can't help but further explore your own. Your feelings become more and more identifiable as you share what's going on inside, especially when love is present and you sense you can be completely open. That's also a point where self-love can grow. It is the essence of what openness can bring.

Still another variation is the love of God, nature, or anything that is larger than we are. That also means sending our love out into the world and having it return in kind. The larger our capacity to love, the more of it we will receive. As we consider the variations, we might also think of how we can make love grow in our lives. Maybe we can learn to see others not in the roles in which they serve, but rather as mirrors where we can see parts of ourselves. When we feel that interconnectedness, perhaps we act differently and be more empathetic. Look deeply into the eyes of someone and it seems eyes do indeed serve as windows to the soul. As barriers disappear, we can see how much we are all alike and how important love is. It's easy to come from love once we decide to do so, because we are made in the image of God, and God is love. You simply have to be yourself, love yourself and consciously offer love in all its variations.

Where's my Soulmate? How to Attract That Special Person

You may want to share your love and life with one special person. If she or he is not in your life, where are they? You've already learned a great deal about how to attract and enrich relationships. I will not go deeply into the intricacies of dating or relationship-building, but will mention a few verbal and nonverbal techniques of attracting another person. Some of the Dale Carnegie methods are useful for your early interactions, as are the SOFTEN (Smile, Open body, Forward leaning, Touch, Eye contact, Nod) techniques reviewed in a previous chapter. Beyond that, you can use approaches that might transmit a deeper level of interest, let the other person know you're attracted and interested in becoming closer. By the way, none of these exercises should be used to be dishonest or manipulative – they should be used ethically.

<u>Verbal:</u>
"I like to call my boyfriend Sweetie," said Summer. "It's a nice way to tell him I care and hold him in a special place. By verbally expressing myself to him and asking questions, I continually let him know that our bond is deepening. As a result, we love talking for hours, now share each other's interests more and the relationship continues to flourish."

• **communicate using "we" statements.** For example, when you and your partner are enjoying a museum, say, "<u>we</u> really picked a great place to visit." The more shared experiences and mutual enjoyment brought to her or his attention, the better.

• **share a private joke.** It could be something you've previously laughed about or experienced. It's something that only the two of you have enjoyed, and it brings back shared laughter.

• **use terms of endearment.** "Sweetie," "baby", "love-of-my-life" all transmit your feelings of like and love. There's no need to overdo it, but a few well-placed terms of endearment can bring someone closer.

• **be captiva<u>ted</u>.** And let the other person see it by being highly interested in what she or he is talking about. Find out as much as you can about your friend. Make certain that you relate, empathize, compliment and keep the spotlight on her or him. If you want a date, you must appreciate and initiate a pleasurable time together.

• **be captivat<u>ing</u>.** Make yourself seem like the kind of person she or he could very much love. Extenuate your good points. Generalizations should not be taken too seriously because everyone is different, but to mention a few, women are sometimes more interested in feelings, intuition, the arts, personal growth and other people. Men are sometimes more interested in their jobs, sports, and non-personal interactions. (Both, however, may be interested in love and sex.) Use a hook, something that makes you both want to talk further. Expand the conversation whenever possible.

<u>Visual</u>:
Use this sense to achieve maximum results.

• **gaze** into her or his eyes, and hold on to that look even after the eye connection has been broken. Be hesitant to take your eyes off the other person, think loving thoughts, and finally drag your eyes away, slowly like when chewing gum is stuck to your shoe. Act like you never want to look anywhere else and he or she will perceive that you very much like them and are interested in learning everything you can about their fascinating lives. You can practice this in the mirror and watch your pupils get larger, which is often perceived as an attractive visual attribute.

<u>Sharing of Feelings and Maximizing Connectedness:</u>

One of your most prominent childhood messages was *don't talk and don't feel.* This survival technique helped you cope as a child, but today it can be preventing you from self-understanding, self-esteem, emotional/ spiritual health and experiencing generosity of spirit and emotional bonding. In contrast, allowing yourself to <u>feel</u> your emotions and to <u>express</u> them accomplishes multiple purposes and can achieve positive results.

"We went to a Kenny Loggins concert on our third date," remembered Sylvia. "I'd been to many concerts… but never to a better one. And **Celebrate Me Home** generated memories of how I *wished* my childhood family had been — but also of how I've transformed my live as an adult. The song brought me to tears - joy-filled ones that recognized a new spiritual and emotional home I've created for myself. Kenny Loggins was clearly singing to my heart and it prompted me to take a chance by letting my new boyfriend Steve see the real me. That's because I've learned some important lessons through my recovery. Everyone needs to feel connected, cared for, valued and accepted. But in order to feel these things, one must be in touch with his or her emotions and open enough to be seen. One must be self-aware, accepting and have the desire, courage and ability to deeply share with others. Then you begin cultivating relationships with people who can respond with love. That's what I was doing. We spent the night talking about our experiences, dreams and feelings. It was a remarkable time for both of us and reminded me that healing from childhood wounds is possible. And that night began the formation of what turned out to be a wonderful relationship. *Celebrate Me Home* spoke to my spirit, mind and heart while reinforcing the fact that emotions, especially love, always have been and always will be inside me; they weren't destroyed by an alcoholic parent – only temporarily hidden."

Certain songs or events may trigger emotions. When that happens, ask yourself what you're feeling and try to determine the origin. *Each day*, work on increasing awareness of what you're feeling and then practice expressing some of those emotions. Controlling or suppressing feelings prevents you from being truly authentic and connected. Instead, free the inner child. You'll learn who you really are, be free of emotional baggage and obliterate chains from the past. Loneliness, self-alienation and frustration can be overcome once you do the work - and that's exactly what you, and like Sylvia in this example, have been doing.

Here are other ways to help build a relationship:

• **share an exciting experience.** When physical or emotional responses are high, they can carry over into a pleasurable, sometimes unforgettable, time together. Sharing the excitement of a sports competition, concert or play for example can certainly generate more feelings of involvement than reading two different books at the same time, each in your own world. The more intensely you are able to enjoy your time together, the more you will learn to feel the excitement of being together

• **similarity.** When two people discover they share common interests, standards, humor, temperament and ways of looking at the world, a solid foundation is established along with a desire to find out more. When you're almost exactly alike, things can get boring so as with everything else, moderation is important. But overall, complementary belief systems are a big plus.

• **analyze, analyze, analyze.** Whether we realize it or not, when we enter into a relationship with anyone, we consider what's in it for us. We subconsciously calculate a cost benefit analysis. Is this person going to bring more positive experiences to my life than negative? Will this be low maintenance but high return? By letting her or him feel like they're getting a great deal with you, you'll be pursued. The other person many have a wonderful personality, kindness, intelligence, consideration, physical looks, maturity, money, adulation, a loving attitude, or even status that could be attractive to you. Keep in mind that some of those things can easily disappear, so it's always advisable for you to give extra weight to internal values that will be less likely to change such as kindness and intelligence.

• **be open and share yourself.** Talk about your dreams and fantasies, ask what qualities she or he liked in a previous relationship, and later casually mention how good you are at them – *but only if you're being truthful.*

• **have goals.** You should sound like you're going someplace with your life. That makes you more attractive in the eyes of another. It also presents you with an opportunity to further explore where you're headed. You can get useful feedback and probably some encouragement regarding your journey.

Love is what almost everyone searches for, but it is within your grasp at all times. It starts internally, with yourself and your spirit. It's the greatest gift you can give to another. Feel the Love inside, share it with others and you will be loved in return.

Sensuality and Sexuality, What's the Difference?

What's the difference between the two, or are they essentially the same? Some people would say that sex by itself could be unemotional and meaningless. Sensuality, however, brings love, openness and usually a commitment between two people into the equation. It can be a physical and spiritual connection of two spirits; two bodies joined into one in a spiritual and emotional bond like none other. It may transcend all other types of connections between lovers, because it incorporates many different aspects of your being.

When you share yourself sexually with another human being, your emotional and physical barriers are gone. You are in a state of mutual surrender. That's why it can be the best or the worst of experiences. One of the most essential things to keep in mind, is to never hurt another. If you're horny and find someone to give you relief, make sure you fully understand where she or he is coming from. If you both are unattached and find it okay that sex simply be a physical, non-emotional use of each other's sex organs, each of you has the free will and freedom to decide to bang your brains out. Consulting adults have to decide for themselves, but it's seldom the best thing to do. You are using each other, and feelings can unexpectedly develop when you're sexually involved, even though that wasn't the original agreement. One person may end up being hurt and the other confused about what happened.

If there is *any* reluctance by the other person to begin a sexual relationship with you, there is potential to cause serious damage all for just a few minutes of physical pleasure. It's not worth it. In that case, the best thing for all concerned would be for you walk away.

The most sensual of times occurs when two people are in love. It can start with a soft caress, a certain look, or the smelling of a rose. All of your senses can be included in a gradual buildup of sexual tension. You can involve play, such as the use of whipped cream, strawberries, blindfolds, or include a mischievous massage and the sharing of fantasies. You can share a bubble bath while surrounded by candles or make love under the stars.

How to best enjoy sensuality can be determined by talking with your partner. Ask her or him what is most enjoyable and be reciprocal with your information. There's nothing to be ashamed of. Our physical bodies can be shared with someone who loves us without worry of condemnation or put-downs. Love also means that the well-being of your special person is equally as important as your own. So in sharing sensuality and sexuality in a healthy relationship, your feelings, safety, and desires are honored in a positive manner, for both of you.

Better Safe than Sorry

You know it - there are diseases out there that are incurable and can be sexually transmitted. This is a very serious problem. With a long-term monogamous relationship, you can avoid becoming infected. However, if you haven't found that person yet and choose to have sex with your dating partner, certain safeguards need to established. They include the use of condoms, periodic physical exams (for both of you), awareness and avoidance of risky behavior, and an honest discussion about previous sexual partners. Because your partner has had only one or two sexual partners doesn't mean that they haven't been infected. So one of the best things you can do is to have medical checkups and continue to use protective gear. Talking with your doctor or visiting an organization such as Planned Parenthood can obtain further information. Herpes, AIDS and other sexually transmitted diseases require that you have all the information possible. Unplanned pregnancy should also be a great motivator to be careful.

Sensuality can be a wondrous experience but before you decide to move ahead with one partner, you must be careful. When you protect each other, then you can be around a long time to enjoy those romantic bubble baths together. And let's not forget the strawberries.

One final comment that bears repeating: no one is ever obligated to have sex with another person, nor should they be pressured to do so. You owe it to yourself to have self-respect, to respect others, and to make responsible choices about when and with whom to share your sexuality.

What's in Your Heart... Is It Gold?

Do you have a healthy self-love and compassion for others? Good intentions at every step can lead you through life having positive, productive and love-filled relationships. Appreciation for the people in your life and expressions of love can make a tremendous difference.

Unlike material resources, you can continue giving your love to others and never run out. In fact, you'll always get back, in one way or another, all of what was given and possibly more. And while you're doing that, the lives of others are dramatically changed for the better. They'll have the strength to attempt goals they never thought possible, be energized by your acceptance and caring, and envision great accomplishments for their future. Everything changes when love is present and shared. So listen to what's in your heart and be generous in expressing your feelings of love *when they're real*. The lives of others and also your own will blossom as a result. And don't put it off. None of us knows how long we'll be here on earth. There have been many instances where guilt and sorrow haunt people for years because they didn't say the words "I love you" before a loved one passed away. The time is now for self-love and expressing, especially to people you care most about, your love for them. Just do it, because you'll see positive changes in them and yourself. You'll be thankful you did.

You are Lovable No Matter What, and We are All One

"This Thanksgiving and Christmas season was the first I've spent not being in a relationship," said Maria. "Surprisingly, I was okay with it. Friends and family who supported my decision to leave my husband surrounded me. Oh, sure, I cried a few times, but was constantly reminded that I was valuable and loved even though single."

Sometimes we are not in a relationship for whatever reason. But the fact remains that you were created in the image of God and are very lovable. You have tremendous attributes to offer to this world. Even if that significant other is not present, the rest of humanity is. You can be open with friends, enjoy the company of coworkers, or simply brighten a senior citizen's day by visiting her or him. We are all brothers and sisters in life, and each and every one of us is magnificent in our own way.

You are entering the best years of your life. There have been lessons and skills to learn, belief systems to adjust and lots of healing that has happened. You deserve to forget your past difficulties, let happiness in and enjoy all of life's blessings. That's the subject of our final two chapters. Learn how to live real and authentically, bring prosperity your way, enjoy the ride to unlimited success and joy and also see what your future will look like. You deserve the best, and it's coming.

Five-Day Action Plan for Growth & Success:
Place a checkmark in each box as you complete the associated action:

❏ List as many things about yourself that you like and love. Give yourself credit for all your accomplishments.

❏ Express your love, verbally and by your actions, to a friend or significant other.

❏ Remember your five most sensual memories or fantasies. Consider what made them so special, and how you added to the experiences.

❏ Look into your eyes in a mirror, and repeat these affirmations aloud in the morning and evening, as many times as it takes until you feel confident about what's being said:
  • My openness brings new opportunities.
  • I'm lovable and open to being loved.
  • I'm free to love myself.
  • I make my own decisions regarding sex.

Summary:

✔ You don't have to be open 24 hours a day to connect with others.

✔ Breaking down walls helps minimize loneliness and self-alienation.

✔ There are many more benefits than drawbacks to being open and honest with friends and loved ones.

✔ The more trust you have, the more open you can be.

✔ There are various types and levels of love. By loving people, our interconnectedness becomes more apparent.

✔ Various techniques can be used to attract people to you. They can be categorized as visual, verbal and feeling.

✔ Love is always within your grasp; it begins with loving yourself.

✔ Sensuality can especially be enjoyed when love is present.

✔ Care must be exercised when sex is involved - for various important reasons.

✔ You are a lovable individual, created in the image of God, whether you are currently in a relationship or not.

✔ We are all brothers and sisters in life, and are all magnificent in our own way.

✔ You deserve to be happy, enjoy love, sensuality, unlimited success and joy.

Chapter 17

The Best Years of Your Life
New Skills, Beliefs and Attitudes

"I've transformed my scars into strengths," observed Susan. "As a child I was damaged. My father was a drunk and the lack of nurturing brought me low self-esteem, a fear of abandonment, shame, anxiety and more. But now, after addressing irrational beliefs through self-help books and support groups, a few years of therapy, and mastering new skills through sheer determination, I've emerged a self-confident and accomplished woman. And I'm using everything that I've experienced in life—even the traumatic events—to move on to a higher level. For instance, as a child I was overly sensitive, often cried and could feel pain even when others were the ones having problems. But I've transformed that *negative* to a *positive*. Today I use my sensitivity and empathy as a physician to connect with my patients in a way that most doctors can't. The strongest life lesson I've learned has been that *it's not what happens to you in this lifetime, but what you do with it afterward* that really counts."

This chapter summarizes what's been learned and developed through the *Transformation for Life* program. You now have the courage, perseverance and openness to change and grow. The ACOA issues that once were so overwhelming have mostly been eliminated or minimized. False beliefs and attachments have been exterminated, like mosquitoes in a bug zapper. The waiting is over; it is time to begin a self-actualized life. You're free to form a clear picture of where you're going and have the newly found abilities to get there. And in the process you've turned scars into strengths and transformed limitations into high expectations. Through self-examination, positive self-talk, acquiring new skills and beliefs, you now have everything you need to create and constantly improve a life of growth and achievements.

Congratulations! Some of your emotional clouds are clearing as a direct result of your hard work and willingness to grow. You probably are experiencing increased self-esteem, effectiveness, and interpersonal success. Your skill level has risen higher than it's ever been and is affecting many different areas of your life. Issues have been resolved by among other things, connecting what was problematic in your present life to your past, revisiting those times and dealing with them. Your *history* no longer dictates your present and your future is now unlimited. You've replaced most counterproductive beliefs with more realistic ones, opening up new possibilities. You've accomplished a great deal already but this is an ongoing process—there are lessons to learn throughout life. I urge you to continue your efforts for personal growth, rebuilding and healing, always striving to improve.

You've had the courage, perseverance and openness to grow by progressing through this book, possibly supplementing it with a support group or therapy. As a result, you're on your way to experiencing the best years of your life. This chapter will review how you've arrived at this very positive place and consider where to go from here.

Self-Interview Taping Exercise:
Use a tape recorder to record questions and answers to the following. Then rewind and carefully listen for the feelings along with meanings behind your responses. Summarize important insights into a notebook for reflection or action.
- What are the three most positive things that have happened to you since you began your recovery? Why have they been so impactful?
- What are the false beliefs and attachments that you have most enjoyed zapping?
- How can you go about enjoying happiness more? What are the things that delight you?
- What do you think you're here to accomplish, and how will you succeed?
- Which of your scars have you turned into strengths?
- Who are the two most significant people in your life? Why are they so important? How would your life be different without them?
- Talk about the people who have saved you from taking the wrong path.
- What are some of the positive things that have developed as you've grown and improved. How has your life changed?

False Beliefs and Attachments Eliminated

If only we could be born with a "false belief" zapper, similar to the one that's used for insects our lives would be much simpler. At the first hint of our believing that we were inadequate, shameful, lacking or any other irrational judgment, we'd be brought back to reality by that electric zapping sound.

Anthony DeMello, author of *The Way to Love*, recognized that erroneous beliefs are a root cause of unhappiness. He also felt that most people have, at any given moment, everything they need to be happy. But when the focus is on *what's missing* (money, talent, looks, a loving partner who you may have pushed away because of your own inability to trust or express/accept love, etc.) rather than what we have, it's natural to become frustrated and unhappy. Being attached to the false belief that you need so many dollars (or anything else external to yourself) to be happy, you're destined for discouraging times. There are millionaires who feel insecure and empty, proving the old saying that "you can't buy happiness" correct. There are many people who have almost no money but manage to experience lives that overflow with love, contentment and joy. What's the difference? Mostly it's the realization that while it's nice to have the best of material comforts, the things that are really important and last are non-materialistic in nature. Some of these include knowing and loving yourself, building positive and fulfilling relationships, being with a group of like-minded people, enjoying nature, nurturing your self-worth, having a sense of purpose and direction, pursuing a connected relationship with Spirit, learning, growing and being your best.

Your good looks can disappear with age, but your character is always present. If you're an investor and the stock market crashes, you can say goodbye to your net worth, but you always remain a much loved child of God. A belief that you're not happy until you have a house, a million dollars, etc., is simply counterproductive and wrong-minded. Attachments to material objects or false beliefs can cause you to take the wrong path, so they should be rejected.

In addition, happiness is not some *future event* – it's within your grasp NOW. Waiting to be happy for when and if you buy a new house, get a better job, win the lottery or any other future goal is a sure way to short circuit today's potential joy. Phrases such as "life is a journey, not a destination" and "life is not a dress rehearsal" contain a great deal of wisdom. Don't put happiness on hold waiting for some future event. Instead, live in the present and focus on all that you can be thankful for right now.

The point is to replace your antiquated negative emotional programming and belief system and that's what you've been working on. Perhaps today you see the world and yourself in a clear and honest manner. If so, now you can begin to experience your life anew—living in the present with positive, constructive, healthy relationships and beliefs. You're beginning to live fully alive because you've changed your emotional programming by using positive self-talk, being kind, considerate, loving and forgiving to yourself. Of course, you'll have problems like everyone else, but they no longer have to seem bigger than they really are. You can approach life one day at a time, keep things in perspective and deliver much happiness into your present life by using your new skills and belief system.

Effort Brings Results – The Waiting is Over

Whether with therapy, development exercises, the expansion of skills, positive affirmations, addressing your belief system or other approaches, personal development and healing have required effort, time and perseverance. Your start may have been delayed because of ACOA issues, but the wait is over. Now you have taken the time and energy necessary to compensate for previous setbacks. You probably already realize that *examining* what happened in your past *does not mean staying there.* It simply helps you acquire insight into what may have contributed to some prolonged difficulties, and identifies what needs to be addressed. These difficulties can be overcome, and if you've utilized some of the techniques illustrated in this book – a self-interview process, affirmations, information to better understand yourself and skill-building to name a few - you have already made significant progress. But highly traumatic experiences in your alcoholic home may call for additional therapeutic assistance. Whatever is necessary to acquire your healing and growth, pursue it without delay. If you have occasional setbacks, know that you will succeed as long as you continue working on yourself.

Through self-examination, positive self-talk, and the understanding of your feelings and self, you discover that you're a lovable and complete person. Those are fundamental truths about yourself. There's nothing holding you back. If you decide to build your self-confidence, there are methods to do so. You can increase your social competency and find new friends by following previously explained methods. And you can practice effective ways of constructively expressing your anger or other feelings. Nothing worthwhile comes without effort, so revisit the skill-building sections of this book if you falter, and practice techniques until you feel good about your proficiency. Remember, we are all constantly growing and none of us can ever reach perfection. Therefore if we do our best, whether the outcome is 100% successful or not, we can have the satisfaction of knowing that improvement is happening.

Why am I Here?

"I've realized how the major experiences in my life have come together to teach and guide me," said Tamia. "Since my mother was consumed by alcoholism during my childhood, it fell on me to nurture and guide my younger sisters. I enjoyed it and did an excellent job if I do say so myself. After entering college, I met my future husband Willie in a psychology class and went on to a corporate job while he became a practicing psychologist. One of his clients was Clara, a teenager with no guidance in her life who entered the criminal justice system at age 13. It made me wonder how many other children were making bad life decisions and I remembered how fulfilled I felt coaching my sisters during their formative years. And it prompted me to make a career decision of my own. No more corporate crap - I wanted to do something that I enjoyed and would make a difference. So I returned to college, took the necessary classes, became a school counselor and now love it. I know I'm doing a good job from the letters and kind words of appreciation I've received. I've found my calling and am doing what I was born to do."

We are all here at this time for a reason. Each of us was born with special talents or gifts. We have the opportunity to respond to this calling and by doing so, may affect people's lives in a positive way. All of our interactions, good or bad, work in unison to mold us into the individuals we've become or will become.

We can learn valuable life lessons (or we can avoid learning and make the same mistakes over and over again). One of the most valuable lessons is that we need to forgive in order to find peace. It doesn't mean that you condone another person's actions or necessarily reconcile. Forgiveness is for your benefit, not anyone else's. The greatest present and future are fundamentally based on our positive, constructive thoughts. So we learn to let go and consider whatever happened during childhood as a past experience that enabled us to learn something. In some cases, it may have even helped us develop or discover a talent. So we let go of resentment, knowing that the bad experiences can be transformed into good, and we remember that the greatest revenge consists of lives in which we reach our potential.

So what do you believe you're here to accomplish? Think about what's calling out to your heart. Where can you make the greatest contribution? What are your best talents, gifts and the attributes? Are you using them? Go to a quiet place and think about these questions and your life's direction. Nothing is impossible for you. Be happy right now, and with every step along your journey. Have faith in your dreams and believe in your future.

Do I Deserve Happiness?

"Sometimes I feel unworthy of the happiness I feel," said Meryl. "Times when I make mistakes, I replay the old, outdated tapes that were self-critical and formed during childhood. Being an ACOA, perhaps they will never entirely go away. But I now know how to turn those messages off and replace them with positive ones by using self-talk and challenging irrational or critical beliefs. I do deserve happiness – everyone born to this world does."

You deserve to feel a positive, loving connection and to also have a support system consisting of people who care very much about you. In turn, you can use your happiness to touch the lives of all around you. There are no limits to what and whom you can affect with your positive influence. We are all interconnected. Mitch Albom's book *The Five People You Meet In Heaven* is illustrative of this.

The universal law of cause and effect is always present and working. But no person or occurrence external to you has the ability or power to globally make you happy or unhappy. You have the power to replace negative thoughts or self-limiting belief systems with positive ones that can bring success, health, prosperity, intimacy, fulfilling relationships, and more.

I See What I Want, and I Know It's Coming

Are you keeping your eye on the target/goal? Are you enthusiastically acting as though you already have it? That sets into motion forces that will bring it to fruition. And that's true of both positive and negative things. Therefore it's important to remember the dynamics and keep your thoughts positive, so positive outcomes will be delivered. Conceive, strongly believe what you want will come to be, and you will achieve it in God's time and if it is for the greater good.

Sometimes it's helpful to act as though the condition, or whatever seems to be missing, is actually present. For example, if public speaking is new to you, but you're called upon to make a speech, think "as if" you are an expert at it. Vividly picture yourself doing an outstanding job. See your audience responding favorably. Have the confidence and presence that an accomplished public speaker might have. Another example comes from someone I once worked with. Vince was on vacation at the beach, coming out of the ocean with his wife when he saw a thief take their radio and start to walk away with it. Vince was much smaller, but he remembered hearing that if you act like a crazy person, it can intimidate almost anyone. He "acted" like a madman, running up to this individual screaming. The thief was shocked and didn't know what Vince was capable of, so he returned the radio, apologized, and ran away as fast as he could. I wouldn't recommend this approach in every circumstance, but in this case it worked. So if you're feeling a little blah today, try acting as if you are happy and excited to be alive. And keep your attention on where you'd like to be. These universal truths can really work for you. Try them out and see.

Turn Your Scars into Strengths

Reverend Robert H. Schuller first coined the phrase "Turn you scars into stars," recognizing that bad things happen to everyone but also that we can make sure disappointments don't emotionally paralyze us. In fact anytime we're dumped on, we can turn it around as this old fable illustrates nicely:

A farmer's donkey fell into an abandoned well. The animal cried for hours as the farmer tried to figure out what to do. Finally, he decided the animal was old and that the well needed to be covered up anyway; it just wasn't worth it to try and rescue the donkey. He invited his neighbors to come over and help him. They each grabbed a shovel and began to shovel dirt into the well. Realizing what was happening, the donkey at first cried loudly. Then, a few shovelfuls later, he quieted down completely. The farmer peered down into the well, and was shocked at what he saw. With every shovelful of dirt that hit his back, the donkey would shake it off and take a step up on the new layer of dirt. As the farmer's neighbors continued to shovel dirt on top of the animal, he would shake it off and take a step up. Pretty soon, the donkey stepped up over the edge of the well and trotted off.

The message is that life's going to shovel dirt on you, all different kinds of dirt. The solution is to shake it off and take a step up, rather than let it bury you. Each of our troubles is a stepping stone. We can get out of the deepest wells by never giving up. Shake it off and take a step up!

As you begin the best years of your life, what new ways have you discovered to deal with adversity? How does that differ from the way you used to react? Being proactive means that you no longer wait for things to happen to you, but instead take actions that can keep your best interests in the forefront. You can be proactive, but occasionally bad things will still occur. What happens then?

September 11, 2001 is a date that will never be forgotten. It was very sobering, especially for the people who were directly affected but also for the general population of the United States. Numerous individuals were affected with depression, extreme anxiety, and/or post-traumatic stress syndrome; a few even committed suicide. Others chose to adopt fear, hate, violence and intolerance. But for many, it was a wake-up call to do something of substance with their lives. A corporate manager with a disability left his well-paying job to work with disabled children. An ACOA decided to lead support groups for people going through heartache and turmoil. An accountant who had grown up in poverty left her job and returned to school to become a social worker so she could help those in the inner city who were in need. The list goes on and on. Adversity can be responded to by turning your "scars into stars" as Dr. Schuller suggests. Anyone can do it. Find a need - and *fill it* doesn't just pertain to marketing. It also can give you some ideas on what to do with the remainder of your lifetime. What hurt have you experienced and lived through that you'd now like to help others with? What can you bring to the table of life?

Turn Your Limitations to High Expectations

Having high expectations for your accomplishments affects how successful you'll be. If you have low expectations of yourself and meet them, you may simply stop growing. So aim high instead. Expect occasional disappointments, but firmly believe that you will attain what you wish as long as you just keep trying and believing. A movie called *Rudy* was based upon a true story. No one in Rudy's family had ever gone past high school but it was his dream to go to college and to play football at Notre Dame. His family lived in a steel town and had little money. After being discouraged from even thinking about college by his high school teachers because of his poor grades, he went to work at the mill. He never lost sight of his dream, and when a friend perished in an accident after giving him a prized birthday gift of a used Notre Dame jacket, Rudy decided to travel to the university and do anything necessary to achieve his dream. He tried harder than most, and even though he was very small in stature compared to the other football players, he participated in a championship game where he was carried off the field on the shoulders of the team as a hero. Rudy also graduated with a degree—in fact so did every one of his younger siblings. It's a remarkable and inspiring film about persistence and having lofty goals. You can follow in Rudy's foot-steps and also inspire others in the process. You can reach your dreams because in reality, your potential is unlimited.

The cycle of life demands that we either grow or die. This is true physically, emotionally, spiritually and intellectually. Nobody should live in a dead zone. So why not fully live, grow every day in every way?

Loving Arms Embrace You

God is love: Whether you realize it or not, His arms are around you, especially during the times when you might feel abandoned and alone. As sure as the sun is behind clouds that may occasionally gather, He is always there for you. When you're afraid or feeling abandoned, invite God closer to you and you won't be alone. Things may not immediately change – natural disasters happen, as do the abuses that some people perpetrate on others. But God will be there to support you and to provide healing. His arms will surround you. Connection with Spirit may best be accomplished through such methods as meditation and prayer. But you can also communicate by being quiet in a field of wildflowers or virtu-ally anywhere you could possibly think of as a restful, serene place. God is everywhere. That fact can offer much peace to your inner being.

Things seem to come together at predetermined times. As you have been learning, all your experiences, both positive and negative, can be used to form you into the person you are becoming. You're the only one who has the potential to accomplish what you've been born to do.

Trust that you are exactly where you should be. Don't forget the infinite possibilities that come from faith; use your gifts, and pass on the love that you've been blessed with. Let His presence settle into your spirit, and allow your soul the freedom to feel it along with the music in your heart. God truly loves you and will never quit on you. Welcome and feel His embrace.

I Will Always Remember You

"My friend's parents, the Minnellas, changed my life," stated Robert. "I was a teen growing up in an alcoholic family and had no clue what living in a normal family was like. And I had never talked to anyone about the inner me. Mrs. Minnella, a kind and disarming person, took me aside and I finally shared my feelings and thoughts. For the first time, I felt accepted and loved. Mr. Minnella told bad jokes and we laughed, but also demonstrated loyalty and commitment when his wife became critically ill by always being at her side. I witnessed how a normal family interacts through good times and bad, learning a good lesson for my future relationships. And through it all, they set my life's course in a new direction by instilling a sense of acceptance and esteem. The Minnellas both loved me, called me their adopted son and I felt the same way. That love changed the way I felt about others, my life and myself. I'll never forget them and will always be grateful."

Who transformed your life? Everyone has special people who have emotionally touched them, whether they are teachers, a parent or other individuals. Who are the three most significant people who have changed your life for the better? How have they specifically impacted your life's journey? What did you learn from them? Think back on how your life might have turned out differently.

Good memories can sustain us during difficult times. They are important to remember. When you consider the positive impact that others have had upon you, it becomes clear that you too, can have such an impact on others. Be a driving force behind the emotional development of a teenager. Or say an encouraging word to someone who's struggling. Touch somebody's life and you will be remembered long after you're gone.

Celebrate Your Transformation and Magnificence

Think of where you were before, and how you've grown and improved. That's a major cause for celebration. The butterfly has emerged from the cocoon. Even if you haven't fully reached your dream yet, the progress should be joyfully appreciated. Honor your efforts and achievements – even the smaller ones, because they constantly add up. Celebrate your life every day, knowing that your growth and happiness will continue. Your best years are here, but there's still much more to come. The best years will be comprised of single days and moments, one by one, throughout the remainder of your life. Empower yourself with thoughts of love, joy, peace, faith, acceptance and transformation. Envision them written on stones that you can toss into the pond of your own consciousness. Watch the ripples move throughout your life, constantly awakening your spirit to these wonderful attributes and conditions. You can make your best years truly magnificent.

Our last chapter will focus on your future. It's your life, ten years from today. What have you accomplished? Raised a family, fed the poor, loved someone special, attained your full potential? How have you affected the world? What will be your legacy? One thing is for sure - you are a wonderful success.

Five-Day Action Plan for Growth & Success:
Place a checkmark in each box as you complete the associated action:
❏ Make a list of all the things you are thankful for.
❏ Consider what your life goals are or should be. Then make a short-term and long-term plan on how to get there.
❏ Look into your eyes in a mirror and repeat these affirmations aloud in the morning and evening, as many times as it takes until you feel confident about what's being said:
• Nothing can stop me now.   • My life touches others.

Summary:
✔ It's fruitless to try to ease unhappy feelings by acquiring or changing things outside of you.
✔ All of our interactions, good or bad, work in unison to mold us into the individuals we've become or will become.
✔ You can achieve what you conceive of in your mind and strongly believe that you'll accomplish.
✔ You can turn your "scars into stars" by refusing to let disappointments stop you.
✔ Keep your expectations *high* and don't be afraid to achieve them.
✔ God has His loving arms around you, and with Him, not *some* things, but rather *all* things are possible. Allow your soul to feel it.
✔ Celebrate how much you've grown. Celebrate every day as your development and happiness continue. Your best years are here, and there are still more to come - years comprised of wonderful single days and moments throughout the rest of your life.

Chapter 18

A Decade Later, Your Legacy Revealed
Plan to Reach Your Potential

"I never thought I'd get anywhere in life," said Marsha. "When I was a little girl, my drunken father's critical voice always reminded me that I was stupid and would never amount to anything. He said I should look for a guy who might keep me *pregnant and barefoot* but taken care of. As I grew older, my friends told me it was only my father's booze talking. They were instrumental in convincing me to attend college. While there, mental health services helped me recover from many ACOA issues. Then I learned about visualization and also how to go after my life's goals. Next semester I'll receive my doctorate in psychology; I plan to open my own office and eventually write a book. I'm not stupid by any means, and by *planning* to have a wondrous future, I've brought it to fruition."

In this final chapter, you will imagine your life ten years into the future by answering focused self-interview questions. This visualized life will be as wonderful as it could possibly be. An overwhelmingly success-ful existence is a certainty for many reasons. After all, you have acquired skills, established high self-confidence and constructed a reality-based belief system. You bring tremendous value to other people's lives, form positive relationships and have developed extraordinary skills. You are at peace with spirituality and have discovered God-given talents that have brought success beyond anyone's wildest dreams. Energized and focused, you live in the present and have reached self-actualization. The chapter concludes by returning to the present so you can make detailed plans to reach your 10-year goals. You are changed, unstuck, recovered, devel-oped and have begun a new life overflowing with possibilities, happiness and self-actualization.

The taping or writing self-interview exercise will ask you to project the brightest future you can visualize for yourself. The magnificence of this future is quite possible, and we'll help construct an exciting look into what your legacy can be. As you're answering these questions, you can assume that you've given your best effort to your own growth and development. It's the most favorable outcome for your life. Assume you've made incredible progress, because since you first began your self-development process, you already have. Add ten years and you have the opportunities and the time to accomplish anything.

If you have difficulty answering these questions, consider your dreams for the future. Sketch out an idea of what you'd like to accomplish and what your destiny should be. Take breaks as often as you wish. There's a lot in your future to recognize and appreciate. You need to discover how you got there.

Good Friends and Good People

Now here we are: ten years have passed since your courageous decision to pursue personal growth and recovery. And you've really made it. There have been some tough times along the way, but you persevered by believing in yourself, you responded to the healthy belief system you created, and you used your acquired skills.

From the time you learned how to communicate effectively, you have formed new relationships that have flourished and endured through the years. Concurrently, some old friendships were strengthened and made more substantial. And there were some who did not like your healthier emotional lifestyle and may no longer be a part of your life. Let's see who your good friends might be in ten years. They all surround you with love, laughter and caring.

Self-Interview Taping Questions:
(Remember – it's ten years in the future)
- Who is your best friend and how long has it been that way? What makes that relationship so close?
- Which friends have disappeared and why?
- What new friends have entered your life? How do your friendships differ from those you had a decade ago?
- Look at a photo taken at your last birthday. You're ten years older but still look fantastic. Who are the people surrounding you? Describe your relationship with each one of them.
- What do you emotionally, intellectually, spiritually, or physically give to them, and what do they give to you?

• How have you changed in what you bring to/seek from a relationship?

Surrounded by friends and family, you can feel confident that no matter what happens, you will always be loved and supported. You're able to make new friends easily, but cherish and nourish the important relationships you currently have.

Your Family Structure and Sense of Belonging

Depending on your age, you may have lost or gained family members over the last decade. If you were unmarried or without a significant other, that may have dramatically changed. Some family members may have died. Babies could have been born, and perhaps you have adopted new roles in your life. The structure of your family can dramatically change over ten years.

Self-Interview Taping Questions:
• Do you now have a significant other in your life, and if so, what is he or she like? What made you fall in love with this person?
• What changes have happened in your family structure and who are the current members? Describe how you relate to each of them.
• How did you resolve left-over issues with those who have passed?
• What is the greatest joy in your family?
• Talk about your extended family. What groups do you consider yourself a part of? What do you derive from being a member, and what do you give?
• Consider your sense of belonging. How has this affected you?

Your isolation is a thing of the past. Now you're part of a family unit and also a member of an extended group. You've become proficient at building and sustaining a quality support system.

Your Soul Mate

There's a special person whose soul connects with yours in an intense, spiritual way. Perhaps this strong connection can be experienced a few times throughout your life, but not many. In most instances, this relationship develops into a strong and vibrant love. There is such a person who has come into your life. It may have been someone who was there ten years ago, but had been considered more of a friend at the time. Or it could be someone who has entered your life over the last decade.

Use your imagination if the latter is the case and answer some questions about your soul mate.

Self-Interview Taping Questions:
- Describe this person. What does he or she look like? Describe your soul mate's personality traits, personal attributes and how you relate.
- You may feel that you've somehow known this person much longer than you actually have. Explain the spiritual connection between the two of you.
- How do you feel about this person? In what ways do you complement each other's lives?
- What does being in love mean to you now, as compared to years ago?
- How has your life changed as a result of having a soul mate who loves and cares for you?
- By expressing your love and caring fully and completely, what has happened, what have you learned?
- What do you see, when you look into his or her eyes? What do you feel when you see what you see?

Love is the greatest gift we can give to another and also receive for ourselves. It's a life-changing experience. Over the last ten years, you've consistently increased your daily dosage. As a result, it's much more prominent in your life. You've witnessed how love can exhilarate people's lives. It's brought you great joy and strengthened your spirit. And it's attracted a soul mate to you. Two lives have been unalterably changed for the better. What a phenomenal and beautiful thing to happen.

Your Impact on the World

There's a story out of the New York area about how one person's act of kindness changed everything.

It started on a Friday afternoon with a high school student watching one of his classmates carry home a huge pile of books. He couldn't help but think "what a nerd that kid must be, taking all that homework home on a weekend." He was happy he didn't live such a dull life. As he was watching his classmate some bullies came along, knocked the boy over, scattered his books, kicked off his glasses, and ran off laughing after hurting him physically and emotionally.
Having watched this happen, he felt sorry for the nerdy student and went over to help. He assisted him to his feet, picked up his books and helped him carry them home. On the way, he asked if he'd like to hang out for

a while over the weekend. The story goes on about how this was the beginning of a wonderful friendship. The nerdy kid became an outstanding student, the other a popular athlete.

When graduation time arrived, the boy with all the books ended up being the valedictorian of his class and gave a speech at commencement. He told the story of how he had been knocked over by bullies on that Friday afternoon, carrying the huge pile of books. He had so many books because he had cleaned out his locker. He didn't want his parents to have to empty it after his planned suicide that weekend. It would have happened, had it not been for this classmate who came along, helped him, and became his best friend. As the friendship grew he found meaning for his life. The friend listened to the speech in shock. He had never known how that little act of kindness saved a life.

You've done some little and some big things over the last ten years that have changed lives.

Self-Interview Taping Questions:
• What would have been missing if you were never born? What would have happened to your loved ones? How has your love and presence made a positive difference in their lives?
• What are some things you did or said that have made a difference?
• In what ways has your gift or special talent contributed to the lives of others?
• How, after working on your personal development, have you been better able to impact your world?
• What acts of kindness have you performed, and what do you think the impact has been?

Pay It Forward is a movie based upon a fifth grader's assignment; a plan to impact the world. He theorized that if one person was the recipient of an act of kindness and agreed to repay it by doing the same for three other people, kindness would envelop and change the world. It can. Give, knowing that your gift counts. Go into life today, this week, ten years from now, always knowing that the things you do, including the little acts of kindness, are instrumental in building a better world.

Your Life's Calling

Everyone is born with a gift, a special calling. Maybe you're a great singer who can move people with your songs. Or maybe (as in my case) people move away from you when you sing, but you have other gifts. All our gifts are different but important. Your special gifts and talents may have been buried before you decided to heal past hurts, embrace new belief systems and learn new skills. But after working on your personal development, your gifts and talents began to surface, slowly at the beginning but then at full force. Like ripples in a stream, building into a raging river, your creativity and life's direction became clear and a decision was made to fully welcome and develop them. These actions provided you with a new direction for your life, doing what you were born to do.

Self-Interview Taping Questions:
(Remember – it's ten years in the future)
• So what did you discover your gift to be? How did you decide to fully accept and develop it?
• How did you become an authority in your field, or an expert at what you do?
• Describe what you were brought to this earth to accomplish. How has this helped people, and how has its discovery helped you?
• What do you think the purpose of your life is?
• How are you using your new life to achieve your potential?

Discovering your gifts and talents is probably one of the most life-alternating experiences. Suddenly, you rediscover yourself in many ways and become excited about your direction. Mortality limits the amount of time you have to accomplish everything, so you no longer waste time with counterproductive activities. You do what you love and are not only focused but also thrilled about what you're achieving. These ten years have allowed you to discover and develop your gifts. You've listened carefully to hear what calls you, and had the courage not to walk away from it.

Prosperity in Spirit and Earthly Things

You've prospered in all areas of your life. And you've evolved to a mature comprehension of what responsibilities come along with your prosperity. Some people would argue that the more we have, the greater the tendency to worry about if it's enough. But sharing with those less fortunate has become a very happy part of your existence, and you may have become deeply involved in giving back. You are grateful for your prosperity and use it for good.

Self-Interview Taping Questions:
• How did you become prosperous? In what ways have you prospered over the last ten years, materially, emotionally and spiritually?
• What has your prosperity allowed you to do?
• How has your affluence helped in making the lives of others better and in what ways has your own life been improved?

Having overabundant resources can produce varying behavioral results. A few years ago, a nationwide pizza chain reported that those people who lived in the most expensive homes gave their pizza delivery drivers the poorest tips. But then there are others who earned millions and decided to use their resources to make this a better world. Several plan to give all their money away for good purposes before their lives are over. You have evolved over the last decade. What have you decided to use your resources for?

Your Home Base

There's no place like home. You now live in an environment that is conducive to your personal growth and development. In fact, it complements the road you've taken. Your comfort and peacefulness enable you to access your creativity, spirituality and universal resources.

Self-Interview Taping Questions:
• Describe the geographic location where you're living now. In what part of the country do you reside? Has that changed from 10 years ago? If so, what made you decide to change?
• Talk in detail about the structure in which you're living and describe every room.
• Who lives with you if anyone?
• In what ways is this house truly a home?

You have chosen a special place to reside. It best reflects your good feelings about yourself and your world. By living in such an environment, you feel you're finally home.

Your Belief System

What a difference it makes when you believe in yourself. Those ridiculous beliefs about being inadequate or undeserving were conquered a decade ago. There's been nothing holding you back.

Self-Interview Taping Questions:
• When did you really start believing in yourself?
• What do you do when self-doubt creeps back? How do you maintain a good self-image?
• What's been your greatest triumph, and how did your new belief system make it possible?

What you can believe, you can conceive and what you can conceive, you can achieve – and that also refers to self-esteem and self-worth. Destructive beliefs about yourself can certainly diminish your effectiveness and success. Where there's no hope, there's no life or vision for a better future. But your critical self-talk has been replaced with talk that is positive and affirming. And it now serves as a motivator and empowers you to grow and flourish. Your belief system is a substantial ingredient in the creation of optimism and success. The past ten years has been a time to embrace a positive belief system, and to nourish it.

Your Miraculous Spiritual Connection

Over the last ten years, you've found the best way to communicate with God and nourish your spirituality. There were many different forms of spirituality and religion to consider, but you were able to clearly see what spoke to your heart and soul. Now you unquestionably feel the love, guidance and support that God has for you. Your spirit is energized and fully connected to the Source of all being. You're at peace with the universe and reflect that serenity to the world. You joyfully feel the interconnectedness with the spirits of other people and your loving spirit touches them in miraculous ways. Most importantly, you've come to realize why you were born.

Self-Interview Taping Questions:
• How do you connect with your soul? What environment works?
• What's your perception of, and relationship with, God?
• How has the knowledge that you have been guided and supported by Infinite Spirit changed your life? Describe your faith in God.
• How do you share your spiritual side with others?
• What were you brought to this earth to accomplish?
• What is your gift, and how are you using it?

You've discovered what happens when you're plugged into the Spirit that created the universe. You've found that all things are possible with God's help. You've reached new heights, and Spirit is within you at every moment guiding you to achieve remarkable things.

Love Runs Through You

It radiates from your being. You made the decision to love a long time ago, and now your life overflows with it. Whatever you've given out has increased exponentially and returned to you. There are others who revel in your love, taking in the sustenance that only your love could provide.

Self-Interview Taping Questions:
• How has your capacity to love others been related to your willingness to love yourself? How do you express your love?
• When did you give yourself permission to love yourself? What made you decide to be open to love? Was there a person who helped you?
• What happened to the people around you after you began to be more loving? What happened to you?
• In what ways has love transformed you?
• What has been the most touching change?

Love is kind and generous and life-changing. You've seen it happen – you're an eyewitness. God is love. And you also have become, in human form, a source of this wonderful force for good. Even though the power of Spirit's love is indescribably bigger than your capacity, you still have enough to change the world for the better. As you move forward, you share it as often and with as many people as you can. We all need it just as vitally as we need food and water. Feed someone with your love, and receive it from yourself and others.

Back to the Present - Making a Power Connection in Time

The answers you provided to this chapter's questions should give you an idea of where you're headed. Everything is attainable. But in the here and now, how will you arrive at where you'd like to be in ten years? You can get there by devising a strategy and then taking one step at a time. In each of the categories listed above, you can methodically construct a detailed plan for what would be needed to get there. Taking as much time as you'd like, review the tape or your writings. (After all, a 10-year strategy will take some planning.) It's essential to remember that nothing is impossible for you. Hockey star Wayne Gretzky once observed that "you miss 100% of the shots you never take." In other words, you have to take the risk, believe you will succeed and act on your dreams for them to come true. And we have to be proactive in making changes, otherwise they may be thrust upon us and be changes we might not necessarily welcome.

So, with an objective of successfully realizing all that you've projected for yourself in ten years, construct your action plan. Prioritize what goals are most important to you. That's where you'll concentrate most of your effort at first. For each target, write all of the small steps that you'll have to take. Some will take longer than others to achieve, but as time goes on, you'll find yourself always getting closer to your goal until you actually achieve it.

You can establish short, intermediate and long-term goals. Reward yourself and take the credit for succeeding in each step along the way. It's best to concentrate on no more than two or three goals at a time; otherwise your direction may be too fragmented. But persevere, and as you accomplish one goal, move on to another.

And you can get spiritual help for this too. Prayer can produce impressive results. In his book *With Open Hands*, Henry Nouwen writes, "To pray means to open your hands before God. It means slowly relaxing the tension that squeezes your hands together, and accepting your existence with an increasing readiness, not as a possession to defend, but as a gift to receive. Above all, therefore, prayer is a way of life which allows you to find a stillness in the midst of the world where you open your hands to God's promises, and find hope for yourself, your fellow man and the whole community in which you live." Reverend Andy Rienstra, one of the greatest preachers from the Reformed Church in America, referenced this quote and then added, "God has a future for us – we can trust that we have an open and wonderful future. Henry Nouwen wrote these words in an article in *Weavings*: 'When our gratitude for the past is only partial, our hope for a new future can never be full. As long as we remain resentful about things that we wish had not happened, about relationships that we wish had turned out differently, about mistakes we wish we had not made, part of our heart remains isolated, unable to bear fruit in the new life ahead of us.' Now let us move on to that new future God has for us with grateful hearts," said Pastor Andy Rienstra.

Your Legacy

Hopefully you have many, many more years to enjoy your life. But have you ever noticed some of the strange things that are written on tombstones? In New Orleans there's one that reads: This is what I expected... but not so soon. It's funny but true. What if you reached your time to die, and discovered that you had not lived? This chapter has enabled you to take a glimpse into your future. It's a very positive future because you have exercised your right to live life fully. You have taken the time, the effort and the necessary steps to grow, heal and become the best you can be.

Your life experiences are what brought you to where you are today. You've challenged false beliefs that were damaging and counterproductive. An enhanced belief system is part of your new personal foundation. Your self-esteem is now healthy. You have control over your own actions and you are competent as well as effective. Relationships are now based upon mutual respect, caring and love. You have everything you need to make your dreams come true. There are special people in your life, individuals with whom you have regular, intimate contact. You've learned skills that will take you far, and you can use them for the rest of your life. You're free to pursue anything and likely to continue to achieve great accomplishments. Where do you go from here?

My mother left me a legacy that included lessons such as "treat others as you'd like to be treated," and "God is Love." Today you're a living legacy. Will you be a role model who teaches children to always try to do their best? Will your success impact the world? What kind of direction can you give to those you love? You can't redo the past, but you can do something about your future. You can choose, today and every day, to be the best of whoever you are, believe in yourself, use your skills, give to others and maintain a strong relationship with people and Spirit. Your contribution to the world is vitally important. There is no better time than now to assist humankind, to love and to be happy. God gives us one day at a time – long enough for laughter to follow any tears, time enough to help someone in need, plenty of time for prayer and to notice beauty. Certainly we have sufficient time over the many days of our lives to build a bridge of forgiveness, to tear down walls of resentment, to embrace friends, to smile at strangers, to enjoy the shining sun and to give thanks.

Live the rest of your life as though this day might be your last. Don't put off your dreams. Don't waste a minute listening to pessimistic thinkers, hate-filled radio personalities or others who promote the dark side of humanity. Instead, be a beacon of light. Free your heart from hatred and your mind from worries, live simply, give more, and never forget that you are a marvelous child of God. You deserve to live a meaningful and complete life that's fully alive.

A wonderful movie called A Walk to Remember illustrated how powerfully one person can change the life of another and be remembered for their gentle influence after they're gone. What would you like others to say about you after you've passed to the spirit world? How will your life have affected others? Perhaps people will treasure you for the laughter you brought to their lives, or maybe for the way you've impacted them with love and caring. It's what kind of person you are each day that will be remembered, along with how you emerged from failure to become victorious. Ways your kindness and consideration touched others and how you became your best by declaring a half-lived life as unacceptable and doing something about it will also be remembered. All this and more will become a part of your legacy.

As you live your new, enriched and improved life, know that many other ACOAs join me in sending each and every one of you our love. I hope this "transformation for life" has helped you develop yourself or at least initiate growth, so that you can significantly impact humankind. I wish you great joy and fulfillment for the rest of your life and beyond.

Roland Petit... holds a Masters Degree from Fairleigh Dickinson University, has led and continues to lead scores of support groups, has served on the presidential award-winning CONTACT crisis intervention hotline, is an ordained Elder in the Reformed Church of America, a Minister of Pastoral Care and an Interfaith Minister. He has been a training and development manager at one of the world's largest corporations, a speaker at the Crystal Cathedral's International Conference on Care and Kindness and has been featured on TV in 2009 and also in print.